CW01649047

THE COMPLETE GUITAR GUIDE

THE COMPLETE GUITAR GUIDE

David Lawrenson

Virgin

Virgin Books

David Lawrenson is a journalist who has spent a significant proportion of his career writing about the musicians' end of the rock market. Fascinated by guitars from an early age, and inspired by the Shadows, he began learning Spanish guitar with Bert Weedon's *Play In A Day* guitar tutor. In 1977 he joined *International Musician and Recording World*, one of the leading musicians' magazines, and subsequently became editor. Now a freelance writer, he covers many fields, but still specialises in "musician" type interviews.

Acknowledgements
I should like to thank **Gary Cooper** for all the work he has done to make this book possible. Gary has been responsible for the majority of the reviews in this book, and is one of the major guitar reviewers around today. In addition to his work with *Sound International* magazine, *Music Week* and *Sounds*, he also edits his own musicians' monthly, *Music UK.*

I would also like to thank, the editor, Catherine Cardwell, without whose cajoling, persistence and hard work, this book would never have been completed.

Thanks are also due to Chris Tomkinson and Neil Brockbank for their contributions in the reviews sections and to the many companies who provided instruments for review, the shops who also helped out and the numerous individuals who contributed in however small a way.

First published in Great Britain in 1982 by Virgin Books Ltd, 61-63 Portobello Road, London W11 3DD.

Copyright © by David Lawrenson/Virgin Books

ISBN 0 907080 391

All rights reserved. No part of this book may be reproduced in any form or by any means without the prior permission of the publisher.

Designed by Tim McPhee

Book Production Services by Book Production Consultants, Cambridge.

Typeset by Laura Beck, Portobello Typesetting
Printed in Great Britain by The Thetford Press, Thetford.
Bound by The Garden City Press, Letchworth.

Line drawings by Steve Downend
Photography by Barry Plummer, Terry Lott, Gary Cooper, Michael Greenwood

Distributed by Hamlyn Paperbacks

Contents

Introduction

Guitars by and large are expensive luxury items. Whether you buy acoustic or electric, new or secondhand, if you want a good instrument then you usually have to pay for it.

Despite the popularity of the guitar over the last 20 years particularly the electric variety, the prospective buyer has had little help in choosing from the vast range available, save for his own ears and the depth of his pocket. There are a number of magazines on the market who do review instruments, although the market is by no means as well covered as other luxury goods such as cameras, hi fi and video. Also, there is the problem of seizing on the issue which has the review of the guitar which you are considering, and many of the reviews anyway tend to concentrate on the newer models.

The purpose of *The Complete Guitar Guide* is to give the would be guitar purchaser some idea of what is available, and what he can expect from that particular instrument in terms of sounds, quality and value for money. It has been called the "Complete Guitar Guide", because we have set out to review as many instruments by as many manufacturers as possible. Of course not every instrument is covered, but any manufacturer of significance will have an entry.

Some names have been omitted either because the models weren't readily available, or because distribution in this country is under review. Some manufacturers were reluctant to have their products reviewed, but nevertheless we have endeavoured to give them space.

In some cases the models reviewed might have been discontinued, but they remain important instruments and often become collectors' items, so we thought it worthwhile to include them. The Guide has also tried to give significant space to the ever growing ranks of British guitar makers, who thanks to some fine designs and the current rise of the dollar are offering a real alternative to Japanese and American instruments.

All the instruments found in these pages are generally of a high standard, so while we give each model a rating, none are absolutely abysmal — there would be no point in reviewing such an instrument.

Having said that, guitars are very personal things and the sounds which delight one player may well be entirely unsuitable to another. Therefore in the reviews we have tried to describe the types of sounds which are available from the guitar, and what kind of music and player they are best suited to.

How to use the guide

After every review you will find a panel which gives a star rating of the instrument, and another which gives a list of specifications.

Star Rating — the star rating for each category is out of five, and you must remember that the rating can only be of the particular sample under review. For instance, the sample may have a particular fault whereas others may not. Therefore great care has been taken to stress that such faults may only occur on this particular sample. The mechanics of the guitar may be fine, but it may not have been set up for playing too well.

Finish — the finish of the guitar refers to the way the guitar actually looks and is presented.

Sound — indicates whether the sounds produced by the instrument are satisfying overall.

Playability — whether the instrument is easy to play or awkward and ungainly.

Value For Money — obviously it is very difficult to rate something which although may be very expensive is the finest example of its kind. However, there are very obvious bargains to be found.

Specification Table — the kind of materials which go into the construction of a guitar are vitally important to the way the instrument plays and sounds. Where possible we have listed these materials although in some instances they are unknown and would require us to scrape away the varnish!

We have also included the name and address of the distributor or manufacturer and an approximate price, which would be accurate at the time of going to press.

The history of the guitar

The sight of a guitar produces some very strange reactions in some people. You only have to walk down the street or get on a bus with a guitar tucked under your arm to attract a few odd looks and funny comments. The guitar has come to symbolize pop music and fame and fortune, so there's every chance that the bedraggled youngster on the bus might be the next Paul McCartney!

The guitar has become one of the most important and influential instruments of the 20th Century. Without it, many of the more popular forms of music today would be vastly different — can you imagine the blues, folk music, country and western or rock and roll without the guitar? In the case of rock and roll it has been a prime factor and became very much a symbol of youth culture and the whole social upheaval that went with it.

The instrument can be all things to all men. In the hands of the classical master it becomes an instrument of rare beauty, to the blues players it was an extension of their emotions and to modern electric guitarists an instrument of immense power. Segovia and Hendrix may seem like uneasy bedfellows, but the common bond of the guitar is indisputable.

Although the guitar is often regarded as a modern instrument, its origins can be traced back to ancient Egypt and their crude stringed instruments. Indeed, it is from ancient Greece that the guitar derives its name, because their stringed instrument was called a *kithara.*

However, the guitar in the form we know today, was probably developed and refined by the Spaniards in the Middle Ages. They were responsible for the traditional guitar shape and the addition of a sixth string, giving the instrument a range of three octaves. This instrument is essentially the same acoustic guitar we have today, hence the basic model is often referred to as a "Spanish" guitar.

Guitars remained virtually the same for centuries and enjoyed fairly wide popularity, but with the advent of the 20th Century things began to change. Acoustics had already changed slightly, with steel strung guitars being offered which were bigger and louder than the Spanish instruments, but the real breakthrough was the emergence of the electric guitar.

Apart from its obvious use by solo performers, the guitar in the 1920s and 1930s was being used in jazz bands and orchestras alongside many other instruments. Competing with drums, pianos and brass sections, the lowly guitar was drowned out and the musicians needed more volume.

The early part of the 20th Century was one of great technological pioneering, and many people began experimenting with the idea of amplifying the guitar. Almost all were working on the principle of a magnet wound with wire which when electrified would convert the vibrations of the steel strings into electrical signals which would then be boosted through an amplifier.

Much of this research was being carried out by individuals in America, and it was an American, Adolf Rickenbacker, who is credited with creating the first commercial electric guitar in 1931. However, Rickenbacker's instrument was really a Hawaiian guitar which was played flat on the lap. The famous Gibson company of America, who had been making acoustics since the late 19th Century, went into the electric field, but their instruments were essentially hollow-bodied guitars with pickups attached.

However, these semi-acoustics were not the complete answer, because the pickup mounted on the acoustic body presented many feedback problems at volume; feedback being the howling high pitched whine when part of the sound output of the loudspeaker is returned to the instrument.

However, it was left to a radio repairman from Fullerton, California to design the first solid electric guitar to go into production. Leo Fender was not a guitarist, although he had an interest in music, his main preoccupation was electronics. During the 1940s he had his own radio shop, and noticed that many of his customers were guitarists who were bringing their acoustic amplified guitars in for repair.

Fender saw the need for a better instrument and set about designing a solid bodied guitar. The first one he built in 1944, but it wasn't until 1948 that he had refined it sufficiently to go into production. The first model was called the Fender Broadcaster. The shape was very simple and straightforward, and it had two pickups which had been specially designed by Fender.

The Broadcaster was an immediate success, but there was one slight hitch concerning the name. Another musical instrument company, Gretsch, pointed out that they used the Broadcaster logo for the drums, so it had to be changed. The name Broadcaster had reflected Leo's background in radio, so he called upon another technical marvel of the age,

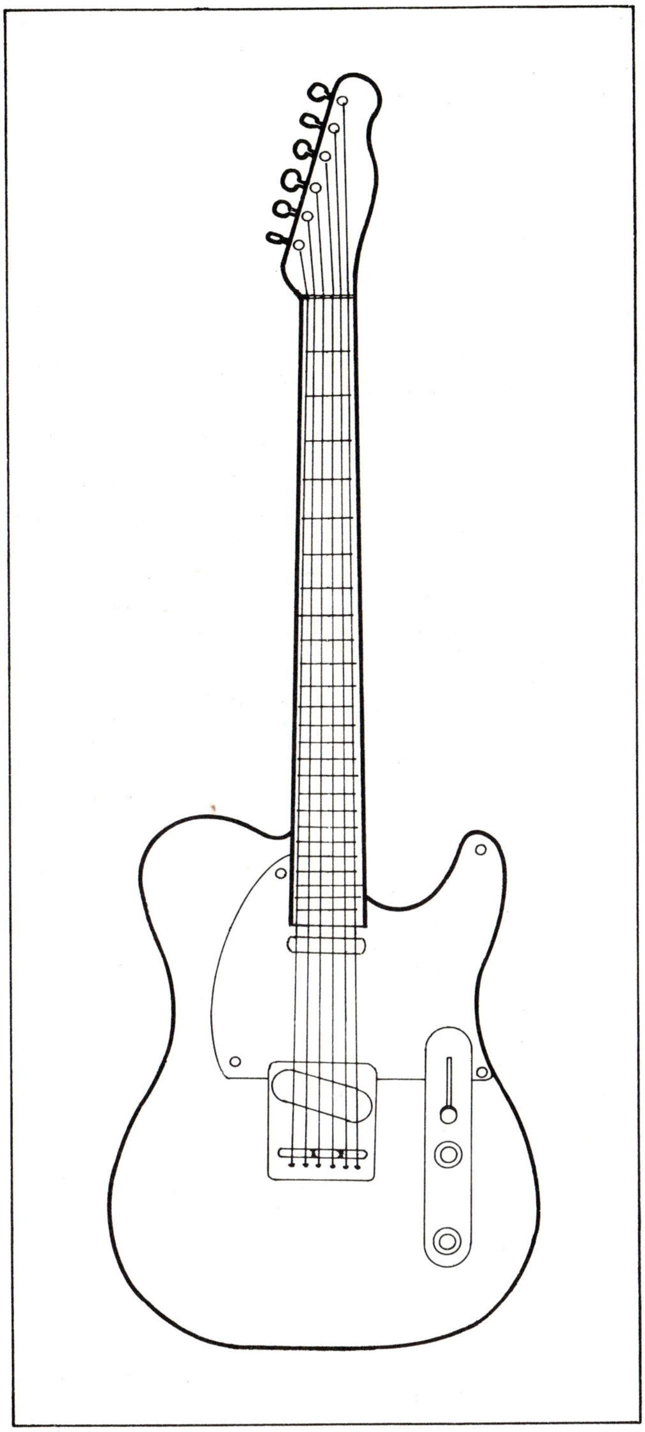

The Fender Broadcaster/Telecaster was the first solid bodied electric guitar to go into production in 1948.

The Fender Stratocaster which went into production in 1954.

television, for the new name. From 1950 the guitar became the Fender Telecaster.

Having sorted out the problems of the guitarist, Leo Fender was soon confronted with a whole army of upright string bass players who were not only finding great difficulty in being heard over the new electric guitars, but they were still saddled with a great monster of an instrument which was both unwieldy and cumbersome. By 1951 Fender had again solved the problem. He incorporated much of the design skill and technical know-how learned from the Telecaster to produce the Fender Precision bass — the world's first ever electric bass.

Not content with the giant steps he had already taken, Fender worked to improve on his electric guitar, and in 1954 came up with the Fender Stratocaster. The Stratocaster differed in a number of ways from the Tele. To begin with it had three pickups instead of two, giving the guitar even greater tonal variety. There was also a tremolo arm which moved the strings up and down to give a vibrato effect.

Overall, Fender made the guitar easier to play, he

sculptured the body shape to make it more comfortable and balanced, and positioned the tone and volume controls nearer to the playing hand. It is a tribute to the man's ingenuity and design brilliance that if you go into any shop today and ask for a new Stratocaster, or Telecaster the guitar you will get is almost identical to the first models the man designed.

The Telecaster is arguably the most popular and versatile of all electric guitars today. It found a particular niche in Country music, but now you're just as likely to hear rock bands such as Status Quo playing them. The Stratocaster has been a classic rock guitar for a long time being featured by such luminaries as Buddy Holly, Hank Marvin, Jimi Hendrix, and more recently Mark Knopfler of Dire Straits.

After Leo Fender's great breakthrough, other companies saw the commercial possibilities of electric guitars and began their own research and development in earnest. Among the early innovations was the truss rod, which was a metal rod inserted in the neck of the guitar to strengthen it and help withstand the tremendous pressure of the strings.

Much work was also done on the pickups, making them more sensitive and developing them to give a wide range of sounds. One of the most significant developments in this field was the "humbucking" pickup. This was developed by the Gibson company in the mid-Fifties and was basically two magnets instead of one, wound with wire in opposite directions. The result being to reduce hum from the pickup (hence hum-bucking) and giving a much warmer sound.

Gibson had entered the solid electric guitar market in 1952 when they enlisted the help of guitarist Les Paul, and produced their first solid which went out under the name of the Gibson Les Paul. While it was much different in shape and sound to Leo Fender's instruments, the Les Paul was to carve out just as important a niche in the history of the electric guitar as those early Fenders.

While the Telecaster and Stratocaster have remained in steady production since their inception, the Les Paul has had its ups and downs. A number of different models were produced, and in the second half of the Fifties, Gibson were experimenting with all kinds of different shapes including the arrow-like Flying V, and the angular Explorer and Firebird. The Les Paul probably seemed quite old fashioned by comparison, and by 1960 production had ceased.

That might have been the end of the Les Paul story, if it hadn't been for a young art student from Ripley in Surrey. Eric Clapton did more than anyone to resurrect the Gibson Les Paul. At the beginning of his career in the early Sixties he was immersed in the blues and found that the ideal guitar for playing electric blues was a Les Paul.

Clapton became a guitar hero and his instrument, the Les Paul, became a much sought after model. Endorsement by other guitar giants such as Peter Green, Jimmy Page and Jeff Beck established the Les Paul as the Stradivarius of the electric guitar, and by the end of the Sixties they were in production once more. It is still probably the most copied guitar shape around.

The Gibson Les Paul which entered the market in 1952.

Other US guitar makers have made inroads into the electric guitar market at some stage, with varying degrees of success. Guild, Gretsch, Epiphone and Rickenbacker have all built quality guitars, and indeed the Beat groups of the Sixties used a varied collection of instruments, but none of these companies were to dominate the scene like Fender and Gibson.

However, the history of the modern instrument hasn't been entirely dominated by America. In 1957 a Swedish company called Hagstrom began making electrics, and many British guitarists who started playing in this era will remember their Futurama models. Another favourite of youngsters who couldn't afford an American guitar was the instruments of a German company, Hofner. Models like the Galaxie and the Verithin were important in that they gave youngsters their first opportunity to play electric.

Several British companies, fired by the success of British music in the Sixties, have dabbled in guitar production, notably two names who made their mark in amplification, Vox and Watkins. However, one British guitar maker who really stands out is Jim Burns. Often dubbed the "British Leo Fender", he never emulated the American's widespread success, but he was an extremely inventive and talented guitar builder.

Burns began his electric guitar building in the Fifties, but really came into his own in the early Sixties when he designed a guitar for Hank Marvin of The Shadows which was named the Burns Marvin. Many musicians played Burns guitars during this period, even Elvis Presley, but in 1965 Jim sold out to the Baldwin company of America and by 1970 production had ceased. Early Burns models have now become something of collectors' pieces and Jim has made several comebacks into the guitar business, but he has yet to firmly re-establish himself.

If the youngsters of the late Fifties and early Sixties had Hofners and Futuramas as their first instruments, there's no doubt what the kids were playing towards the end of the Sixties and into the Seventies — Japanese.

Popular music instruments were yet another area where the Japanese felt they could score with their extraordinary production techniques. They flooded the electric guitar market with "copies" which looked identical to the famous Gibson and Fender models, but were often at about a third of the price. While many of them weren't particularly good, there's more than one musician who has liked the sound of his "copy" and decided to keep it.

The significance of these guitars, was that they brought electric instruments within the price range of those who normally would never have been able to afford one. However, as has been seen in many other fields, the Japanese weren't content simply to churn out cheap copies. They learned the craft of guitar making extremely well, and by the middle Seventies were producing high quality instruments which were exceptionally well made.

Manufacturers like Aria, Yamaha and Ibanez have brought design and quality onto a higher level, and now some of their instruments are gaining the respect which used to be solely reserved for American models.

Today, the guitar scene remains as interesting and diverse as ever. On the acoustic side, most of the major guitar manufacturers are producing a high quality range of instruments stretching from Spanish acoustics, through steel strung "jumbos" to semi-acoustics and companies like Guild and CF Martin have enviable reputations in the acoustic field.

One important development in the acoustic guitar over the last few years, has been made by the Ovation company of America. Although they manufacture both acoustic and electric instruments, it is their acoustics that really demand attention. They introduced a range of acoustics whose sound boxes were made out of a special glass fibre called Lycrachord which became very popular.

Ovation also went on to develop a unique system for amplifying their acoustics which has met with great success and would surely have Leo Fender himself applauding.

Speaking of the great man, he's still around designing guitars. After selling out to the giant CBS corporation in 1965 because of ill health, Leo eventually found a cure for his ailment and came back into the guitar making business initially with the Music Man company. Like many manufacturers today, Music Man are incorporating modern day technology into their instruments.

Active electronics is a fairly recent development and involves using active circuitry in the tone controls of the guitar to produce an even greater range of sounds and tonal blends. Experiments have also been made with a variety of materials for making guitars from Perspex and glass fibre through to aluminium.

New companies have sprung up like BC Rich, Alembic and Kramer to offer guitarists a wider choice, and it is significant over the last few years that bass players are being catered for more and more with many superb instruments finding their way onto the market. The British guitar industry is still surviving although it remains on a relatively small scale. What they lack in quantity they seem to make up for in quality and companies like Shergold, WAL and Gordon Smith produce some of the most impressive instruments on the market.

The modern day picture of guitar building wouldn't be complete without reference to the vast army of independent guitar makers who specialise in making instruments to the exact requirements of a particular customer. They are often very expensive, but people like John Birch, Tony Zemaitis and Peter Cook have become luthiers to the stars.

Another new direction in guitars over the last few years has been the development of customising. Companies like Schecter, Mighty Mite and DiMarzio can offer you replacement bits for just about everything on your guitar. So if you like the way your guitar is made but don't like the pickups, then you can replace them with whatever you want. Some companies have gone the whole hog and offer a complete guitar kit, so you just decide what body shape you want, what neck you would like, what kind of pickups etc, and make your own.

So the wheel has turned full circle; from the efforts of a few people struggling in workshops in the Thirties to develop an electric guitar, we now have a situation whereby anyone can assemble their own guitar at home.

However, despite new technology and the advent of synthesizers, the guitar is still a dominant force in modern music and is likely to continue to be so for a long time.

Buying a guitar

Buying a guitar whether it is your first or your tenth, always creates a little buzz of excitement. It may be the fulfillment of a long-standing dream, but the dream can quickly turn into a nightmare if you choose the wrong instrument.

For a beginner, it can turn him or her off the guitar for life, while for the more experienced player acquiring an expensive model, it can mean money down the drain. Buying anything is something of a risk these days, and instruments are probably more of a risk than most, but there are a few guidelines you can follow to help minimise these risks.

To begin with, where possible, enlist the help of someone who knows something about guitars. This may sound an obvious statement, but you'd be surprised by the number of people who believe that all guitars are the same just because they are the same shape and have six strings. You may be lucky to find a shop with knowledgeable, helpful staff — but remember their basic aim is to sell you a product.

For the beginner it is essential to buy the right instrument to learn on. The best one to go for is the simple Spanish acoustic. It will usually have nylon strings, a wide fingerboard and a gentle, mellow tone. For a youngster you can get them in slightly smaller sizes, although remember they will eventually grow out of it. Avoid one of the steel strung jumbo models, not only are they bigger and more of a handful to play, but the steel strings will make the initial discomfort of fingering that much harder.

The guitar should have a nice wide fretboard, which enables you to get your fingers across easily when playing chords. The neck itself shouldn't be too chunky, if you can't get all your fingers onto the fretboard easily, then it's not the instrument for you. The fretboard should be nice and smooth as you run your fingers over it; if it feels rough and uneven you could end up with very sore fingertips; if you are in the slightest doubt, go on to another model.

One of the important points to check, is whether the neck of the instrument is straight. This can be done by simply holding the guitar up to eye level and looking along the edge of the neck from the beginning where it joins the body to the nut. A warped neck will result in all kinds of tuning problems and make the instrument virtually unplayable.

On the subject of tuning, always ensure that one of the shop assistants tunes the guitar for you, and then play it yourself for a while (or have a friend play it). Always be suspicious if it takes a long time to tune, and then appears to go out of tune again a little later. If you are in a shop with a lot of guitars, leave the instrument for a while and play some others, then go back to your original one and see if it has kept in tune.

There's nothing more frustrating than having a guitar which constantly goes out of tune, or worse still is impossible to tune in the first place. It is hopeless to try to learn how to play on such an instrument, so the tuning aspect should be a high priority. There are many reasons why tuning problems occur in an instrument, almost all instruments will go out of tune over a long period, and the changing atmosphere has much to do with it. Other problems are minor and can be put right by a knowledgeable shop assistant, but there are always some guitars which are badly designed and will never play well.

Try and play each individual note on each fret, listen out for any that don't ring clearly and also be aware of any rattles and buzzes coming from the instrument as you play, particularly from the sound box and the machine heads. Make sure the machine heads move easily and don't creak when you turn them.

Another important feature of your guitar is what is called the action. The action of guitar is the distance between the strings and the actual frets. A low action means that the strings and fretboard are close together and this makes for easier playing, a high action is one where the two are wide apart and this can make playing difficult.

The string height will increase as you move from the first fret down towards the body of the guitar. If at any time you feel your finger is searching for the fretboard when you have made contact with the string, then the action could well be too high, and this instrument would present you with enormous difficulties.

Always try to play several different models before deciding to buy one. If the shop has some expensive versions of the type you want to buy then try one of those. Ask yourself what the difference is between that and a cheaper model and try to get as near to that as your budget will allow.

If you're buying a new guitar you will presumably get some kind of guarantee, but it's always a good idea to have a chat with the people in the shop, so you can come back to them if you need further help. Finally if you haven't got a piano at home, it's worth investing in a set of pitch pipes to tune your guitar, also make sure you leave the shop with a spare set of

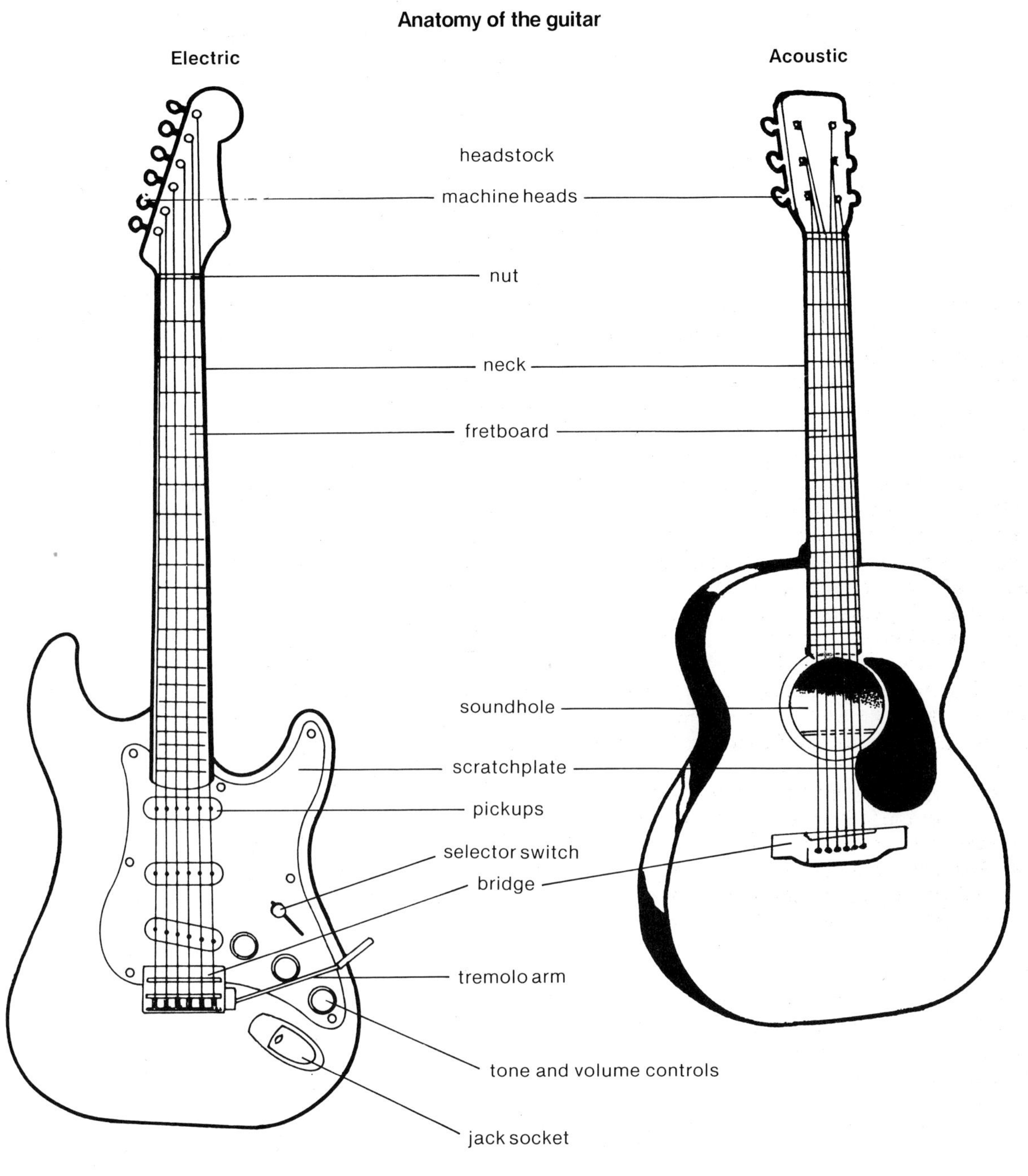

strings and ask the shop assistants to show you how to change them.

Buying an electric guitar

Buying an electric guitar is more subjective. Almost certainly you will have graduated from an acoustic model, and will be of a reasonable standard, so you will know something about the instrument. Nevertheless, it is all too easy to get carried away with the flush of excitement of owning your first electric.

Many of the criteria mentioned in the buying of an acoustic guitar, still apply to the electric, although you will have to plug into an amplifier to get any sound. Obviously you will be limited in your choice by the money you have available, so you must tailor the instrument to suit your needs.

Don't pick a model simply because it looks like the one your favourite guitarist uses. Decide what kind of music you will be playing and try and choose a guitar that will give you the sound that best suits it.

Obviously the amplifier will play an important part in this sound, so when you are trying the guitar in the shop, where possible play it through the amp you will be using.

Make sure all the electrics on the guitar work perfectly and there are no crackles or buzzes. If the guitar has a range of volume and tone controls make sure they all work smoothly. For instance, does the tone control really make a significant difference to the sound, and would it be noticed when playing at volume? Once again, if there is more than one pickup, check that all work perfectly, as do any switches that are connected to them.

One of the major features of an electric guitar is how well it sustains. Sustain is much sought after by modern electric guitarists, and it means the length of time that a note rings out after it has been played. Sustain also varies in actual sound quality. Sustain is a combination of many things like the pickups, the wood of the guitar itself, down to what the fittings are made of. This will probably be the major difference between a relatively cheaper beginners' electric and a top quality instrument. If you get the chance, try to compare the two, and you'll notice the difference.

Always remember when dealing with electric instruments and amplifiers that you must treat them very carefully. If anything goes wrong, don't go poking about with a screwdriver, take the item to a reputable dealer or guitar repairer.

One of the more interesting aspects of the current guitar scene, as has already previously been mentioned in this book's introduction, is the vogue for customising guitars. So if you start off with a cheap electric, you can if you wish, improve it by adding better pickups and other hardware. See p.187 "Guitar hardware" for suggested buys in this category.

Most of the points made about buying an electric can be applied to buying a bass guitar, although this is a specialist field and expert advice is really essential. However one particular point is that it is important to play an electric bass through the right amplification, you can't hope to get by using ordinary amplifiers which aren't specifically designed to take bass frequencies.

The old adage of "you get what you pay for" is certainly applicable when it comes to buying guitars. Nevertheless there are increasing numbers of top quality instruments for both beginners and professionals available today. It doesn't follow that your first instrument has to be cheap and nasty, so use your head and buy wisely. Don't forget, a guitar can be a good investment for the future if well looked after.

Taking care of your guitar

Having bought a guitar, the chances are that it will have cost quite a bit, so you will want to look after it. To get the best out of any instrument it is very important to maintain it regularly, and if it is an expensive or rare instrument, you may well be protecting a very worthwhile investment.

Looking after your guitar is very much a matter of common sense, but there are a few basic points which should be born in mind.

★ Make sure you buy a decent case. Your guitar may well see a fair bit of travelling, so it is wise to invest in a strong, sturdy and well fitting case. If you're going to be doing a lot of gigging, then a flight case is essential, your instrument will probably have to go in a van with all the other equipment, and only a good flight case will ensure survival.

★ Keep your guitar away from excessive temperatures e.g. fires, radiators or strong sunlight. This could seriously affect the wood and cause warping.

★ Always keep your guitar clean, particularly the strings and fingerboard. You will be surprised just how much dirt accumulates there, and just think of all the sweat that is being deposited from your fingers during a gig. Always try and wipe the guitar down thoroughly after a gig.

You can buy cleaning agents for the guitar, and one famous one is Boogie Juice which is a formula created by master luthier Stephen Delft. Boogie Juice gets rid of all the dirt and grime from fingerboards and helps keep them in good condition. It is available from Gigsville, the Aria guitars' distributors.

★ Change your strings regularly. If you're playing a lot this is essential as old strings will give you all kinds of tuning problems.

★ Buy a good strap. The strap is all that holds your pride and joy from crashing to the floor so make sure you have a good one, and that the strap buttons on the guitar are secure.

★ Invest in stands for the instruments when you're not using them. Guitars propped up against amplifiers have a habit of keeling over at the slightest knock.

★ Machine heads. Keep them well oiled so they always operate smoothly.

★ Find a reliable repairer or dealer who you can trust to carry out any repair work that may be needed. It only takes a slip from a screwdriver for an amateur to ruin a guitar's paint finish. Any electrical problems should be dealt with by a qualified repairer.

A to Z of Makers, Manufacturers and Distributors

A

ALEMBIC — Based on the American West Coast, the Alembic company were one of the first specialist guitar makers to concentrate on developing sophisticated, highly crafted electric basses.

They were one of the first to promote active electronic circuitry in their instruments, and use only high quality woods and components. In the Seventies, they undoubtedly set the standard by which other bass guitars were judged, although only the very rich could afford them. Over the last few years, bass guitars have advanced enormously and Alembics have become quite rare instruments although their quality and reputation remains.

ARIA — The Aria Company, who produce Aria guitars, was founded by a Japanese concert guitarist named Shiro Aria in 1956. They were launched in the UK by Gigsville towards the end of 1977, and since then have earned an excellent reputation for producing top quality products at reasonable prices.

The initial success of the PE1000 was followed up very rapidly with a whole range of electrics, which expanded through to basses and acoustics. Along the way, Aria picked up some important endorsees including former Boomtown Rats' guitarist Gerry Cott, and jazz players Ike Isaacs and Herb Ellis.

Their bass range has been particularly successful, with the SB1000 drawing universal praise from players and critics alike, and a major endorsee is the legendary Jack Bruce. Over the last few years, the Aria range has expanded to incorporate just about every type of guitar, and they have become one of the most important Japanese names on the market.

ARMSTRONG — Kent Armstrong, son of guitar maker Dan Armstrong, is rapidly gaining a name for himself in the pickup world. Based in Brighton, Kent's pickups can be seen on Manson guitars among others.

B

BARNES and MULLINS — One of the old established British distributors based in Grays Inn Road, London WC1, they handle a range of the British made Shergold electric guitars.

BARRATTS of MANCHESTER — This Northern based company are the UK distributors of the German Hofner guitars.

BALDWIN PIANO & ORGAN CO — This British arm of the American company are based in Dagenham, Essex, and were responsible for distributing Gretsch guitars in this country. However, the future of these guitars seems to be in some doubt and at the time of writing they were no longer available in this country.

BAILEY — One of the leading lights of the British guitar business, John Bailey wrote books and ran courses on guitar building and repair.

BIGSBY — Paul Bigsby was an early electric guitar pioneer from America but he is better known for the vibrato or tremolo units which he developed for electric guitars.

BIRCH — John Birch was a British guitar innovator of the late Sixties and early Seventies who custom built guitars for many leading players.

BURNS — James Ormston Burns is probably the most famous British guitar maker. His Burns guitars were popular in the early Sixties particularly when the Shadows started to play them. Jim Burns eventually sold out to the American Baldwin company and the range was discontinued. Jim has made various comebacks into the guitar market, but as yet has failed to firmly re-establish himself.

C

CBS/ARBITER — The British distributor of Fender guitars, the giant American company CBS took over the production of Fender guitars in 1965.

CHANDLER — The company formed by Doug Chandler, they are the main agents for Schecter hardware and are also authorised to put together "Schecter" guitars. In their shop near Richmond in Surrey they also carry out guitar repairs and have a stock of rare and vintage guitars for sale.

COOK — Peter Cook is one of the new generation of British guitar makers. As well as making his own highly praised instruments, he is also employed by Rosetti and Co to set up each Gibson guitar brought into the country. So when you buy a new Gibson guitar, look for Peter's certificate of authenticity.

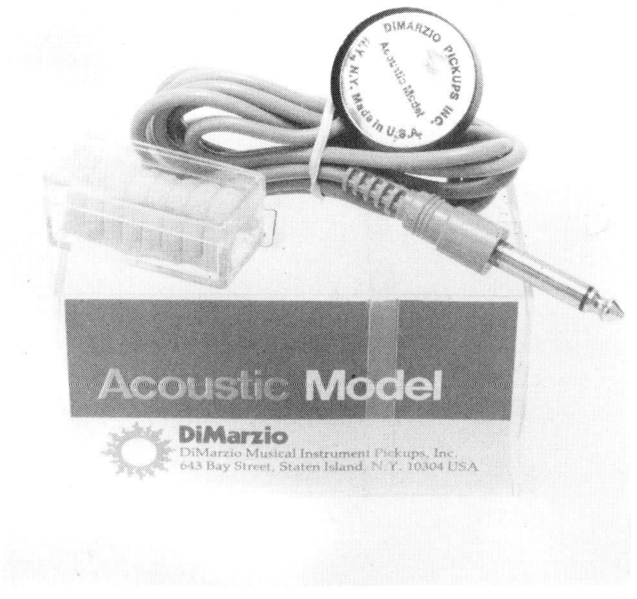

D

DiMARZIO — Larry DiMarzio was one of the early pioneers of replacement pickups and his company are now one of the leaders in the market, offering an infinite range of hardware, and also complete guitars. They are distributed by the Rose-Morris company in the UK.

E

ECCLESHALL — Another of the British guitar makers, Chris Eccleshall's work is detailed elsewhere in this book.

EKO — Made in Italy and distributed by Rose-Morris in the UK, Eko acoustics have a long history of being inexpensive but good value-for-money instruments. The Ranger 6 is probably the most popular model, and is played by students and stars alike.

ELECTRIC WOOD — The name of the company who produce WAL bass guitars.

EPIPHONE — Another venerable old American name in guitars which has always been around but has never seemed to develop into a major force. For the most part existed in the shadow of Gibson, who took them over in the Fifties. Rarely seen in the hands of rock performers, yet John Lennon is seen playing a beautiful blonde model in the Beatles film "Let It Be", and at one time Epiphone Rivoli basses were quite popular. Production was eventually moved to Japan.

EVERBIMES — A comparatively new company based in Nottingham and distributing Leo Fender's latest guitars, the G&L range of six string solids and basses. Unfortunately they were not able to supply us with any guitars for review.

F

FCN MUSIC — The Kent based company of Fletcher, Coppock and Newman are another UK distributor of long standing. They distribute a wide range of instruments including Kapok, Kent, Kimbara and Lorenzo acoustics and Columbus and Satellite electrics although the new Westone range looks likely to dominate the company's electric products. The company also distribute Bill Lawrence pickups.

FENDER — Leo Fender was the inventor of the modern electric guitar and the guitars that he designed in the early Fifties are still being made today, and remain among the most popular instruments. More recently, the CBS company have taken to re-issuing "vintage" models of the early Telecaster and Stratocaster.

Leo himself went back to guitar making with the Music Man company in the Seventies and more recently left them to produce his own G&L guitars.

FENTON WEILL — Henry Weill worked with Jim Burns producing electric guitars before Jim went on to found his own company. Henry carried on into the Sixties and produced quite a range of guitars before closing this side of the business to concentrate on lighting products.

FYLDE — Roger Bucknall began making guitars in the early Seventies and was based on the coast near Blackpool, lending itself to the name of his instruments. Many top folk players possess Fylde acoustics, and Roger even went into producing some electric guitars under the name of Pack Leader — John Miles used to play one. Roger now concentrates on acoustics, which are distributed by Keith Hand.

G

GIBSON — One of the big two of American guitar makers, for many players a Gibson represents the ultimate in electric guitars. Originally started as a one man operation by Orville Gibson to make mandolins, banjos and ukuleles, the rise of the guitar saw the change of emphasis within the company.

From their Kalamazoo factory has come the Stradivarius of the electric guitar, the Gibson Les Paul, in addition to many other classics including the Explorer, the Firebird, and the SG. The company have tried to keep pace with modern development, resulting in the active powered RD Artist and the synthetic Sonex series, but compared with the older established lines, these have met with minimal success.

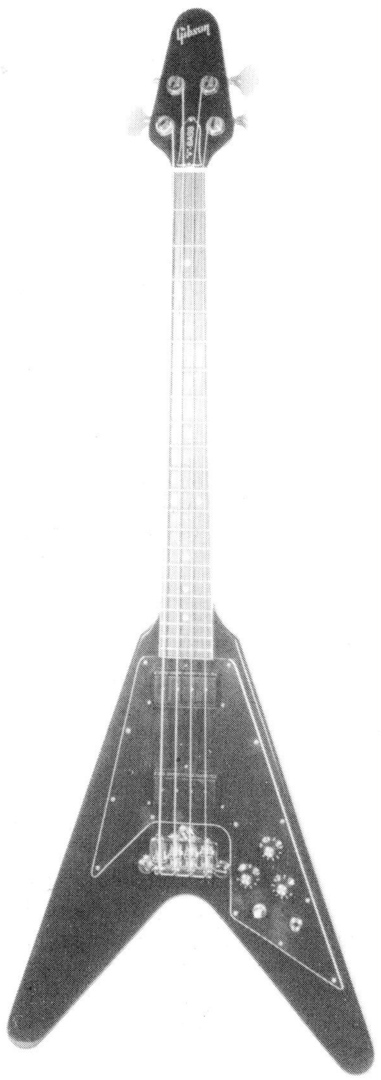

Gibson Flying V

GIGSVILLE — The company formed by Pete Tulett and Terry Mabey in 1977 to distribute Aria guitars in the UK. An important member of the Gigsville team is quality control manager Johnny Joyce, who is responsible for setting up the instruments. The quality of his work has earned Aria top marks in the finesse stakes, and an ever increasing slice of the UK guitar market.

G & L GUITARS — Leo Fender's latest excursion into the guitar market, they are still very much of an unknown quantity in the UK.

GORDON SMITH — The brand name for a group of British guitar makers based in Lancashire. Over the last few years, Gordon Smith guitars have established themselves as one of Britain's leading manufacturers, although their instruments remain hand crafted to a very high standard.

GRETSCH — Another of those old established American names which has always been around but never quite managed a period of sustained popularity. They became synonymous with country guitar star Chet Atkins when he had models named after him. Gretsch guitars have always been expensive and at one time the Gretsch White Falcon was considered the most expensive guitar in the world.

Throughout the Sixties and Seventies you would find odd guitarists using them, but for the most part they just didn't seem to fit in with the image and kind of music that was being played. Apparently production of these guitars has now ceased, so it is likely that they will become highly prized collectors' items.

GROVER — An American company specialising in machine heads and used on many guitars including some Gibsons.

GUILD — The Guild company was founded in New York in the early Fifties by Albert Dronge. Acoustic electrics were among the first instruments he made for jazz players, although some of the up and coming rock and rollers adopted them, including that early guitar hero Duane Eddy.

However, the vogue was increasingly for thin solid bodied electrics so in the early Sixties they introduced the Starfire followed by the Thunderbird, Polara and Jet Star. At present they produce a range of good quality electrics which sell steadily, but the name of Guild today is more associated with steel-strung acoustics.

The acoustics began to take off in the Sixties with the revival of folk music, and the company introduced a range of flat tops including the F-50, D-40 and F-210. Guild acoustics have a very strong reputation, and as well as the flat top six strings, they also make 12 strings and a classical range.

H

HAGSTROM — The Swedish guitar company, Hagstrom, was founded in the Twenties by a farm hand called Albin Hagstrom. He began by making piano accordions and within 10 years was exporting instruments all over the world. During the Fifties, the accordion business began to stagnate and Albin's son Karl saw the potential in providing guitars for the new pop music that was becoming increasingly popular everywhere.

They began making guitars in 1957 and benefited from the music boom of the late Fifties and early Sixties; producing the Futurama guitar which was one of few cheap electric guitars available to young players at that time. Despite Hagstrom guitars cropping up in all kinds of unlikely places (Jimi Hendrix featured an eight string bass on "Spanish Castle Magic" from the Axis Bold As Love album) they never really established themselves in the big league.

They were one of the early pioneers of the guitar synthesizer, but a couple of years ago production of Hagstrom guitars ceased.

HAMER — Another comparatively new American guitar company, founded by Paul Hamer and Joel Dantzig in Illinois. They began by producing a reproduction of the Gibson Explorer which was often used by Rick Neilsen of Cheap Trick, and many others found their way into the hands of top guitarists. They make interesting instruments and are imported into the UK by Guitar Grapevine, Denmark Place, London WC2.

HAND — Based in Bury, Lancashire, Keith Hand is a guitar distributor who specialises in handling British handcrafted products like Gordon Smith and Fylde.

HAYMAN — A British made guitar of the early Seventies, the Hayman was the result of a collaboration of a number of British guitar talents. Jim Burns joined forces with Bob Pearson from Vox, and together with Jack Golder and Norman Holder produced a number of models. The 2020 looked very much like a Telecaster, and the instruments distributed by the Dallas Arbiter company were impressive, but after a few years production stopped. Golder and Holder of course went on to form their own Shergold company.

HOFNER — Together with Hagstrom's Futurama range, the Hofner electric guitars of the Sixties were very often the first electric instruments that a young musician played. Influenced by the American makers, the President, Galaxie and Verithin models were particularly popular, and of course the Violin bass was a firm favourite with Paul McCartney for much of his time with the Beatles.

Despite offering a full range of acoustics, six string electrics and basses, Hofner guitars are rarely seen on stage.

HOHNER — Another German company, they are noted more for their keyboards and harmonicas than guitars. However they do have a range of acoustics, electrics and basses. The electrics have tended to be copies of American instruments, although a new range of guitars is due to be introduced soon.

HONDO — A budget price good value-for-money line distributed by the Leeds based John Hornby Skewes company. Hondos cover quite a range stretching from six string electrics and basses through to acoustics. The Professional Series are made in Japan while the De Luxe tend to be made in South Korea, and it appears that the Japanese-originated products tend to have the edge.

I

IBANEZ — One of the major Japanese guitar manufacturers, Ibanez offer a considerable range of instruments. They have earned a reputation for quality products, and are used by a number of top players. players.

Ibanez have a very strong range of semi-acoustic "jazz type" guitars, and a major coup was endorsement by George Benson, in fact the company went as far as to develop a special George Benson model. However, they have kept their finger on the pulse of the younger player with models like the Destroyer, the Iceman and the Blazer series.

J

JAYDEE — The brand name for John Diggins guitars which he makes in Birmingham. Another excellent British maker, John specialises in adding some imaginative touches to his instruments, like fibre-optic position markers, or markers designed to resemble rings of Saturn.

K

KAMAN — Charlie Kaman is the man behind the revolutionary Ovation acoustics, which have become a prominent feature in the hands of rock players, particularly for stage work. An American, with an aircraft design background, he invented an acoustic guitar which had a bowl made out of a Fibreglass substance called Lyrachord.

Apart from straightforward acoustics, he also developed an Ovation with a built-in pickup and pre-amp which has become almost de rigeur for amplified stage work.

KLUSON — Another American company specialising in machine heads, at the time of writing it appears that the future of the company may be in some doubt.

KRAMER — One of the newer American instrument companies who incorporated new ideas into electric guitar making, offering instruments which had aluminium necks guaranteed against warping or twisting. However, their success was limited, and UK distributors Brodr Jorgensen no longer handle them.

L

LAWRENCE — Bill Lawrence is an American who offers pickup replacements. His products in the UK are distributed by Fletcher Coppock and Newman.

LEVIN — Levin acoustics were popular during the folk boom of the Sixties, in particular the Levin Goliath model. The company became part of the CF Martin organisation in the Seventies and seems to have suffered from the influx of Japanese made steel strung flat tops.

LOWDON — George Lowdon is a home grown guitar maker based in Northern Ireland producing some fine quality acoustics.

LYS — A new name in acoustics these instruments are apparently made in Canada. UK distributors are Tip Top Musical Supplies of Norwich.

M

MACCAFERRI — An Italian born guitar maker, Mario Maccaferri built some very famous instruments in the early Thirties which were used, among many others, by the legendary jazz guitarist Djano Reinhardt. The instrument has a very distinctive shape and originals are much prized collectors' items today.

A number of companies and individual guitar makers have made replicas of the Maccaferri guitars. In fact Maurice Summerfield, the British distributor had a range of Maccaferri guitars made in Japan which the great man himself endorsed.

MANSON — The Manson brothers Hugh and Andy are two of the better known UK guitar makers. Andy is a product of the London College of Furniture's Instrument Technology course, while Hugh qualified as a teacher in Design and Technology.

They make every kind of instrument from electric six strings to lutes and mandolins at their workshop in Crowborough, East Sussex. Needless to say their work bears all the hallmarks of top quality craftsmanship, and their Flying V model, which appears in this book, has to be one of the most stunning guitars ever seen.

MARTIN — The most famous name in the world of acoustic guitars, CF Martin was born in Saxony in 1796. He learned the trade of guitar making there and emigrated to New York in 1833, where the first Martin guitars were made.

Almost every guitar player of note will have a Martin in his collection. Old Martins have, of course, become collectors' items, but the new models have maintained that high level of craftsmanship which makes them among the most expensive acoustics you can buy. Incidentally, the company is still owned by the direct descendants of CF Martin, and is based in Nazareth, Pennsylvania. The UK distributor is Philip York of Frinton in Essex.

MAYA — A range of acoustic and electric guitars made in Japan and distributed in the UK by Stentor Music.

MIGHTY MITE — One of the original spare parts manufacturers, Mighty Mite are still one of the important names in the replacement business. They offer everything from replacement pickups to complete guitars, and are distributed in the UK by Rosetti.

MUSIC MAN — The company which saw Leo Fender go back into guitar making in the mid Seventies. Leo incorporated active circuitry into his guitars, but only the Stingray bass made any real impression on the market. Production of guitars eventually stopped and Leo Fender moved on to G & L Guitars.

O

OVATION — Formed by Charlie Kaman for his Lyrachord backed acoustics, the company also produce a range of electrics including the Viper and Preacher models, but current hopes are riding on the UK II.

OVERWATER — A new British instrument company formed by luthier Chris May and based in Cumbria in the North of England. In keeping with the great instrument making traditions of this country, Overwater go for quality not quantity, and already their basses have gained a considerable reputation. We are likely to hear a lot more of this company in the future.

P

PANGBORNE — Ashley Pangborne is another British maker whose guitars have earned quite a reputation. Distributed by Pangborne Guitars of Reigate in Surrey, the range comprises six string electrics and basses, and models which incorporate active circuitry.

PAUL — Les Paul was an American recording star and guitar innovator when the Gibson company approached him to endorse one of their new electric guitars in 1950. The model wasn't wildly successful in the Fifties and was eventually taken out of production, but in the Sixties Eric Clapton, Jeff Beck and a host of other top guitarists turned it into a much sought after instrument.

Gibson went back to producing the Les Pauls, and they remain one of the most popular models of electric guitar. The two names of Gibson and Les Paul have become entwined in rock and roll history.

PEAVEY — Peavey were well established as amplifier manufacturers before they went into the guitar market in the late Seventies. The company spent considerable time and effort on research and development before they introduced their electric guitars, and much emphasis was placed on their use of high precision manufacturing techniques. A recent innovation has been a guitar case with a built-in amplifier.

R

RICKENBACKER — One of the early pioneers of the electric guitar, Rickenbacker have never been able to challenge the supremacy of Gibson or Fender. Still their products have sold steadily, the 4001 bass being particularly popular. There have been sporadic upsurges of interest with the likes of John Lennon and Pete Townshend playing their guitars in the Sixties, and more recently Paul Weller of the Jam championing the cause.

For a long time the guitars were handled by Wing Music of Bromley in this country, but that association has ended, and the future of the guitars in this country seems unsure.

ROLAND — A Japanese company specialising in keyboards and synths, they have been at the forefront of the development of guitar synthesizers. Their UK outlet is based on Brentford, Middlesex.

ROSE-MORRIS — One of the major wholesalers/ distributors of musical hardware in the UK, Rose-Morris handle Ovation and Vox guitars in addition to DiMarzio hardware. Based in North London they have a modern outlook to the business and in Adrian Legg a guitar technician of the highest order setting up their instruments.

S

SCHALLER — A German company noted for their high quality metalware such as machine heads and bridges.

SCHECTER — Another of the replacement pioneers, apart from a vast catalogue of spares, the company are now putting together their own guitars and many top players are switching to Schecter built instruments.

SHERGOLD — Shergold are probably the biggest and longest established of British guitar makers. Having said that, the company formed by Jack Golder and Norman Holder is still a relatively small operation and owes much to hand crafting.

For a long time Shergold have kept the British guitar flag flying, and their products continue to sell steadily. Among Shergold users can be numbered Mike Rutherford of Genesis, who is often seen sporting a Shergold double necked instrument.

SKEWES JOHN HORNBY — A Leeds based distributor carrying Hondo guitars as their main range, although in the past they used to distribute the S.D. Curlee models. They also have a range of JHS Encore acoustics.

STENTOR — A British distributor based in Reigate, Surrey, Stentor handle a range of Japanese guitars including Maya electrics and Asturias and Hokada acoustics. However, Stentor are also well known for providing parts and tools for guitar makers and enthusiasts. They also handle a range of guitars made by the Manson brothers.

T

TOUCHSTONE — Specialise in providing woods, parts and tools for guitar makers. They are based in Reigate, Surrey.

TRAVIS BEAN — Another innovative American guitar manufacturer, the Travis Bean had a through neck made of aluminium. A number of noted players used them in the Seventies, but they are quite a rarity in this country.

V

VANTAGE — One of the newer Japanese makers, Vantage have quite a wide range of six string electrics and basses in addition to a few jumbo flat tops. They are distributed in this country by Stack Music of Peterborough.

VOX — One of the great old names in British rock music, their amplifiers are legendary and in the Sixties they tried their hand at electric guitars. They didn't meet with a great deal of success but many enthusiasts remember their much vaunted Organ guitars.

Rose-Morris re-introduced the name of Vox to guitarists recently when they launched a range of instruments which were designed by their own Adrian Legg, and manufactured in Japan.

W

WAL — Wal basses are the brainchild of Ian Waller, a well known British musician who turned his hand to guitar building in the Seventies. He teamed up with bass player John Perry to form a company, Electric Wood, in 1977, to produce high quality basses. The company and the product are still going strong, and many top bassists have a Wal instrument in their collection.

WASHBURN — The Washburn company are interesting in that the original George Washburn began making guitars in Chicago about a century ago. An enterprising pair of Americans, Rudy Schlacher and Rick Johnstone took over the name and designed a completely new range which are now built in Japan.

The company make folk, classic, electric acoustic and fully fledged electric models. They are distributed in this country by Roland (UK) in Brentford, Middlesex.

WESTONE — A new name to hit the market over the last year, these Japanese made instruments are set to take the market by storm because of their tremendous value for money. Distributed by Fletcher, Coppock and Newman in Tonbridge, Kent.

Y

YAMAHA — One of the all conquering Japanese manufacturers, they approached the world of guitars with the same thoroughness and professionalism as they did with countless other products.

One of the first Japanese companies to get away from the copy syndrome and produce their own highly individual guitars. Their SG 2000 is now regarded as a classic, and their range of instruments and high quality remains impressive.

Z

ZEMAITIS — Tony Zemaitis was one of the early pioneers of custom built British guitars, He made many guitars for the stars and is noted for his highly individual mother-of-pearl inlays.

Buying Amplification

If buying yourself a guitar seems like a major operation, involving a process of elimination which might have daunted even Sherlock Holmes, buying an amplifier to match it could be just as time consuming — unless of course you plan out your purchase logically beforehand.

The key to picking an amp suitable for your needs is not just to find a sound that you like, at a price you can afford. There are many other factors to be taken into account, like whether it will be small enough for you to be able to transport, whether you can add extension speakers to it or whether it wil take a "slave" amplifier to increase its volume for larger gigs. The list of possible options is as great as the list of amplification equipment available — and there are almost as many amps on the market today as there are guitars.

But, in some respects, the choice should be simpler than that of guitar buying. Amplification doesn't call for that tactile sense of "rightness" which makes you finally buy a guitar and which often leads you to buy an instrument you never thought you would consider. Buying an amp can be a purely cold, logical decision, provided your criterion of a good sound is met. So, how do you go about it, and what is on the market today that is worth considering?

Probably the first exercise should be undertaken sitting down with a piece of paper and a pen. Ask yourself some key questions. Once you've answered them you'll be in a position of having narrowed the field down to at least half the equipment on offer.

What you have to consider first is the purpose to which your new purchase will be put. Will you be taking it on the road for massive world tours (well, we can all dream, can't we!), playing country and western gigs in pubs, practicing at home? Establish what you want your amp to do and you're far less likely to be disappointed with it later on.

As a guide it might be suggested that a practice amp would certainly be a combo and would need no more than, say, 10 watts rated output power. Many manufacturers offer equipment of this type and so the choice becomes a matter of finding the right sound at the right price, although facilities such as built-in reverb, effects and possible future up-grading of output power will also be factors worth considering.

The next type of amp is one for smaller gigs, pubs and clubs, rehearsals etc. and will, again, almost certainly be a combo amp. These days you're going to have to invest in about 50 watts of power for a guitar if you want a reasonable sound without the distortion of an overdriven amp (suitable for some purposes, of course, but it should only be there when you want it there) and at least double that for bass guitar. Bass is always a problem, the lowest frequency of a bass being difficult for the ear to detect at equal volumes when compared with a higher (guitar) note. Furthermore bass frequencies are relatively hard for speakers to reproduce, so bass amps will be discussed separately.

A typical choice for a pub and club guitarist would be a 50 or 100 watt combo amp with the power delivered into two 12" or two 10" speakers. If portability is a problem then advantage can always be taken of the better quality of modern speakers and the same load be delivered into a single 12" speaker. Whether you actually *need* a 2x12" or 2x10" or would find a single speaker amp sufficient can only be a matter of personal choice, largely based on sound and transport questions.

Moving up the scale from there, we come to the rock player who either needs the sheer muscle power of a bigger amp to get his sound across to a larger audience or to give him that characteristic "overdrive" tone beloved of rock musicians since its discovery by players like Beck and Clapton back in the early 1960s. For this sort of work there is really a wide choice of equipment, ranging form high-powered 100 watt 1x12" combos through twin speaker jobs and then up to the "stack" — a four speaker (or more) cabinet driven by a separate "head" with an output rating of at least 100 watts. Beyond that we're in the dizzy heights of multiple linked stacks, say four 100 watt valve heads, each with two 4x12" speakered cabinets — the typical set-up of a heavy rock professional player.

Bass players, as we've seen, have their own quite definite set of general needs. Their problem is to obtain sufficient dispersal of their sound, free from distortion, to a venue which may have many acoustic problems (like hollow wooden floors, stages which cause loss of frequency transmission etc.). Furthermore, bass players are often rather poorly served by the equipment makers, some of whom take the basic circuitry which they have developed for guitar use, put this into a combo, adjust the tone frequencies and replace a 12" speaker with a 15" model — calling the result a pukka bass amp. It isn't, of course. Bass calls for specially designed cabinets (sometimes with acoustic designwork such as reflex

General shot of a selection of H H gear.

porting and folded horn construction) and pre-amplifier circuitry which will enable the player to compensate for any specific problems his gig might present.

Beginners, or those who just want to play at home, will often have problems finding good practice bass amps, so I will recommend some suitable amps a little later on.

As with guitars, there really are no rules at all for amplification. There are too many brands to choose from, each with their own very special qualities and ranging in price from around £35, to set-ups for fully professional use costing several thousand. Likewise you may feel that your own style calls for a louder or quieter amp than I might have suggested earlier. That's fine, but the golden rule (and I would suggest that there is just this one) is never buy an amplifier on impulse. Think, first, what you'll be needing and then shop with that in mind.

Practice amps for general guitar use come in two very distinct types: those which offer excellent sounds and wide ranging tonal facilities (often at a very high price) and those which cater for the absolute rock bottom of the market. Often the prices of the luxury mini-amps seem extortionate but it must be appreciated that it costs almost as much for a manufacturer to make a small amp as it does a large one. The components which actually produce the volume in a power amplifier stage cost relatively little, as a proportion of the selling price. What costs the money are the myriad little things like potentiometers, knobs, wooden casings, aluminium chassis, and these are required in small amps just as much as in larger models — hence a 15 watt amp doesn't cost proportionately less than a 50 or 100 watt one. Each extra facility costs much the same to add, whether it's going to be built into an amp delivering 10 or 100 watts. So don't be surprised if it seems hardly worth buying small amps with up-market features.

Of the basic practice equipment currently available there are several rather gimmicky devices which, contrary to their appearances, can be useful. Powered headphones (for example) enable you to plug straight into your guitar's output socket and play through to the "cans" with total security. They may not have the sound of a 100 watt Marshall top but they can have their uses, especially for hotel rooms, tuning-up, holidays, coach travel and suchlike. Quite a few players find these devices useful.

There are also a few tiny Oriental amps which plug directly into the guitar and contain a mini-speaker. These are no larger than a matchbox and have a jack built-in. In my experience they are often so quiet as to be inaudible in anything other than a totally silent environment and tonally are usually very poor.

However, two Japanese makers offer exceptionally good amps in ultra-small packages, these are **Aria** (whose Loco range has much to commend it, especially price) and **Roland**, whose Cube series of mini amps even caters for 100 watts of bass in a small package with a remarkably good sound. Of the practice amps that I've come across I'd have to say that these two ranges are probably about the best — better by far than the legendary (but frankly less than impressive) American-made Pignose. Both the Loco range and the Rolan Cube series are loud enough to be used for rehearsals and recording, but there are other choices available, especially if one is prepared to opt for a physically larger package.

There are several UK manufacturers of

amplification equipment catering for players whose requirements are for a good sound at low volume levels — equipment which sounds professional enough to be used for full rehearsals and yet can produce a good rock lead guitar sound at relatively low volume levels when required.

The first to spring to mind are **Carlsbro** whose all-transistorised amplification range covers just about every need from the rankest beginner to the complete professional. At the bottom of their line are two amps, the Hornet guitar combo and the Cobra bass combo. These are both very reasonably priced and can get astonishingly close to the sound of a full-powered amp on solo overdrive whilst actually delivering low sound pressure levels. The Hornet features a single 10" speaker and has some very useful extra qualities, such as a mid-frequency tone control section which operates on a "parametric" basis. Parametric equalisation systems (as they are properly known) employ two, rather than one, controls. The first selects the *individual* frequency to be altered and the second gives the level at which it is to be reduced ("cut") or raised ("boosted"). The idea behind this is to offer a finer degree of precision in tone settings and, more importantly, a far wider range of sounds. Many of the best studio mixing desks employ this general principle and to find it on an inexpensive guitar or bass combo is a pleasant surprise.

Parametric equalisation is becoming increasingly common on modern amplifiers and is always a good sign. Traditional tone controls merely squash or raise one frequency and sound quite dull by comparison. They are fast losing out to "active" tone systems, of which the parametric type is one of the best. Extremely basic amps may still offer no more than two controls — volume and tone, but better can be had if one is prepared to spend just a shade more money and it would certainly be well worth stretching one's budget a little.

Another UK manufacturer who offers a very creditable series of amps suitable for the beginner or those with more modest needs is **Custom Sound** who produce the Trucker series, a range of equipment aimed specifically at this market. Whilst the actual Custom Sound amps are on a par with those of such well known lines as HH and Carlsbro, the Truckers offer exceptionally good value for money and would suit a lot of players. In the Trucker line is the 2-5 Lead combo which delivers 25 watts into a single 10" speaker and can be had with or without reverb built in. Currently the recommended retail price of the 2-5 with reverb is around £134, which makes it good value for money.

Even the technologically "up-market" **HH** can provide good equipment for those whose needs are rehearsal and practice but who are short of cash, and the recently launched Studio Series from this maker is a conscious attempt to cater for this market. Although more of a rehearsal/stage amp than a rehearsal item, I've recently spent quite a bit of time using an HH Studio Sixty combo and found it to be one of the best sounding amps that this maker has offered.

By the time one gets into this sort of volume level (50 watts and above) the whole market opens out, as just about every maker offers at least one amp (and usually far more) in this market sector. Here's where the task becomes daunting as there is such a wide choice.

It may be advisable to set your requirements on the bare minimum of facilities you require and then start listening hard to the sounds which other players whose work you admire are using. If you are working in a vacuum it should still be possible to get close to the sounds that you want, certainly it will be easy enough to find out what people use (musician's magazines regularly give such information on interview subjects) and a good music shop will be able to guide you if you can tell them the type of sound you require.

Many amps these days will give you several basic sounds which can be widely varied — but all amps have their own distinct "voices" and you'll find that however close you can get, the best way to get *exactly* the sound used by such and such a player from a Fender Twin is to go out and buy yourself one! Of course this may well be beyond your financial resources and so you will have to find the sound you want by another route. This is the old principle of trial and error and will entail you going round the music shops, guitar in hand, trying amp after amp until you find what you want. Here there are a few definite rules to follow; by and large if you stick to them you won't go too far wrong. Firstly, get to know the *type* of amp you want. Let's set a few more very rough guidelines which may, provided you don't regard them as 100 per cent fixed, help you in your choice.

A practice amp should be lightweight but sturdy. They can be run from the mains but some will work with batteries as well. Regrettably, to give reasonable battery life when delivering power of about five watts or above, manufacturers are often forced to use large and expensive batteries. A case in point is the **Vox Escort** practice amp which can be obtained in a mains/battery version. This uses two PP 9 batteries which cost over £1 each. Other battery powered amps will also cost you a fair bit to run so bear that in mind. If a totally portable amp is what you need then perhaps you should consider buying a set of Ni-Cad batteries which are rechargable. Most battery sizes (but *not* PP 9s) can be bought in this form and, although the initial cost is high you can save a small fortune with them over a few years. Basic facilities you will require are a volume control and tones plus a speaker capable of handling the delivered power. There have been some really *terrible* practice amps made over the years and you should check yours in the shop by running it flat-out to see that it will actually do what it's supposed to.

A major plus factor on the best type of small amps (and this applies to larger amps too) is some type of built-in distortion system. Some amps offer this via an integral fuzz effect (which goes under a variety of names depending on who is offering it) and others do it by supplying a twin gain system whereby you can turn up the gain on your pre-amplifier, turn down your main volume and overdrive the amp that way, giving a vaguely similar sound to that obtainable from a fully driven amp. These vary from the highly effective to the highly repulsive and your ears should be the best guide. If you don't need that effect, fine. Most players these days, however, do and it should be there on your practice amp to accommodate that need.

In may well be that this provision obviates the whole necessity for buying a practice amp at all. The ability of many stage amplifiers to reproduce their distortion tones at low output power levels by employing fuzz effects or pre/post gain settings means that they can be used as quietly as you like whilst still sounding pretty reasonable. If you're looking for an amp which will work on stage at, say, 50 to 100 watts and it will double as a practice amp, so much the better because, as we've already seen, the economics of production costs nearly always make the bigger amp better value. The only advantage of the out-and-out practice unit is its portability, when compared with the value for money and stage use potential of a modern combo.

Let us assume that you are looking for a guitar amp which you can use at medium sized gigs, which has good facilities for practice and rehearsal use and which will give you the sound you're looking for. Think carefully about your requirements. Are you ever going to need more power than this? If you anticipate playing bigger gigs then is it worth going beyond the 50 watt level, and if so, where on earth does one stop? For the time being stop here. You know that you want a 50 to, say 75 watt amp. Next ask yourself whether it will be used solely by you or whether another musician will have to share it. This is something to be wholeheartedly avoided, of course, because few amplifiers will comfortably cope with more than one instrument at once. If you *must* do it, however, then you'll need a twin channel amp. That's, at least, one question answered!

Secondly, do you have size problems? Fifty watt amps can come in many sizes and many different speaker configurations. If transportation is limited to public means, then a 1 x 12" combo is all you'll be able to manage. Bigger than that and you'll be rather unpopular with the conductor, and that's not to mention the other passengers! But is a single speaker 50 watt combo as good as a twin speakered one? Well, it all depends on how the cabinet has been designed and, of course, on how good the speaker is. Provided the speaker quality is up to scratch, 100 watts can be quite a reasonable figure for a single 12", so don't worry too much about that aspect. The reason why some makers use single speaker set-ups and others don't, indeed why many offer both types is simply to do with taste. Some guitarists feel that twin speaker amps sound louder, some sound better — it's all down to personal taste.

Having established whether size matters, and to what extent, whether you need single or twin channels, what money you can afford to spend etc. it is now time to start thinking about sound quality. Here too you should ask yourself what you want your amp for. It you intend to play Heavy Metal lead guitar then, frankly a very cheap transistorised 1 x 12" combo with no fuzz facility and no pre/post gain arrangement on offer is *not* going to make you sound like Ritchie Blackmore. On the other hand, it may be perfectly suitable for a player whose needs are simply for a good clean sound to play jazz or country and western.

Now you should be in a position to know roughly what sort of amp you're after. You have the output power, size, number of channels (or inputs on a single channel amp) thoughts about how many speakers you will need and that's quite a lot of data to be going on with.

So how do you decide which brands to look at? I would strongly recommend asking any musician friends you may have what they've used. If a friend uses an amp that you like then go ahead and buy one. Your experience of hearing opinions about its reliability and performance will be worth far more to you than any trial in a noisy, crowded shop could ever be.

Likewise, read reviews in the musician's papers and magazines, see what brands your favourite players use. Ask local bands whom you know what experiences they've had. If they keep telling you brand X has broken down every third gig and the manufacturer doesn't seem to care, then you too should steer clear of that maker in the future.

Even if you don't know any other bands or guitarists, don't be shy of asking a player you've been to see what he thinks of his amp's performance. Most musicians love shop talk and will be only too willing to be horribly honest with you if they feel they've been ripped-off! Now you have even more data to go on. So perhaps it's time to drop in on your local music store and see what's on offer.

The first thing to beware of here is the retailer who seems over-committed to one particular brand. He *might* have so much of it because he likes it or, equally, he might have a lot of it because he was offered the best discount by this particular firm. Don't be too swayed if he tells you that his brand is the only one that's any good. By all means try what he has to offer but also find another dealer who has other gear and try that too. It's your money, after all.

The particular market we're talking about here (the basic combo) is about the largest in the world and you're faced with trying to pick just one amp out of that. Price will help a lot, the parameters set above will help too — but from here on it's down to your ears. If you know what you're looking for, fine, your own tastes will guide you through all that maze of amplification like nothing else can. But what if you're just starting out? Well, why not take a friend with you, someone who knows more than you do and can act as a guide?

Having spotted an amp which you like the look of and which appears to offer all you want now's the time to try it with your own guitar. That is essential by the way. Every guitar reacts differently with every amp and your's may sound rotten with brand X which sounded fine in the shop with a borrowed Gibson. Insist that you be allowed to take your time over making your choice. Don't be rushed and don't buy the first amp you see. Listen to several makes and several samples from each make. Try the tone controls — will they give you the flexibility of sound that you want? Does the amp sound as loud as it could? Make sure you try it at full power too. Some combos can be badly under-provided for in the speaker rating department and, although they sound fine at low power in a shop, can distort in quite the wrong way when turned up fully on stage or at rehearsal.

After trying several different brands you like, you can start to think about making up your mind. Try to resist the temptation to get a lot of help from one dealer and then go to another to actually buy because he's £10 cheaper — that £10 is probably going to be worth ten times that amount when you have a problem in six months' time.

One point here which you should know about relates to quoted output power figures. Watts are, really, a rather meaningless term. In acoustical theory the figure you need to know is the sound pressure level measured at a fixed distance from the speaker, a fact which, unfortunately, no-one I know of, quotes. An amplifier might well deliver 50 watts average (normally quoted as RMS) into a 12" speaker but some are far more efficient than others. The number of speakers and the size and design of housing can help or hinder here too, so don't be surprised if two amps, both rated ostensibly the same, sound relatively louder or quieter than each other. There is more to volume of sound than a mere figure quoted in watts.

Also don't be puzzled if a trial of a 100 watt amp makes you feel that the 50 watt version sounds almost as loud. Subjectively speaking, 100 watts is not double 50 watts at all — the progression here is not a direct arithmetical one and, in fact, a good 50 watt amp will often only sound marginally less powerful than its 100 watt running mate. Nevertheless professional users playing larger venues will probably opt for at least 100 watts. This could either be in combo form or maybe a "stack", the latter comprising a separate amplifier head riding on top of one or two (or even more) separate speaker cabinets. In the past it used to be true that speakers simply were not good enough to handle 100 watts in a combo, but advances in design have changed this and there is a growing trend for amplification backlines to shrink in size away from stacks, down to high quality combos — some retailing for enormous sums.

For professional use it has to be taken for granted that the potential customer already has some experience of owning several amps and is thus far better placed to make a choice than the absolute beginner. He already knows which brands he likes, which speaker types he prefers, what he needs his amp to do plus what extra facilities he could make good use of. He is possibly more worried than most by absolute sound quality and total reliability — the latter consideration being particularly vital to him. Accordingly you can usually take it for granted that any brand of amp regularly seen on professional stages is capable of meeting these criteria and will be a safe buy — and this can help the less demanding purchaser too.

Facilities these days are becoming more important than they have ever been. The time was when massive guitar amplification was called for by the professional player simply to make himself heard at the back of the cinema venues, which constituted the ubiquitous touring environment of the 1960s. Eventually it was found that (especially in America) it just wasn't possible for a decent sound quality to be obtained this way and so players began reproducing all of their instruments via a PA system, as opposed to just the vocals, as had been the case in previous years. Finding that jamming a mike in front of a cabinet didn't always get the best sound routed to the mixer (especially with bass guitar amplification) road crews started taking direct feeds from amps to the mixing desk. Soon amp makers began offering this feature as standard and most amps will now allow a jack plug to be inserted somewhere on the back panel to feed a signal to a mixer (a system known as "direct injection").

The growing use of effects units created difficulties too, as some highlighted or caused noise problems. Some makers, therefore, have a "send" and "return" facility for effects units, enabling them to be interfaced with the best part of an amp's circuit for optimum low noise qualities. Built-in effects (like phasing, chorus and others) are sometimes offered too but these are generally not popular as most players prefer to choose which effects they want to buy from individual specialist makers. One "on-board" effect that *is* worth having is reverb, the sub-echo sound which is produced either electronically or by a spring device in the back of a combo. Generally speaking, spring echos in combos are nearly always better than electronic ones but the quality of their sound can vary from amp to amp (even if they are all using the same brand of spring like the Hammond or Accutronics type) and it is as well to check this area out when trying various amps.

Tone controls too can be rather more complicated at this end of the market (especially on bass amps) and double or even triple parametric systems or possibly graphic equalisers are offered by some makers to give the widest possible tone flexibility. Again, assess your potential purchase by ear. You may not need or want an amp with 1,000 sounds — two or three might be all that you need, so why buy a model with surplus knobs to twiddle (and pay for)?

People will pay a great deal of money just to get the particular sounds that they want, a tricky choice as it isn't just speaker type or size, tone controls or cabinet design or similar factors which cause the distinctive tone of one particular amplifier. There is one extra major factor which can have an effect on sound in guitar amps and this has caused more controversy during the past ten years than any other single factor, and that is whether the amp in question uses valves or transistors to produce its sound.

Valves are, obviously, the traditional way of amplifying sound. Originally they were the only way of doing it, using technology borrowed and adapted from the makers of televisions and radios. But in the early 1960s transistors evolved which could give power levels as high as those from valves and many manufacturers decided that the cheaper cost of making amps with these "solid state" devices and their theoretical advantages of reliablity, would make them an instant replacement for the cumbersome, heat producing, old fashioned valve of the past. As with all new ideas there were early teething problems and many older players recall the industry's first fumbling steps with transistorised amps with a laugh or a shudder — depending on whether they'd been unlucky enough to buy one. But technology improved the transistor and the reliability problems became a thing of the past. Surely *now*, amp makers reasoned, the guitarist would abandon the valve? Well he didn't.

By this time it had been discovered that an overdriven valve amp would produce that classic rock solo guitar sound which almost every player seeks. This, put at its most basic, comes from overdriving valves so that their output runs into distortion, producing even order harmonics which naturally sound sweet and warm to the human ear — that expressive, creamy guitar sound produced by players like Jeff Beck and Carlos Santana. Until no more than two or three years ago there was still no amplifier using transistors that sounded like a valve when overdriven. So professional rock players were buying them in preference, as soon as they could afford to pay the considerable price difference between the slowly made, cumbersome circuited valve amps and the increasingly easy to produce solid state. Recently, a handful of transistorised amps have appeared on the market capable of such a good imitation of the "valve sound" that it is becoming possible to accept them as reasonable substitutes — but still the majority of professional guitarists stick with the valve which is why some makes (Marshall, Peavey, Fender, Mesa Boogie, Hi-Watt) are still so popular with professional players. These manufacturers make mostly all valve units and their owners usually believe that the sound they give cannot yet be reproduced by transistors. They are probably right, of course, but the gap has narrowed recently.

For all that, valve amps remain an expensive professional tool and will probably become increasingly expensive as their hand wiring costs and the scarcity of valves (fast becoming a problem) counts against them. For all that, there is nothing to touch a fine valve amp for the discerning guitarist who can appreciate the difference between the two and it is unlikely that 100 per cent conversion will ever be made.

One option open to players is to go for a hybrid amplifier — one which uses solid state devices to run the pre-amp (tone controlling and initial amplifying stage of the amp) and which then converts over to valves for the vital power amplification parts. American makers **Music Man** have used this technique for some years and have some notable players (including Eric Clapton) using their equipment. During the past year a new British maker, **Pro-Amp** has come on to the scene using a similar principle and they are fast becoming one of the most important new brands on the market, as there has been, until their arrival, fewer and fewer valve amps available. For the poorer player, or the one who doesn't need the traditional valve sound, transistor amps are good enough — more than good enough in most cases. Either way it's a problem which need not concern all but those who have a lot of money to spend — valve amps do not come cheap!

Before discussing some individual products, it's time to look at bass guitarists and their special (not to say peculiar) needs. As we've seen, the bassist needs a totally different set of facilities to those of the guitarist. He needs more power, he needs a cleaner sound (few bass players use distortion and thus transistorised amps tend to be more acceptable here, even for the pro players) and he needs, above all, a good speaker system. Probably the classic bass speaker is the 15" type. This forms a happy compromise between the guitarist's 10" and 12" speaker and the old fashioned (but far too bassy for modern use) 18" type. Fifteen inch speakers will handle bass guitar superbly well and enable players to play an open E with as much conviction as a higher, fretted note — assuming, of course, that the speaker cabinet around the speaker has been properly designed, and this is an art in itself.

Because of the difficulties associated with amplifying the bass guitar successfully, it is generally true that the better bass amps switch from combos to head/stack set-ups before guitar amps do. True, there are good 100 watt bass combos but, not forgetting our principle of a bassist needing about double the power of a guitar player, 50 to 70 watts might arguably be considered the limit unless one is thinking in terms of luxury equipment where massively expensive speakers and complex housings have been designed for bass combo work.

Bass players, more than guitarists, need tremendous tonal ranges in their equipment and one is accordingly finding more and more makers offering graphic and parametric equalisers for bass use, combined with some very clever types of speaker design. For all that, bass amp buyers must be rather careful. There is a definite strain imposed on any speaker required to handle regular full power bass and so players must be sure that their speakers can take full power for long periods without undue deterioration in their sound. This calls for a full power test in a shop and a careful enquiry to see that the speaker is rated by the maker as being about twice the rated output power which the amp itself will deliver. Hence a 50 watt bass amp should have a speaker capable of taking 75 to 100 watts.

Bass frequencies can rattle cabinets apart and shatter internal components too, so it is well worth thinking hard about a head/speaker set-up if you need loud amplification. If your guitarist can get away with a 50 watt combo, you may need a 100 watt bass head and a speaker housing containing, say, two 12" or two 15" speakers to compete night after night.

When buying bass gear apply all the criteria your guitar playing colleagues use but, above all, question whether a combo is enough for you and go for twice his power. Make sure that even at full whack your speaker compartment doesn't rattle nor does the speaker sound "flappy" or "buzzy". Look also for good tone control systems. These will often be of the active kind and never assume that such features as parametric equalisation or graphic equalisation are gimmicks. They will enable you to shape your sound precisely to what you require with this most difficult of instruments.

So great are a bass player's problems that many professionals have chosen what amounts to a virtual PA system to amplify their instrument, a complex array of speaker cabinets, power amplifiers, pre-amplifiers, just to get a satisfactory sound in large venues. Admittedly we are talking here about fully professional equipment designed for large venues, but some of these player's ideas are beginning to filter downwards into semi-pro equipment.

Professional bass players break their sound down into segments. Their instrument plugs into a separate pre-amplifier and then a lead is taken from that to a power amplifier such as a Crown or HH (some of both types capable of giving out well in excess of 500 watts!). In extreme cases there are actually two or three power amps, each fed with only a portion of the overall tonal spectrum. One power amp will have high frequencies (selected by a device called a "crossover") another mid and another low. The highs will be fed into small speakers, the mids into mid-size units and the bass probably to a specially designed enclosure which uses one of the many patterns suitable for reproduction of the very lowest tones with absolute purity. Armed with this 500 watts, 1,000 watts, even 2,000 watts of power, the modern bass player will be able to get the sheer muscle power and tonal purity which he needs for large auditoria.

So successful have these latest ideas in bass amplification been that even some semi-pro equipment is offering versions of the same idea — most notably the **Carlsbro Stingray Pro-Bass** combo and head amps which offer built-in bi-amping (running two power amps, each driving a separate speaker section but run from a common pre-amp) as a feature.

Another trend is for bass guitarists to go even beyond the power level of twice that of a guitarist to achieve as much tonal integrity as possible. 150 and 300 watt rated bass heads can nowadays be found in even modest equipment ranges; for the most part designed to be used in bands where the guitar player(s) uses 100 watts.

From practice amps to the most advanced fully professional items of gear, the key to what you need is a shared proposition between purely mechanical considerations, like output power, number of channels, effects and suchlike, and the individual sound of one particular amplifier. This last criterion can only really be a personal matter and one would hesitate to give too much advice in that area because of the problems conflicting tastes can cause. On the technical front, however, it is possible to be more definitive.

We've already seen that practice amps at their most miniscule can be either battery powered or can run from the mains. Does one need both? Well, that can be provided. Pricewise the two Japanese brands mentioned earlier (**Roland** and **Aria**) aren't really that cheap, although they both offer first rate quality, probably good enough to use for professional recordings, especially if a clean sound without heavy distortion is all that is needed.

If the price levels of these two amp ranges are off-putting then UK manufacturers **Badger**, offer some interesting practice amps at very reasonable prices and the latest (but not the earliest) amps from **John Hornby Skewes** (the JHS range) are not at all a bad buy.

One of the best practice amps on the market (although its plain looks account rather strongly against it) is the **Satellite** amp available from **FCN Music**. This can be driven rather powerfully into overload and yet will also suit a player looking for a clean undistorted sound at bedroom levels. The current RRP of this battery and mains amp is around £60 and it isn't bad value at all, especially if it can be found retailing at a discount.

Moving on from bare minimum practice amp levels to items which will suit both rehearsal level *and* practice level, one immediately thinks of the two **Carlsbro** amps previously mentioned — the 30 watt **Hornet** guitar combo (currently recommended at around £144) and the 60 watt **Cobra** bass amp (one of the best small bass combos I've tried) which retails around a suggested price of £243. This may seem a big jump compared to the Hornet but that's just the bass player's curse coming in to effect. He needs the sound quality and, regrettably, it costs money.

If the Carlsbro looks like too much money then the **Custom Sounds Trucker** 6-5 bass might be another choice. This offers a single 15" speaker, gives around 65 watts and sells for a recommended £163. Many makers offer good quality lines in these price ranges, **Ohm**'s 60 watt bass combo (about £230) is a well designed and manufactured item as is the rather pleasant **HH Studio** 60 bass at about £217. I am making no claims here to be exhaustive in my suggestions. What I'm doing is covering a few of the makers whose equipment I have tried and whose products have impressed me in their respective ranges. Between the above, for example, there is some difference in sound and you would be advised to listen to all of them before making any sort of decision.

Guitar players will find that they have even more choice than bass guitarists but, as so many of their needs are based on a very subjective assessment of sound, it is very hard to judge their tonal requirements on an advisory basis. Still, most of the major UK makers offer a wide range of combos in this market area ranging from whistle clean transistorised amps to those which offer some provision for forceful rock lead guitar. Of the clean amps, possibly one of the best known lines over here is the **Performer** range produced by **HH**. For guitar players who value a good quality of design and clean sound with impressive technical specifications then this line must have potential. One of the major advantages of a clean, distortion-free sound with plenty of sparkle to it is in the amplification of acoustic guitars and here the HH Performer range would be especially useful. Their recently introduced **Studio Series**, a budget priced line, curiously comes closer to the archetypal rock

The Peavey Classic combo.

guitar sound that the Performer range (which was, I have been told by HH, designed mainly for cleaner sounds anyway). The Studio bass combos are pretty good, as we have seen, and their **Studio** 60 1x12" guitar combo (selling for around £212) or, better still, the 2x12" 100 watt version (about £299) are upholding a reputation HH have long had in this country and on the continent, of providing very fair value for money, coupled with excellent quality of design and manufacture for the semi-pro player. Other famous makers, like **Carlsbro, Custom Sound** and **Peavey** must be considered too.

The next stage of equipment is for those players who really do need something to take out on gigs, which is larger than the 50-60 watt combos suitable for pubs and small clubs. This is getting nearer to a professional level and by the time you're ready to buy this sort of equipment your previous experience should have told you a lot about what sound you personally seek.

Assuming that your band will now be miking-up the amplification backline through your PA it may be that a good 100 watt combo for guitar, or a head with one or two cabs, will be what you need. Bass players now virtually have to abandon combos altogether, and start thinking about separate amps and heads. To ask for a clean 150-200 watts from a bass combo is really going too far, except for one or two specialised pieces of equipment like the phenomenal **Trace Elliot** 150 watt 1x15" combo (selling at £624) or the less luxurious and far less advanced **Fender Studio Bass** combo. Despite the latter's lack of technical sophistication it is one of the very few valve bass combos left on the market and has a warmth of sound which some players may still seek.

If this sort of money is still out of your price bracket, bassists can find a large number of good quality bass heads on the market, delivering the required 100 to 300 watts with good tonal range and reliable performance. Makers like Custom Sound and Carlsbro, Vox, Peavey and HH all offer equipment in this price range and there is often little other than personal taste in sound and the number of specialised facilities on individual models to recommend one over the other. This is a very competitive segment of the market and the intense competition in it has improved the product.

Again, most makers offer speaker cabinets to go with their amp heads but it isn't always wise to feel you must match amp brand X with speaker cabs from the same maker. Look around. You might find that another manufacturer can supply a similar (or even better) cabinet at a lower price. True, it's often hard to tell which speakers are used by which makers, but use your ears and remember that those who use prestige, high-quality speaker makes, will not usually wish to keep the fact quiet!

For guitarists the choice available here is baffling. There are so many good quality 100 watt combos on the market these days that it can only be a matter of personal taste in sound that makes the choice possible — plus available cash, of course! If you are happy with a combo then a great rock guitar sound can be got from **Peavey's VT Series**, especially if one can afford to opt for models using their **Scorpion** speakers. The **Deuce** or **Classic** combos are especially impressive. With these, of course, we're beginning to get into the realms of valve amps and, at last, the real valve overload sound is becoming a practical proposition. As we've seen, this sound costs money but pro guitarists seem to feel it's well worth it. For those who still cannot afford it, or who just don't need it, then combos like the **Roland JC Series** have their supporters. If Roland amps appeal to you but the valve sound is what you want, then this Japanese maker is one of the few orientals who have a valve amp to offer in their **Bolt Series**. These have some excellent features (like effects interface in a loop system for low noise) and sound really good. At £400 the **Bolt 60** may seem over-priced but it has a fine sound and if one is miked-up then it is plenty loud enough.

The classic valve amp comes from makers **Marshall**. Their range runs from newly launched transistorised combos to valve combos of devastating sound quality. The 2x12" valve powered **4104** retails at around £299 (recommended price) and

The Roland Bolt 60.

is quite remarkable value for money. It may only be rated at 50 watts but, like the Bolt, it belies the mere rating of its power by sounding exceptionally loud — ideal for both stage and recording use.

Vox too, have a new 125 watt valve combo on the market, which promises to be interesting. Meanwhile American makers **Fender** and **Music Man** also have their devotees. Music Man are tremendously expensive but have a sound which is quite unique; clean and yet warm at the same time. Fender, on the other hand are the traditional amp of American guitarists and their peculiarly transparent and yet vital sound tends to make them the first choice for players who want that sort of sound.

The very top end of the market, however (which is where we're straying now) is where the field narrows in terms of options, but gets progressively idiosyncratic.

Bass players now can consider bi-amping their instrument, feeding one set of speakers with low frequencies and another with highs. One or two amp heads offer this facility as a built-in option for players who cannot afford to do it by using expensive (often studio based) components. **Carlsbro** are one example. Their **Stingray Pro Bass** head can push out 300 watts and has that built-in crossover unit to feed a separate slave amp which can then, in turn drive a second speaker set. It's excellent value for money at around £372.

To go the whole way, specialised pre-amps can be manufactured or bought off the shelf. Traditionally these are then run through an American power amp (the **Amcron DC300 A**) but there are now other choices such as the remarkably good **HH MOS-FET** power amps like the **V500** and **V800**, capable of delivering massive output power into large bass enclosures and with a wealth of high technology internal devices to ensure reliability. Carlsbro too have recently entered this market with a new line of power amps (too new for anyone of my acquaintance to have tried yet) and American maker **BGW** have their adherents too.

Many of these power amps (and the designers who make and offer the bass speakers for professional use) are originally based in the PA field and a player seeking this type of equipment will find himself dealing out of the normal run of group equipment makers. Just one company, however, **Trace Elliot**, have developed their own range of specialised stacks and heads with luxurious features and rugged constructional qualities. Prices are high compared with semi-pro and even ordinary pro gear, but a set-up like their **GP 11** (pre-amp with 500 watt twin channel power amp and electronic crossover at £596) plus, for example, a matching 2x15" 200 watt cab (£228) is close enough to the ultimate bass system for any professional user.

Guitarists, fortunately, are never called upon to use so much expensive equipment. A 100 watt **Marshall** valve head will cost them only around £311 and matching 4x12" cabs cost approximately £210 apiece. This may seem to be an ultra-traditional set-up but it still holds much attraction for guitarists — especially among Heavy Metal bands. But the choice isn't just restricted to stacks. The **Pro amp** range can offer a remarkably good hybrid valve 100 watt 2x12" for only £363 and there are numerous other high quality valve combos around.

One maker whose reputation seems to be enduring (and whose valve combos and heads are among the most impressive I have tried) is **Burman**. Manufactured in Newcastle they may not be so easy to come by, but the Burman professional quality combos are the equal of anything on the market and are highly favoured by many lead guitarists. The **Pro 2000** gives a rated 140 watts into two 12" speakers and currently sell for £681. Like other specialised equipment (including such esoterica as **Session, Lion, Mesa Boogie** etc) it may take some hunting down, but Burman's equipment is amongst the highest professional quality equipment available.

Despite predictions emphatically made by proponents of the solid state amplifier, it can readily be seen that by the time we start looking at fully professional equipment, valves are still very much alive for the guitar player, even if they are rarely used by bassists. Recently many players were delighted to hear that the famous UK maker **HiWatt** was back in business following the takeover of the company by its employees, after the tragic death of its founder and designer, Dave Reeves. It looks as if the valve amp will just keep on going — whatever the pundits might say. Even old stalwarts like the **Vox AC30** (seemingly overpriced for a very basic 30 watt 2x12" combo) remain ever popular, despite having been on the market for years. Many players maintain that an AC30 just cannot be beaten for sheer sound quality and as most professional bands replay their equipment through a PA system, is an AC30 really too quiet? Some guitarists would maintain that it certainly isn't.

For more modern players the 125 watt **Vox V125** stack could well be just the thing, with a very aggressive — not to say violent — sound. The younger player who wants a professional sound but cannot afford this luxury valve equipment is, thankfully, better served than ever before by the mass market manufacturers like Carlsbro, Peavey, HH and Custom Sound. Year by year their transistorised amps get closer to the valve sound (Peavey offer both types, of course) and it is now possible to get close to the real thing with solid state devices.

Bass players too are getting better and better sound for their money. Who would have dreamed that a bass combo as good as the little **Carlsbro Cobra** or **Ohm** 60 watt would have been possible ten years ago? Despite the apparently bewildering complexity of choice the good gear is all there waiting to be bought. If you plan what you want in advance, listen and let your ears do the deciding between equipment of similar specifications you can't go wrong. Just remember that your amp is as vital a part of your overall sound as your guitar and should be chosen with as much care.

The perfect guitar for you is the one that suits *you*, not one that, necessarily, everyone else likes. The same goes for amplifiers too. And when that perfect guitar and that perfect amplifier mate — the effect for the player is magical. So keep on looking — they're both out there somewhere! **Gary Cooper**

Chris Eccleshall — profile of a British guitar maker

The modern guitar market is very much dominated by American and Japanese manufacturers; the Americans, by virtue of developing the modern instruments, and the Japanese by utilising their high craftsmanship and incredible manufacturing techniques. However, between these two giants, British guitar makers have carved out their own special niche which over the last couple of years has grown substantially.

Britain may never be able to challenge the hierarchy of the big two in terms of manufacturing guitars on a large scale, but the quality of British guitar makers is second to none. And there is a long tradition of British luthiers which is being worthily carried on in small workshops up and down the country today.

The history of the British guitar goes back a long way, to the middle of the 19th Century. Prior to this there had always been very good violin makers, and also craftsmen making citterns which were a forerunner of the guitar. However, one of the first names to register as a specialist guitar maker was that of Louis Panormo. He came from a family of violin and guitar makers, and had a workshop in the West End of London in the early 1800s.

Panormo was making guitars at the same time as C.F. Martin, and apparently rivalled the quality of the American instruments. Panormo's guitars had a distinctive headstock, similar to an inverted horseshoe, and there are still some of these fine old instruments around today. After Panormo, things seemed to go in fits and starts, and it wasn't until the 1920s that a significant British maker emerged.

Jack Abbott was probably the next big name in guitar making, and in the Twenties he was producing Gibson type cello guitars. His son took over in 1935 and carried on until the Second World War. One of the next names to appear was that of Emile Grimshaw, who made banjos and arch top guitars. This period also saw the rise of the Clifford Essex company who were based in London's West End. They had a craftsman named Marco Roccia working for them who turned out some exceptionally fine instruments.

Clifford Essex, like so many old British companies, had established a very good reputation as banjo makers. In the Twenties and Thirties, this was where the great demand lay, and even old Gibson catalogues of this era sport only one flat top guitar amid their many other stringed instruments ranging from banjos to mandolins.

The Fifties saw the birth of the electric guitar, and in Britain this meant Burns guitars. Jim Burns was the designer and Jack Golder was the foreman of the workshop — Jack is still going strong today with his Shergold guitars, and remains the largest British guitar manufacturer.

The music explosion of the Sixties failed to provide Britain with a guitar industry to rival foreign competition, but it did herald a whole new era of British guitar craftsmen. Suddenly many of the top guitarists were going to people like Tony Zemaitis and John Birch to have a guitar custom built. Quite simply, it meant that rather than having to rely on finding a suitable guitar in a shop, the musician could go to a specialist maker and tell him what kind of guitar he wanted, and the craftsman would design and build to these specifications.

One of the major figures in this development was John Bailey. Not only did John make guitars, but he also started classes on teaching other people how to make them, and wrote books on guitar making. Initially John started out as a craft teacher who made a few guitars himself. He began to teach guitar making and as a result courses and evening classes were instigated which were to have a profound influence on many young aspiring guitar makers. Indirectly, this work led to the setting up of many courses and the foundation of the Instrument Department at the London College of Furniture.

Today we are seeing the benefits of those innovations with the great upsurge in British guitar making. People like the Manson Brothers, Peter Cook, George Lowdon, Chris Eccleshall and Ashley Pangborne together with Gordon Smith guitars, the Overwater company and Electric Wood. All these makers produce high quality instruments, but whereas in the Sixties, hand crafted guitars were only for the superstars, today it is possible for anyone to order a handbuilt guitar at a price to suit their pockets. Since the rise of the dollar over the last couple of years, British handbuilt instruments have been able to compete with American and Japanese products. While no one home grown company is likely to swamp the market, the British made guitar is becoming an increasingly important part of the guitar industry.

British guitar making is still essentially a cottage industry, with guitar makers working in tiny workshops. Most of these makers have no wish to produce large volumes of instruments, because it would mean a departure from handcrafting and therefore lead to a decrease in quality. For an insight into this small but important band of craftsmen we take a look at one of them.

Chris Eccleshall has been making guitars full time for about 11 years. He works in a small workship in Ealing, West London and is typical of many who had to struggle first to gain the necessary training for guitar making, and then fight hard to establish himself as a guitar maker during an era when most people were unaware that guitars could be made in this country.

Chris originally came from Gosport in Hampshire and had developed an interest in woodwork from an early age. His interest in guitars also led to him making his first guitar by the age of 11, but Chris faced an uphill battle to use his guitar making ideas in his woodwork classes at school. "The only subjects I was good at at school were woodwork, technical drawing and English, and I used to concentrate on woodwork. The standard test piece if you were doing woodwork was making a firescreen, but as we lived in one of the first centrally heated houses in the road it wasn't really much good me making one so I insisted on making a guitar.

"I made my first guitar when I was about eleven in the back shed with a hacksaw, an old chisel and a screwdriver scrounged from Dad. I've still got it, and it's really not too embarrassing. I think my interest in making guitars, stemmed from my interest in playing, but I was also fascinated, like many little boys, in pulling things to pieces and trying to put them back together again."

Chris was lucky in that the boyfriends his older sister had all tended to be guitarists, and they used to get rid of him by giving the youngster their guitars to have a look at. These were the only guitars that he saw, and the majority of them weren't very good, but he vividly remembers seeing his first really good guitar, a pink Fender Stratocaster.

"When I was about fourteen, my sister went out with a guy who was well in with some of the American Forces and they got him a Strat, which was the first one I'd ever seen. It was around 1962 and it was a pink one, so I started on solid electric guitars by pulling apart a pink Fender Stratocaster — a model which you could name your own price for these days!"

Once bitten by the bug, Chris was hooked and he used to save up his pocket money to go into Portsmouth and have a look in the music shops. There were no such things as Japanese guitars around then, it was mostly Hofner Presidents and Framus guitars. Gibsons began appearing in the Portsmouth shops in about 1964, but by and large Fenders were still virtually non-existent.

When the time came to leave school, Chris decided that he wanted to be involved in guitars, and in particular learning to make them. However, openings in those days were few and far between and none of the instrument makers he wrote to would take him on and eventually he had to settle for an apprecticeship at the nearby government Fleet Air Arm helicopter yards as an aircraft engineer. Although he only stuck it out for a year, Chris found the training invaluable.

"Looking back it must have been a phenomenal training scheme because I learned so much in that one year. It gave me a very good basic training, and I still remember things they taught me. It taught me the principle of precision because being a government training scheme everything has to be done perfectly, they will accept nothing less. So it taught me from an early age, high standards and precision fitting of parts and how to present things properly, which has been very useful.

"However, after a year I got a bit restless and travelled the South Coast, eventually ending up at Hastings with a violin maker called John Howard Lucie. He took me on as a part time assistant, and as well as making violins he also used to repair them, so I learned quite a lot. Eventually he said that he couldn't do much more for me and that he'd put my name down for an apprenticeship with a firm called Hill and Sons in London and I was to go up there the following Monday.

"Hill and Sons turned out to be the number one violin company in the world. They were established in something like 1680 and are still going strong today, and always had a reputation for being the best craft training centre."

Training at Hill and Sons was very much the traditional way of doing things, and Chris came under the influence of brilliant craftsmen. Here he learned the intricacies of instrument making and the skills needed in every process. After a while he left the company to work for another violin specialist, Ealing Strings, who were just starting up in West London.

Despite all his work and training on violins, Chris still found time to make and repair guitars. He was putting his new skills to good use, and more and more friends were coming to him with their guitar problems. Gradually, the musicians' grapevine spread the word about Chris Eccleshall, until he was spending eight hours of his working day making violins, and a further eight hours making guitars.

Fortunately, Ealing Strings allowed him to use their workshop in the evenings to make guitars, but the long hours were beginning to take their toll, and after two years with the company he had to make a decision about his future.

"All of a sudden in January 1971 I got a whole burst of orders for some unknown reason. It was probably only four guitars with a total value of about £90, but it was a lot then. So I left Ealing Strings and my landlady allowed me to use a shed at the bottom of the garden. I stayed there for about three months until a workshop came up in nearby Ealing Common, which is one of those I still have today.

"Everything was in the one room, and I had very few tools, and no power tools. I probably had half a dozen chisels, a few gouges and all the violin making tools. I had very few jigs and patterns and making these is the expensive bit of this business, but I've steadily built mine up over the years."

Things were far from easy in those days and Chris was literally on the bread line to begin with. Business was steady but very slow, and one of the major problems was the very fact that he was entering a

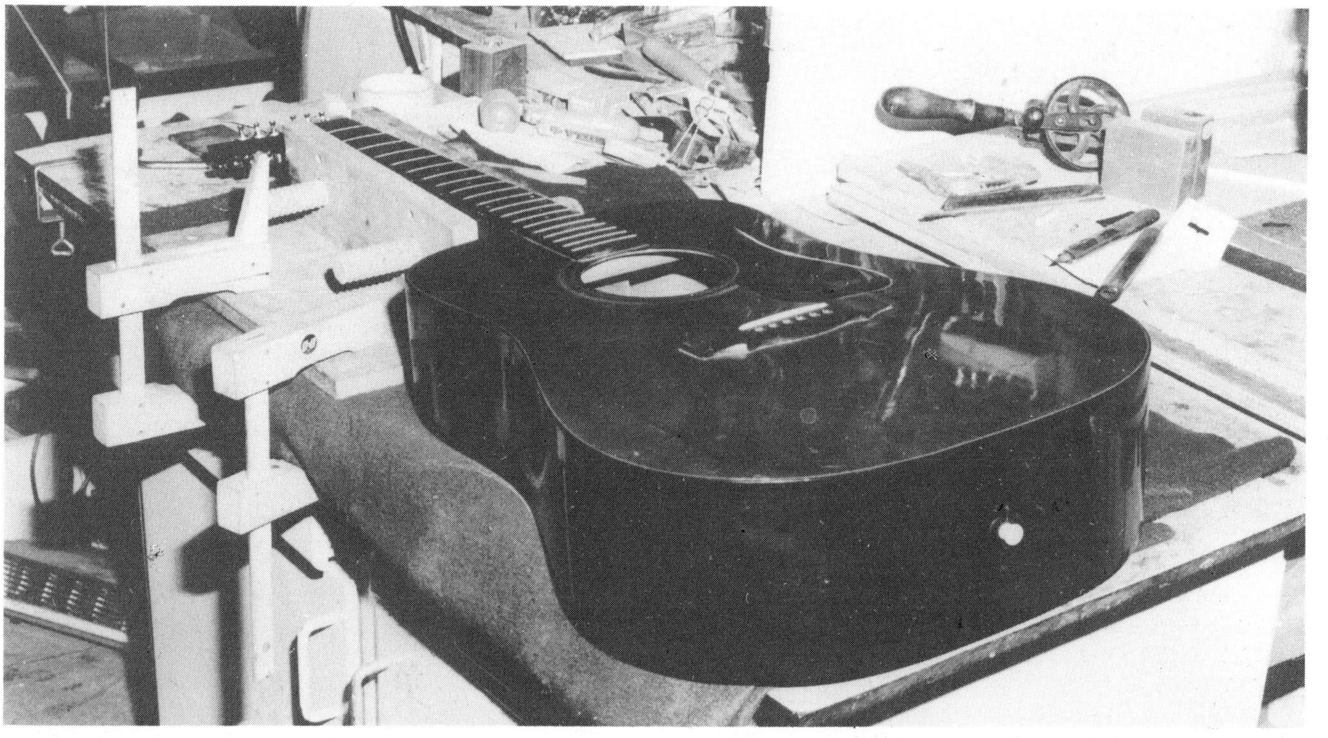

Acoustic body clamps.

fairly unknown field as far as most people were concerned. Tony Zemaitis and John Bailey were still only known to a few people, and there was still the attitude of "nobody in England makes guitars" prevalent among the suppliers of materials.

"The major problem in the early Seventies was to get the metalware and the fittings. The last couple of years has seen a great emphasis on the accessory market, but then you couldn't buy a Tun-O-Matic bridge, replacement pickups or even a decent set of machine heads. Wholesalers just didn't stock them and I've spent a long time battling with people to bring spare parts over. If I've achieved anything in this business, then it's to get them to bring over spare parts, just by being persistent.

"Now it has blossomed into a huge industry in its own right, but I was in there nagging them out of necessity. I couldn't afford to get huge amounts of spares so I had to badger people, but most wholesalers then wouldn't give you the time of day. If you phoned up a firm about some wood and told them you wanted it to make guitars they'd say, 'we don't have anything to do with guitars' and just put the phone down. The pure ignorance of a lot of people was astounding. The difficulty then was not making the instruments, but getting the materials."

There were times during those early days when Chris felt like giving up, but his dogged perseverance won through. He soon learned the importance of getting to know roadies, who often know more about the equipment than the musicians anyway, but more significantly they have a whole information network of their own. So if one brings a job to a guitar specialist and gets good service, he will pass the word around to other roadies and they will bring more work to you.

"I was very lucky in the early Seventies in doing work for the Alan Bown Set and that helped create other work. Then Rory Gallagher just phoned up out of the blue and said he had some guitars that he wanted fixing up, and I've been doing his guitar work ever since. Through his roadie I met other roadies and got into bands like Sweet, Roy Wood and Slade.

"All these bands were on 'Top Of The Pops' in the early Seventies and everyone was trying to outdo each other in the guitar world. It was the era of the silly guitar with John Birch making the Super Yob guitar for Slade. I did a couple of star shaped guitars for the Glitter Band and a really silly shaped one for Sweet. From there things steadily built up, I learned more and widened the range of models."

Although restoration and repair work forms an important part of his business, it is the guitars that Chris designs and makes himself which really make the whole thing worthwhile. The main emphasis is on quality rather than quantity, and more about spending a lot of time on one model rather than seeing how many you can make on a production line basis. Chris and his assistant Kevin Chilcott will probably only make a maximum of a couple of guitars a week.

As far as acoustic guitars are concerned, Chris has some very hard and fast ideas, and from the outset designed his own models rather than copy established ones. Now he finds people adopting some of his ideas into their own designs, while for electric guitars he tends to be more influenced by Gibson patterns than Fenders.

Materials for guitar making are fairly pre-set, the predominant woods being mahogany, maple, rosewood, ebony and spruce with ash and alder used for solid guitars.

"Fortunately now in England there are firms who specialise in cutting and supplying woods. Being well

Assorted hand tools and chisels.

established, I can go to the source and buy wood in board form and then get it re-sawn to specific diameters, which is very important. There's a very good guy called David Dyke who's absolutely brilliant at re-sawing and re-planing to specific dimensions.

"I've discovered other specialist suppliers over the years where I can get things like boards of Honduras mahogany — the best you can buy — and I use that as standard. Gathering the right woods together involves a lot of time and effort and you've got to be prepared to go out and look for it. I've had a couple of scoops where people have rung me up offering Birds Eye maple."

Chris has gone to similar lengths to find the best hardware to fit to his guitars, his choice of machine heads for example, would surprise many people. "I always use Japanese machine heads made by Gotoh because to my mind they are the best you can buy. I started using Schallers, then Grovers and then someone gave me Gotohs to try. I was impressed and so used more, they work beautifully and I've never had any trouble with them so I stick to them.

"I use Japanese-made bridges and tailpieces because they do an excellent job of the finer finishing of metalware — that's for Gibson style instruments. For Fender style I think Schecter make the best Telecaster and Stratocaster bridge units. I generally use Seymour Duncan pickups because I think he knows more about it than anyone, although Bill Lawrence makes some good ones, and I also make some of my own.

"I tend to switch around products, picking out the best bits for a specific end result. I make all guitars to custom order so sometimes people specify the parts they want. If they leave it to me, I shop around and pick the best parts which will be relevant to that specific guitar. The acoustic guitars are fairly pre-set because I make all my own fretboard bridges and all the bits and pieces."

Having assembled all the materials, just how does one go about making a guitar, namely a solid electric guitar? Obviously there is no easy straightforward way, but Chris gave us a brief outline of the processes and stages involved in putting together a solid electric instrument.

Stage One

This first stage is one of design, you've got to choose a pattern to start off with. You can invent your own design or take something like a Fender Telecaster, which is the easiest solid guitar to copy. It's flat, so you can put it on a board and draw an outline around it either on paper or cardboard, although Chris tends to use thin plywood.

With a solid guitar, the thickness and density of the wood under the bridge mounting area, combined with the type of bridge a... ...tal used, affects the sound very noticeably. ... outline doesn't seem to affect the so...

Above ... — an explorer type (left), Fender Te... ... mandolin (right).
... ...tterns showing different guitar bodies.

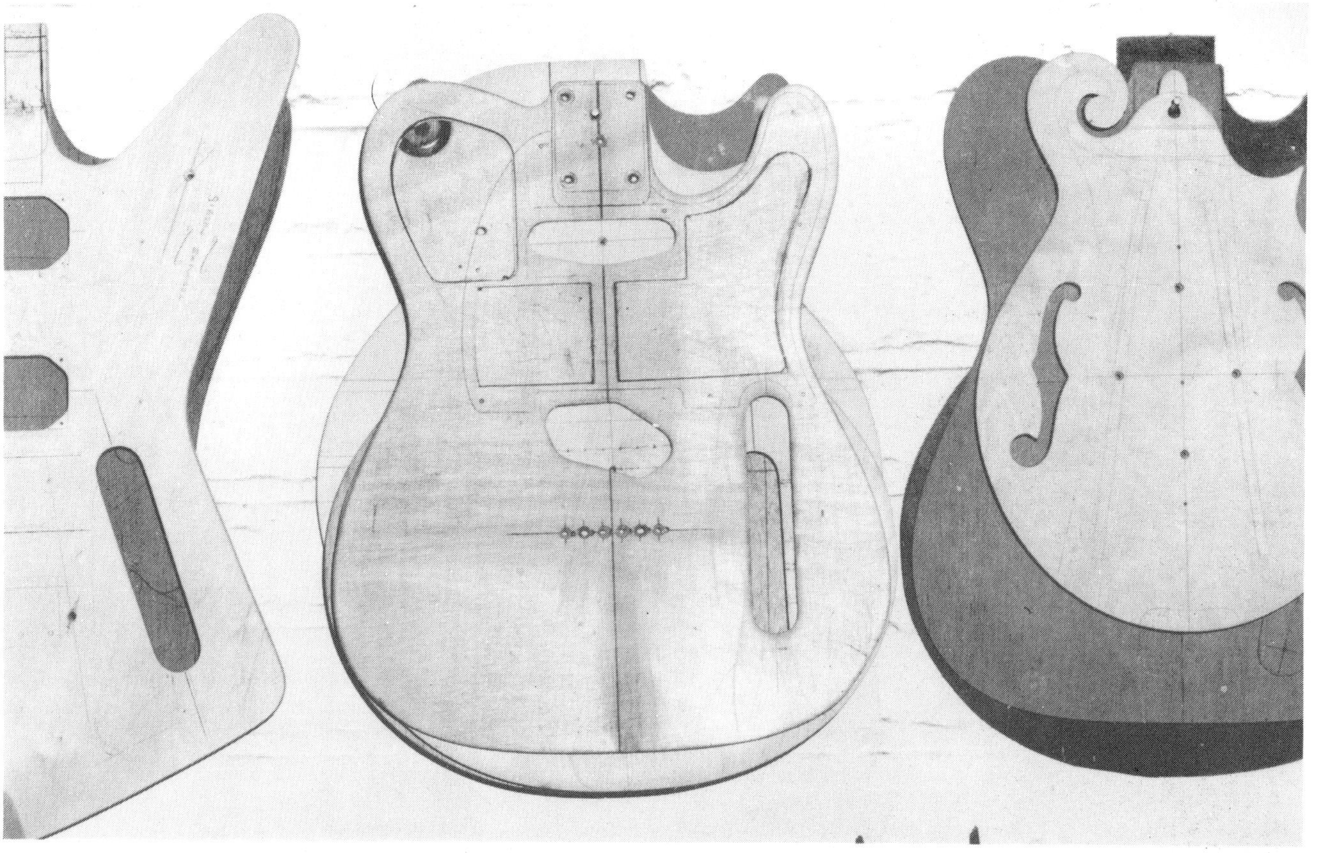

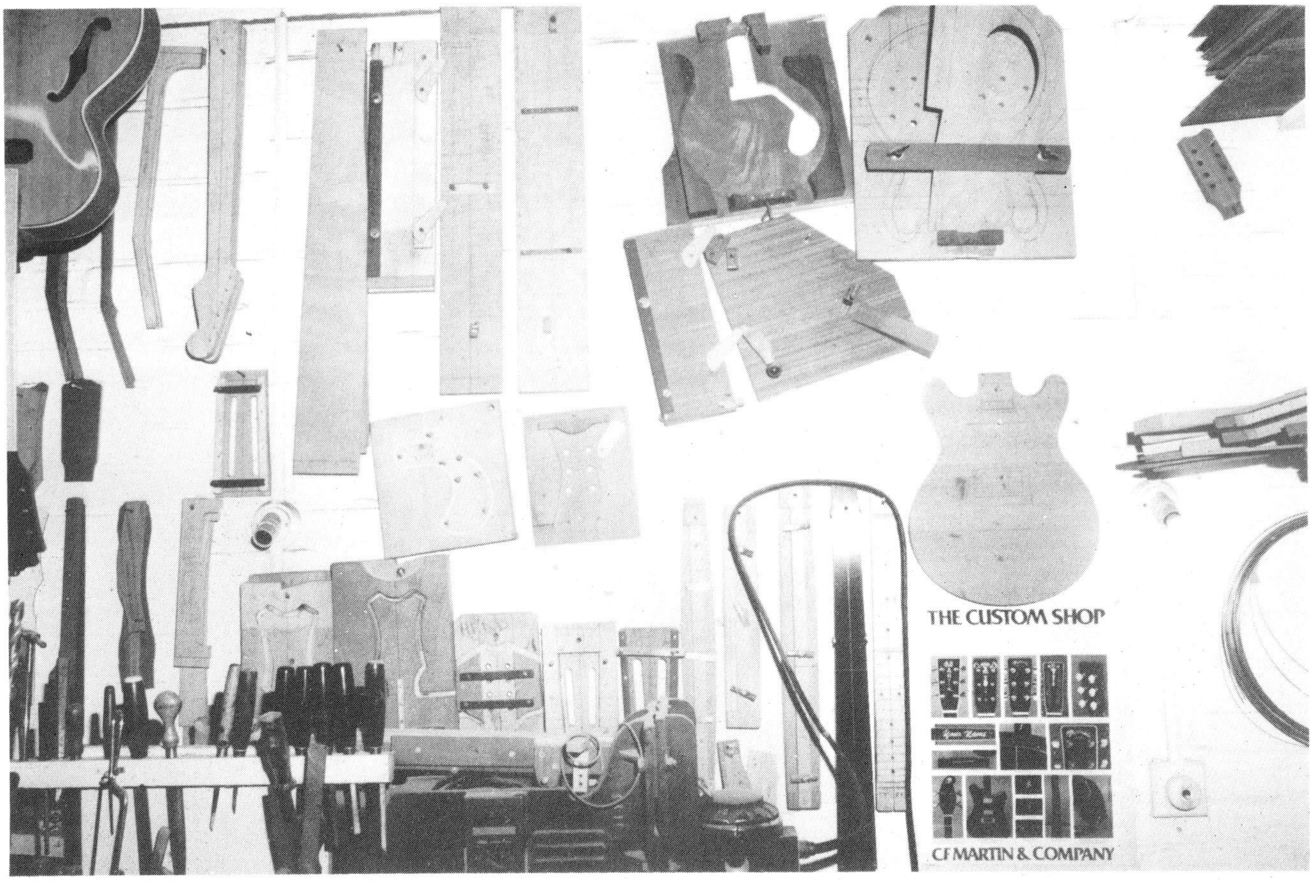

Above: router jigs for profiling necks and bodies, the router machine (at the bottom) cuts them out.

Below: a selection of carved bodies showing (l to r) violin, a 335 type and an F5 mandolin body.

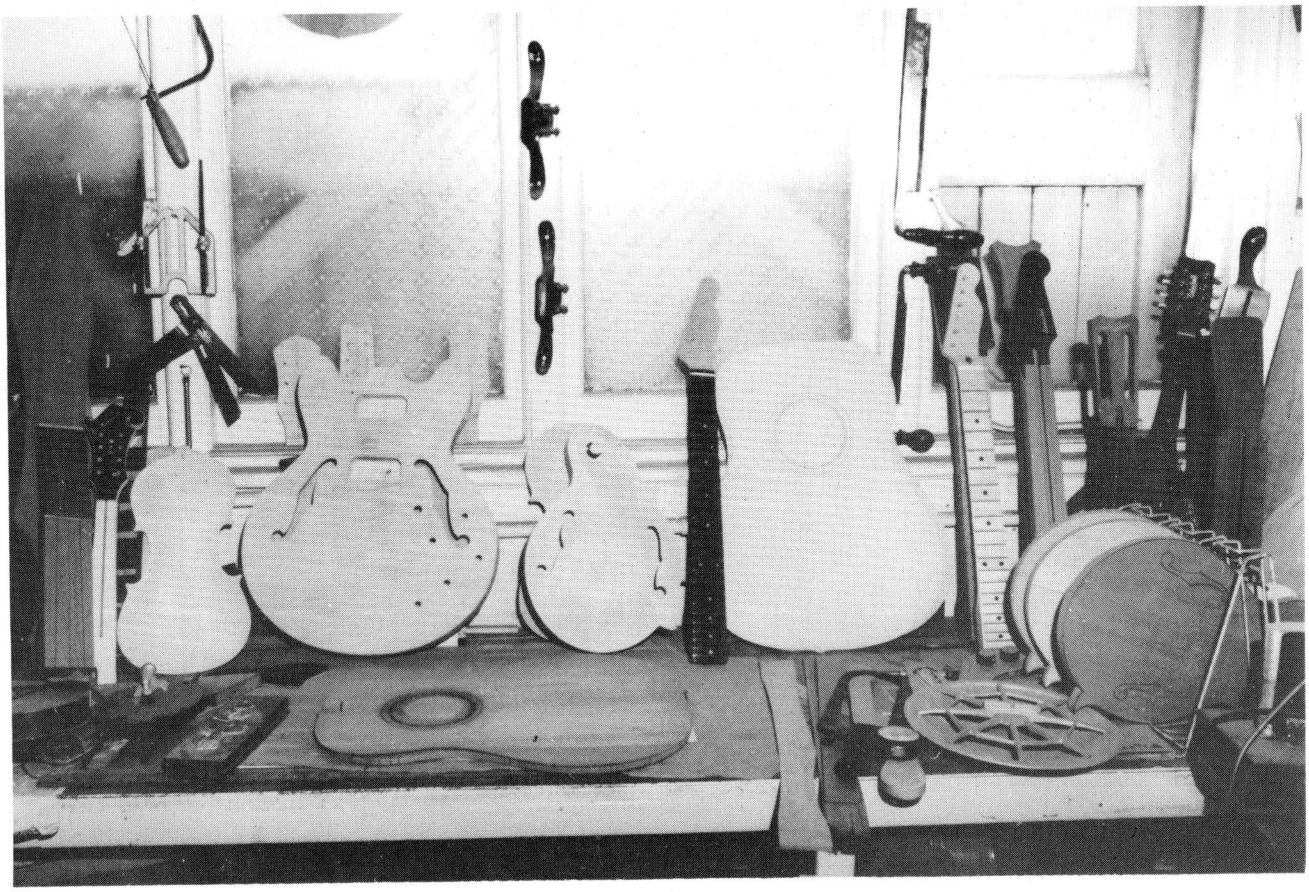

Stage Two

This stage involves the assembly of the materials. For the body you need a blank of wood, either one whole piece or spliced up into various pieces. You draw around the body outline, using your pattern and then saw it into shape using either a hand saw or fret saw. The professional will use a band saw because it's faster and more accurate. The edges have to be finished with a file and sandpaper, and then you begin the neck.

Stage Three

Chris comments, "I've noticed that with all the spare parts available over the last couple of years, people have been making their own bodies and buying in a ready made neck, and then claiming that they've made their own guitar. But the neck is the difficult bit, and until you've made a neck properly you can't say that you've made your own guitar."

For a Fender style neck, the neck is cut from a flat billet of maple, and a channel cut down the middle for the truss rod. You can buy ready made truss rods these days, although Chris makes his own.

Neck blanks — the left is a single side headstock, the right has a three-a-side and truss rod fitted.

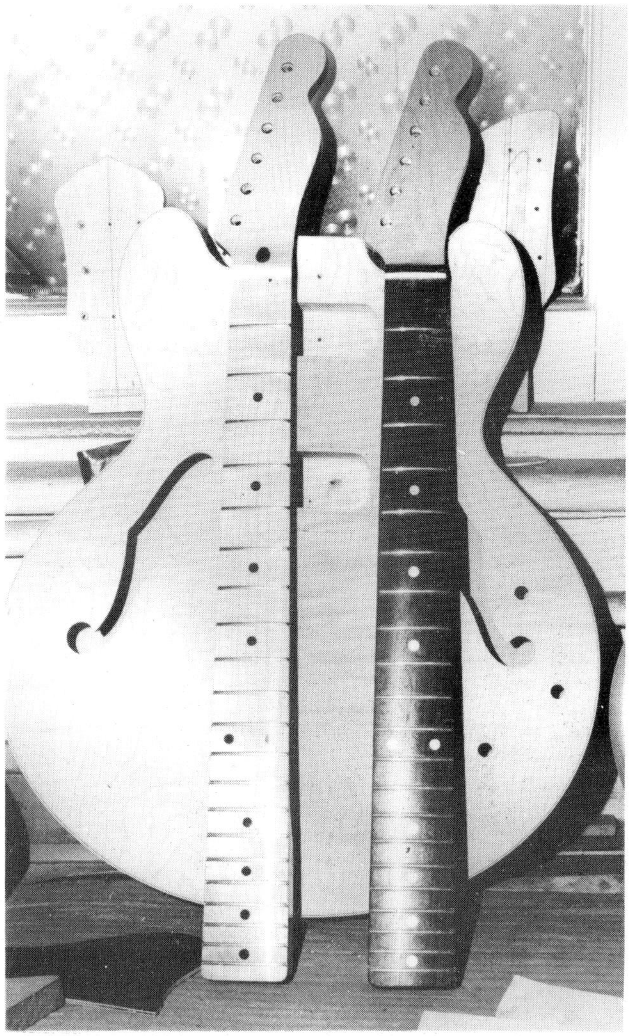

Fender style necks (left: maple, right: rosewood).

Stage Four

The next stage is the fretboard which is usually made of rosewood, but occasionally of maple or ebony. The most complicated part of this is the fret slot positions. The majority of solid guitars work on two patterns of scale length which is the vibrating string length from the top nut to the bridge saddle. The first is 24¾" (as used by Gibson) and the second is 25½" (as used by Fender).

Nowadays you can buy fret caliper rulers (from Stentor Music) which have the fret positions marked on them. All you do is use it as a template to mark the frets onto the wood. There are various ways of cutting the fret slots, and you can do it by hand, but it takes about two hours of very careful work. However, Stentor Music also sell fret cutting gear to help slot the frets square and true. The frets are cut with a fine saw, the fretslot being 25 thousands of an inch.

Naturally, Chris has developed his own tool for this very precise job, which takes the form of a pull-over saw, but the beginner will have to do it the hard way. The width of the fingerboard can then be cut according to the requirements of the individual, and once the edges have been trimmed it can be glued onto the neck blank using ordinary woodwork glue.

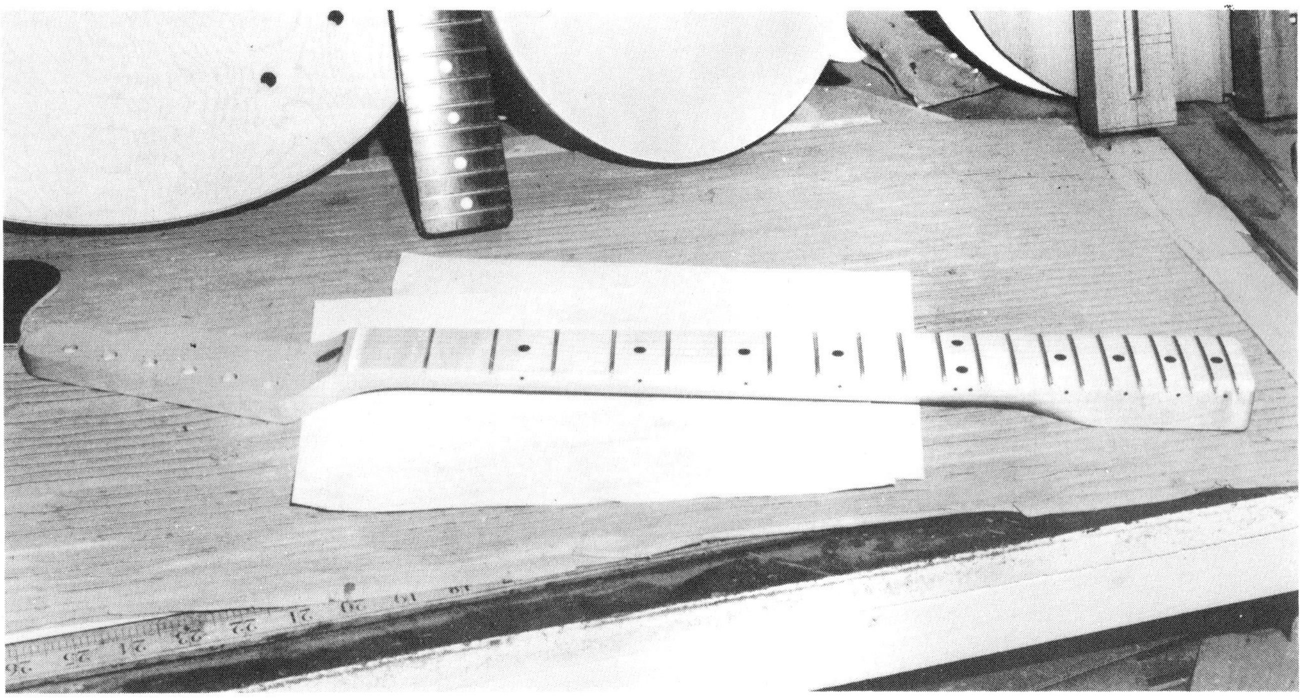

Fully finished Fender style maple neck.

Stage Five

The neck is now cut down to the taper of the fingerboard and the whole thing is cleaned up. The headstock can be cut out next, followed by the shaping of the neck with a spoke shave, rasp, file and sandpaper to a contour which is comfortable to the player.

A range of specialist carving tools custom built by Geoff Mather of Wigan, including planes for carving arch top instruments.

Stage Six

For the actual fretting, fretwire is supplied in long lengths which is flat on top and V-shaped below. The V shape is known as the tang, and has little pointed studs on it. The tang is fitted into the slot that has been cut with the saw, and the studs dig into the end grain of the wood. Normally a fret is held in place purely by this method, although a woodworking glue may be used at each end of the fret to fill in any gaps.

It's best to fret the neck before the back profile is shaped, and with something like a Fender neck it's easier because being flat it can be clamped down onto a flat table for sanding the profile of the fingerboard,

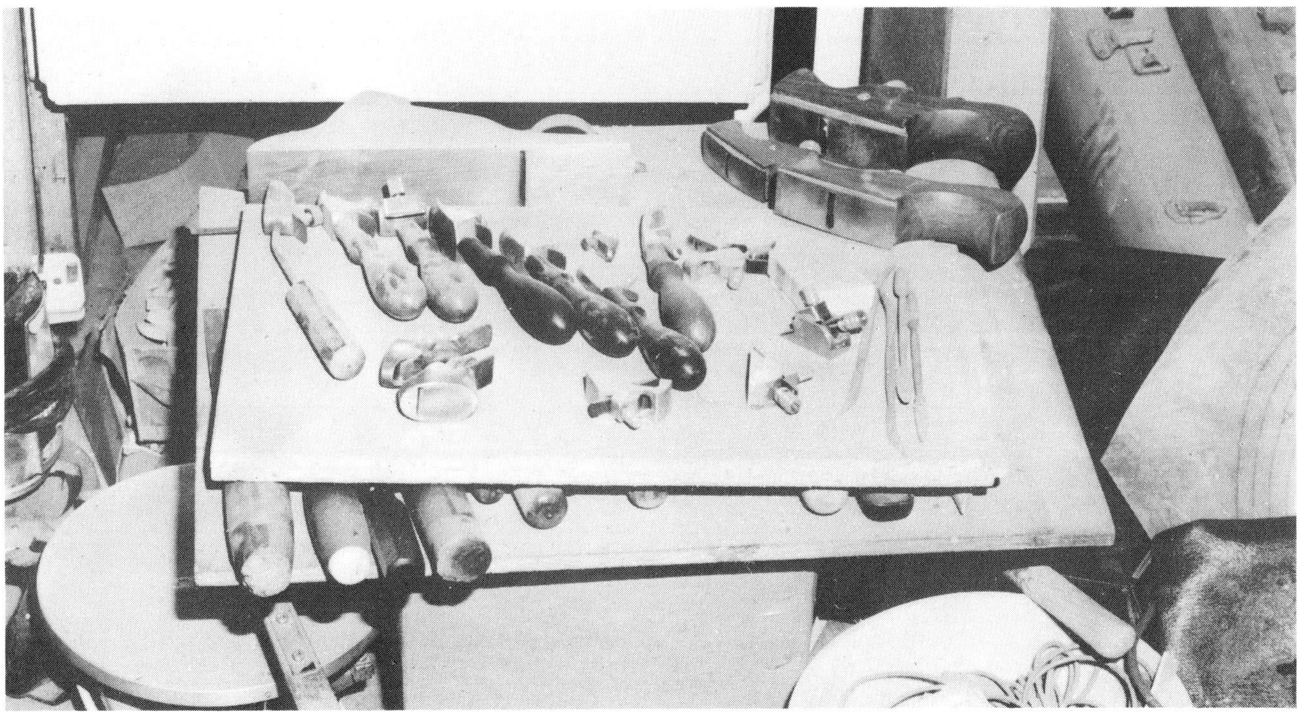

marking the centre for the position markers and drilling the holes for the marker dots. Once this has been sanded smooth, the fretwire must be banged into the grooves so that it fits down flush with a small hammer.

The theory of fretting is very crude; you take a strip of fretwire, slightly oversized, then work the hammer along the length to bed it down. Of course there is quite a fine art in banging them in so they don't get chewed up or bent, and then the edges are trimmed down with a fine file to make them flush with the fingerboard.

At a later date, when stringing, the frets have to be dressed with a fine oilstone to ensure complete uniformity. Flatspots on the top of the frets have to be rounded out using fine sandpaper, then polished.

Chris believes that on most factory guitars, this final polishing is omitted. The frets are merely banged in and when the guitar is assembled and strung it is left with a fairly high action which tends to disguise any irregularities. If any obvious buzzes occur, a file is whipped over the frets to remove the high spots, but they tend not to re-polish.

"You find on most new guitars in shops, if they're set to the correct action, that the frets buzz. It doesn't necessarily mean that the neck's no good, more probably that the frets haven't been dressed, which is the subtlety of making guitars play really smoothly. Some shops now have their own in-house guitar repairer to do the job and set them up. Some wholesalers have people working for them to do this, like Peter Cook who sets up Gibsons and Johnny Joyce at Aria. It used to be a major problem, but standards have improved greatly over the last couple of years.

"It's much easier if the manufacturer leaves the frets alone, because of possible climatic changes from the country where they are made to the country where they are shipped. Necks do move, so it's much better to leave the frets semi-circular to be finely dressed down once they settle in.

Completed front and backs for acoustic models awaiting fitting of sides.

Belt sander. Top section is used for flat sanding fingerboards and neck blanks. Bottom section is a pad sander and can be moved in and out in conjunction with a sanding block and is used for thickening up acoustic guitar fronts. Plus coils of fretwire of various gauges.

"On our guitars we find out what action the player wants and then set it up accordingly. Quite often we've had a situation where people have come to pick up a brand new guitar in the afternoon, and used it for a gig in the evening. In mass production, you can't expect that standard so it often involves taking it to someone to be set up. Setting up is an art in itself, and it takes three to four hours to set a guitar up satisfactorily.

Stage Seven

The next job is to cut out recesses on the body which will house the pickups, controls, switches and any other hardware. While this is generally straightforward, one of the more awkward jobs on some models is drilling a channel through the wood from the pickups to a switch which may be on one of the horns of the guitar. This involves a long thin drill and a steady hand, but as in everything, practice makes perfect.

Stage Eight

The next important step is finishing. The major point to remember here is to make sure the guitar is properly cleaned out, sanded and all the joints are correct before proceeding. Chris uses a spray gun predominantly for his finishing, which he believes gives the best results. For guitars he uses a cellulose based synthetic lacquer, and first applys two clear cedar coats in order to seal the wood.

This is followed by the colour work which either involves staining or spraying. The art is to build up a really deep finish by applying numerous clear lacquer coats, and this is then left for about 10 days. The

Neck patterns and a finished cello guitar, waiting to be sanded for the next coat of lacquer.

The spray shop. Guitars hang from a rail in the ceiling for individual spraying.

surface is then fine sanded, to smooth the surface down and make sure there are no blemishes, and this has the effect of making the lacquer look like a matt finish. Each instrument then has to be hand polished with a cloth and a fine polishing compound, which means two to three hours of hard work. Finally, Chris finishes them off with a power buffer, which is itself a fine art.

One of the most popular finishes for a guitar is sunburst, and this is achieved using a special methonol based dye which stains like ink. You begin by spraying round the edges and then build up with successive coats until you have the depth of colour you want. Fine sunburst is done with the gun, shading a very thin tint of dye, the idea being to have the colour fading away from the centre a though it has been rubbed away.

Stage Nine

The hardware is fitted, the guitar is strung and then set up to the individual requirements of the player.

This is only a brief run-through of some of the processes involved in making an instrument. It involves much time, patience and skilled craftsmanship, but it does indicate just what goes into producing the instruments that you only usually see as bright objects on a music shop wall. One of the reasons Chris is pleased that so many people are now having a go at making their own guitars, is that it brings home to the ordinary musician the amount of hard work as well as the level of skill involved in making a guitar.

The fact remains that more and more enthusiasts

Assorted electrical components including pick guard, pickups and machine heads.

are taking up the challenge. When Chris registered with one wholesale supplier in 1971, there were just five guitar makers/repairers on their list, now there are 205 and those last two hundred have appeared in the past two years. Clearly the pioneering work of those early builders has inspired many and with the growth of numerous building and repairing courses youngsters can now get a good basic grounding in instrument making — a far cry from the attitudes and opportunities which existed for those early British makers.

Another important factor can be seen in the business side of the industry. Those early British guitar builders became synonymous with making very expensive instruments which were mainly for wealthy rock stars. Today's second generation of guitar builders have realised that they must also compete at the lower end of the market, the result being that many are producing superbly crafted instruments, which in some cases are cheaper than their mass produced Japanese or American counterparts.

So while the British guitar industry may not be heading for a mass takeover of the world guitar market, it is certainly among the leaders in quality and craftsmanship. Chris Eccleshall's talent has also been recognised internationally; for he has now been commissioned by a large Japanese instrument manufacturer to work on some guitar designs. A rare accolade from the masters of mass production for the man who still makes guitars in a workshop near Ealing Common.

Chris Eccleshall with one of his completed guitars.

Vintage Guitars

One of the major bonuses for British musicians touring the States in the late Sixties and early Seventies was the prospect of guitar hunting — the chance to pick up a rare guitar for next to nothing. Stories of musicians finding old Gibsons and Fenders in pawn shops for next to nothing were legendary and often such finds proved more successful than the actual tours.

Sadly those days are pretty much over, according to one British dealer who specialises in old and rare instruments. Stuart "Screw" Sawney runs the Guitar Grapevine just off Denmark Street in London's West End, and spends much of his time scouring America in search of rare and exotic instruments.

Like so many in the musical instrument business, Stuart is himself a player but he has developed an avid interest in old guitars. He put his ideas for a specialist guitar shop to the men behind Argent's Keyboards shop and was given the go ahead to open up. Together with Howard from the Keyboards shop, Stuart set about renovating the premises to the rear of Argent's and opened for business at the end of 1980.

Since then, the shop has acquired a reputation as one of the top vintage guitar shops in the country. Stuart purposely avoided stocking many of the newer instruments and Japanese lines, preferring to concentrate on the vintage models and a few specialist ranges, among them Wal basses and Hamer electrics. The biggest challenge he finds, however, is discovering those lovely old instruments.

"I have to go to the States for most of them", explains Stuart, "although occasionally a customer will come in with something for sale or appraisal. In general, though, I have to rely on the States and I'm in contact with a number of specialist shops over there who send me regular lists, pictures and other information which might interest me. They are aware of the type of guitar I'm looking for, particularly models like old Fenders and Gretschs.

I should imagine that ten years ago you could walk into a pawn shop and find vintage guitars going for good prices, because the vintage guitar market wasn't a factor which interested prospective buyers of instruments. Now it has become very difficult to find vintage instruments in good condition anywhere in the States, let alone in pawn shops."

As a result of the publicity surrounding old guitars, and the fact that so many top players use them, people have become far wiser about old instruments. Occasionally, there will be the odd find or the odd bargain, but according to Stuart it is very much a case of keeping your eyes open and your ear close to the ground.

So how does he go about assessing whether a guitar is rare or worth collecting? "You have to possess a basic knowledge of construction techniques, in particular identification marks and signs of when the guitar was made. You also have to know what to look for in the finish, whether the original finish is correct, or whether it has been re-finished. It is a knack you pick up over the years, through seeing so many guitars, talking to other dealers and generally getting snippets of information about particular instruments off anybody you can.

"An instrument in original condition will be worth a lot more than an instrument which has had the body re-finished or the tuners changed. The value of an instrument will immediately decrease if features of the original have been altered. The sound is also very

A typical collection of guitars from Guitar Grapevine. A couple of Fenders, a Les Paul and a plastic-bodied National.

important; the pickups must still put out their full output and everything should be in good working order. Obviously, one doesn't want to tamper with any of the electrics, but if a pickup has lost a little top or a PAF isn't putting out the full 10,000 ohms, this can be rectified by either replacing it or getting the pickup rewound. Obviously it will reduce the value to some extent, but it is something you can get away with."

Serial numbers alone can be misleading and it is important to use the number in conjunction with other traits, among them identifying marks, or changes that occurred in the design and cosmetics during a particular period.

Most people, of course, buy guitars to play and not merely as showpieces. Many musicians like the feel of old guitars which are often far more comfortable to play than new models. There is also the opinion that quality control was considerably tighter in those early days than it is today in many factories.

There is no doubt that the value of certain instruments is increasing over the years, In 1959 a Les Paul would cost about $269 but now you would pay between $10 and $15,000 for one. A number of guitars are particularly highly priced; the D'Angelico jazz guitars will continue to increase in value as will the 1958, 59 and 60 Les Paul Standards and all the pre CBS Fender instruments.

According to Stuart, the most desirable and valuable of all vintage guitars these days is the 59/60 Les Paul sunburst model, because it is considered one of the best guitars ever built. Many of the top guitarists own a sunburst. Another valuable set of guitars to own is the Modern series, built by Gibson and introduced in 1958.

Stuart continues: "There was also a guitar called the Gibson Modern, of which there have only been two or three discovered and one of these was a prototype. Once again they were shaped very radically for the time. The Gibson ES335 range from 1958 to 1968 are also classed as collectable items, particularly the early 335 dot neck guitars. The dot on the neck generally indicates that the neck was a lot wider in profile and shallower in depth, making it nicer to play for some, including people like Larry Carlton and Lee Ritenour. These guys have very big hands, and with that double cutaway, it allows notes to be played high up the neck.

"Extremely treasured are the blonde ones. There were very few made with the actual colour of the maple untreated and they are very rare in good condition. Dave Edmunds uses one, and at a show in Dallas I went to there was only one and that was not for sale, which gives you some idea of how rare they are.

"The Firebirds which are of value these days are those with the original reverse body shape which were similar to chopped down Explorers. The very rare ones are the Firebird Sevens with gold fittings in custom colours. I've come across a couple and they go from between $2 and $3,000. The 1963 reverse models are the only ones really, especially those with three single coil pickups."

But the market is not dominated by Gibson and

Stuart Sawney with a plastic bodied National (left) and a rare Fender Esquire.

Fenders, for old Gretsch and Epiphone models are also highly prized. The Epiphone models made between 1958 and 1968 are particularly prized because they were made at the Gibson factory during this period. Not only are these instruments collectors' items, but they are also of extremely high quality. Models such as the Casinos and Rivieras are probably as good as their Gibson counterparts, and in some instances you can pick them up for less money, which makes them better value.

During the Fifties and early Sixties, Gretsch guitars were among the dearest instruments, and the White Falcon model was the most expensive electric guitar on the market when it was introduced. Naturally, these models fall into the sought after category, and Stuart has had several in the shop. "We had a 1952 model which was one of ten with rhinestones set in the headstock, it's a very attractive guitar and very expensive. It was sold to a star then re-sold to another star.

"They are very nice guitars, and particularly valuable are the single cutaway stereo models made in the late Fifties. These were popularised by people like Steven Stills, who brought them out into the rock

Stuart Sawney, surrounded by Wal basses.

field, and I notice the guy out of BoWoWow uses a single cutaway model. A lot of the other Gretsch models are very good like the Eddie Cochrane models and the Rancher acoustics.

"Gretsch were a company who changed their designs constantly and were always using different configurations of switching facilities and pickups. A lot of the time you will see the same model Gretsch with different inlays in the fingerboard or different pickup configurations."

But it's not always old quality guitars that are sought after, recently Stuart has been delving into what he calls the "cheap crazy guitar market" which is starting to take off in the States. This revolves mainly around those weird and wonderful guitars which were made for huge chain stores like Sears and Roebuck, and include Danelectros, Silvertones and Nationals. Often they are striking looking instruments, like the Nationals, a model of which comes in bright red plastic, but some top guitarists go for instruments such as these. Jeff Baxter is one player who gets good sounds out of cheap guitars, and in most instances these instruments can be set up to sound and play well. This is probably one of the few areas where bargains can still be had from pawn shops.

In America too, there is a small market for some of the old British instruments like Vox, Baldwin and Burns. Certain players will go for them because they may have seen groups like the Beatles using them at some time, but for the most part Stuart doesn't bother with British guitars because he feels they don't really hold up in the value and quality stakes.

Although the vintage guitar market is still relatively small in the UK, there are signs that it could blossom as it is now doing in America. In Dallas, for example, a special vintage guitar show has been held, where dealers came to exhibit and sell their stock, and it proved a useful place for Stuart to make new contacts.

"People in England are becoming very aware of the vintage guitar market and they don't throw up their hands in horror when you tell them the price of some of the guitars. There are always going to be those who think it outrageous to charge over £500 for any guitar, but in the same way it's outrageous to pay £50,000 for a violin. It's the Stradivarius situation on a slightly larger scale.

"It's very difficult to find guitars in original condition in England, if you look in the ads in *Melody Maker* there are a considerable number of Fenders for sale that have been tampered with in all sorts of ways. It has happened, however, on occasions that people have bought quality vintage instruments at very good prices straight out of the trade papers.

"What I do is keep an eye on all the local 'For Sale' columns and buy any kind of random 'For Sale' magazine looking for that one bargain. It's just a question of being patient and having every base covered."

And what makes it all worthwhile is something like the sunburst Les Paul which Stuart had hanging on his wall. It used to belong to Mick Taylor and is worth around £2,500. "In the aging process the sunburst fades and everything turns a lovely golden colour, and the arched top is a lot more arched than on contemporary models. It has a really thick maple top which gives it that sustaining quality and the sound has really mellowed out.

"Everybody who plays guitar and knows anything about them wants a vintage instrument because they look great and they sound great."

Introduction to acoustic guitars

Whatever the ultimate aims attached to learning the guitar, be it the pursuit of riches in the rock world or merely entertaining yourself playing tunes, the starting point is inevitably an acoustic guitar. Even those musicians who have become synonymous with the electric instrument invariably have at least one acoustic to write songs on or merely play for fun.

The acoustic guitar, therefore, is very important and anyone contemplating playing electric should still begin with an acoustic. The acoustic market is as diverse as the electric for although there are probably fewer models to choose from, one rarely gets to hear about more than a few top class instruments.

The acoustic guitar reviews that follow are a selection of the best on the market and should serve as a guide to the types of instruments available and what you can expect of them. But here are some general points to bear in mind when looking at acoustics.

To begin with, different guitars do different jobs, for example, one instrument may have been designed for beauty of tone, ideally suited to the fingerpicking style of playing while another designed for volume and bass power, will be best suited to a busker. Also, a beginners' guitar wouldn't really work in the hands of a top musician and conversely a beginner couldn't do real justice to something like a Martin D45. Many players also insist on using bronze strings for volume and sonority, although these are not always fitted as standard.

The guitars we have chosen are mostly good value for money instruments, or have a particularly good feature which make them worth including. However, bear in mind that of the models we have selected and particularly recommended it is ultimately down to personal choice of what feels and sounds good to you.

Aria Paul Brett PB 30

It isn't often that one has the opportunity, when reviewing guitars to judge how well an instrument will age. But it so happens that this reviewer first came across this guitar a couple of years ago and, as a result of having one to live with for a couple of months, a songwriting friend fell in love with it the moment she tried it. Eventually she bought one and watching her growing familiarity with the guitar, hearing the wood mature, and seeing how she settled down with it has been an illuminating experience as it is undoubtedly true that acoustic guitars (at least *good* ones) do mature and improve the more they are played.

The Paul Brett is a fine looking instrument and one can quite see why my friend fell for it. It comes in a plush lined case and when you open that case you find a guitar with a very pleasing looking top of solid spruce. The back and sides are made of mahogany and, one suspects, the spruce has been darkened a little to match the rest of the body. It has superb inlays up the excellent quality rosewood fingerboard; not of the usual abalone or fake mother-of-pearl but of maple, with the title "Aria Pro 11" inscribed in the last position. The body is bound to a checker pattern of alternating woods which also extends around the sides of the headstock and binds the neck. The name Paul Brett is also maple, inscribed on the headstock. The quality of this work on the sample was immaculate, reminiscent of the finest workmanship of the old American guitar makers.

From a constructional view it was not possible to fault this guitar. The sound of the Paul Brett was also excellent when new, and for once one can report that it has not deteriorated over the past few years of use but has improved with age, as any good guitar should. The tone is phenomenally well balanced with none of the bass boom and weak top one associates with some "jumbo" sized American guitars, nor the treble bias when new which is a characteristic of many superficially attractive new Japanese acoustics.

If this elaborately decorated instrument had come from one of the top American makers one estimates that the current selling price would be around £800-£900. As it is, the current asking price of £277 makes it easily the best Japanese value for money in acoustic instruments that this reviewer has seen to date.

The Paul Brett would suit any guitar player who wanted a fine guitar at a reasonable price. It is a folk/jazz player's instrument, not really a rock guitarist's acoustic, but it is superb value for money and very, very difficult to fault.

Price: £277

Body materials: Spruce top/mahogany back & sides

Neck materials: Mahogany

Fingerboard materials: Rosewood

Machine heads: "Aria"

Pickups:

Construction:	★★★★★
Finish:	★★★★★
Sound:	★★★★★
Playability:	★★★★★
Value For Money:	★★★★½

Distributed by: Gigsville Ltd, Phoenix Way, South Drive, Heston, Middlesex. Tel: 01-897-3792.

Daion Caribou Electro-acoustic

Although not one of the best known brands on the UK market, the Daion range is very impressive and the introduction of the Caribou electro-acoustic is a move which should be taken rather seriously. If it follows typical Daion quality then it promises to be a very good instrument selling at a very fair price.

I suppose you'd have to say that the Caribou has a vaguely Country and Western shape. I wouldn't know how to define that precisely but the rather "flash" nature of it suits the Watford cowboy image quite adequately! Nonetheless it's not a bad looking guitar and it *is* very well made. The Daion boasts a body comprising a solid cedar top with a mahogany back and sides. The neck is also mahogany and both it and the body are very well bound in a surprisingly tasteful plastic pearloid material.

The fingerboard is rosewood of a nice quality and the sample came with very pleasant, accurate and comfortable frets. It also had a good action and reasonably decent strings.

The hardware is also very good, gold plated machines of excellent quality and a solid bright brass nut matched by a staggered adjustable bridge of the same material. The neck on the Caribou is very pleasant indeed, in fact it would come as a distinct revelation to a player who was used to pure acoustics and who picked up one of these for a quick trial. The neck is atypical of acoustics generally in that it is flat, almost concave to look at, and very suitable for both barred chords and rock and jazz, taking advantage of the cutaway in the body.

The pickup on the Caribou is totally concealed, the jack outlet being on the bottom cutaway of the guitar (rather an odd place for it). The pickup is controlled by two *slider* controls (one for volume, one for tone) on a fake wood plate set on the top curve of the body. Here they are accessible in mid number, and easy to use.

Acoustically the Daion sounds surprisingly good, perhaps sharing a brightness born of the brass bridge and nut which is characteristic of other Daions but a very pleasant guitar indeed to play, suitable for guitarists of all styles.

Played through an amp the sound isn't bad but, frankly, the built-in pickup does tend to fail in its attempt to reproduce the natural sound of the instrument. A more natural acoustic amplified sound would, one feels, be produced with a C-Ducer transducer tape pickup, rather than the pickup built into this guitar.

This, however, may not matter overmuch to the prospective buyer especially if he wants that "¼ acoustic, ¾ electric" sound which the Daion provides so well and which would be excellent for Country and Western playing. Although it may not sound 100 per cent like an amplified acoustic, the Daion Caribou is a very nice guitar and would suit any guitarist who wasn't too bothered by this lack of fidelity, and who wanted a very well made guitar, easy to play and with a good sound for both acoustic and electric playing. For the price one would say that it was excellent value.

Price: £275

Body materials: Cedar top/mahogany back & sides

Neck materials: Nato or mahogany

Fingerboard materials: Rosewood

Machine heads: Unidentified

Pickups: Transducer, (concealed, make unspecified)

Construction:	★ ★ ★ ★ ★
Finish:	★ ★ ★ ★ ★
Sound:	★ ★ ★ ★ ½
Playability:	★ ★ ★ ★ ★
Value For Money:	★ ★ ★ ★ ★

Distributed by: Rosetti & Co. (EMI) Ltd, 138-140 Old Street, London EC1 V9BL. Tel: 01-253-7294.

Daion Legacy

Whilst there are many acoustic guitars of Japanese origin currently on the UK market, few have any serious claim to originality, either of shape or tone.

Yet the Daion Legacy, by no means one of the best known Japanese guitars, is very much an individual, both in its looks and its sounds. The Legacy is a large bodied guitar but one would hesitate to call it either a Jumbo or a Dreadnought — in fact it certainly isn't the latter by any standards. It's an original shape, given that there probably isn't very much you can do with acoustic guitar shapes, with a smaller top end than bottom, rather nicely profiled and apparently very well made indeed using this sample as a judge.

The materials used in the Legacy comprise a dark stained cedar top (although you'd probably not recognise it as such, so heavy is the finishing colour) with an elegant rosewood back and sides. It's a fine looking instrument and is likely to improve or, at least, hold its tone on account of the solid wood top, as the makers have not skimped and used a laminate.

The neck on the Legacy is nato; a wood frequently used by the Japanese and one which seems to be very successful in standing the strains of string tension. The fingerboard on the sample was a nice piece of well polished rosewood into which had been set frets of a very good quality, each well placed in terms of accuracy of height and intonation. The fifth fret also bore an inlay of the rather tasteful Daion logo.

The machines on this guitar are gold plated which sets off well the odd use of brass for both the nut and the bridge. Whilst it is becoming very common these days for brass to be used on electrics, it is usually felt to be rather inappropriate on acoustics. And yet, the arguments against it, that it encourages rattles and an overbright tone, are not problems encountered with the Daion. The guitar is *very* bright in its tone but that isn't necessarily a fault, as such, and no rattles were present on the sample whatsoever.

The brightness of the Daion's sound would make it a fine guitar for playing purely acoustically in situations where the audience was noisy; folk clubs, underground stations (busking being what it is!), parties, just about any situation where a guitar with a basically good sound yet the ability to cut through background noise is called for.

Despite this rather bright voice, the Daion's sound is not unnatural, it's just bright — not objectionably so, but bright enough to offer you a serious alternative, if you happen to like that sort of sound, to most other acoustics on the market.

At the current asking price the Daion Legacy is a tremendous bargain for a very well made, distinctive looking and sounding acoustic with a solid wood top and gold plated machines. There are a few other bargains around at present in this particular market but none of them beat the Daion.

Price: £199	
Body materials: Cedar top/rosewood back & sides	
Neck materials: Nato	
Fingerboard materials: Rosewood	
Machine heads: Unidentified (gold plated)	
Pickups:	
Construction:	★★★★★
Finish:	★★★★★
Sound:	★★★★★
Playability:	★★★★½
Value For Money:	★★★★★

Distributed by: Rosetti (EMI) Ltd., 138-140 Old Street, London EC1V 9BL. Tel: 01-253-7294.

Eccleshall Custom Concert

After viewing and playing a plethora of factory made guitars, which all seem to come from either America or Japan, it makes a nice change to look at an instrument from one of Britain's small but excellent band of custom guitar builders.

The model under scrutiny is made by Chris Eccleshall of Ealing, and was made early in his guitar building career. It represents a standard available from many builders who can't afford the huge amount of advertising which often guarantees mass acceptance.

The shape and visuals of this guitar are slightly unusual in that it is "concert" size (smaller than a Dreadnought but larger than a classical) but in contradiction has fairly exotic cosmetics like real abalone block inlays.

From the top, the head is shaped in the now familiar Eccleshall style, and is fitted with Japanese "Schaller type" machine heads, which are fine. The name transfer on the head, however, is messy and belies the overall quality.

A plastic nut guides the strings over a "nought" fret which this reviewer personally liked. It makes for an easier time getting a low action and improves tuning when playing root chords — particularly if you prefer an un-wound G string.

The distinctive feature of this guitar is the neck and fingerboard. The neck is a five piece splice (laminated running lengthways) of mahogany, maple and rosewood, which theory tells you makes for extra stability against bowing. With the curved fingerboard, the shape and feel is exactly like a Les Paul and therefore superb.

After some minimal bridge adjustment, an action was achieved which could grace many an electric. The fingerboard itself is ebony, and coupled with fat electric type frets and large block abalone position markers, makes for a very smooth feel.

On to the body of the guitar, which as already stated, is concert size and tends to preclude loud chord bashing. In fact with the unconventional mahogany back and sides and a solid spruce top, it has to be one of the quietest guitars around. This probably results from a comparatively thick "table" coupled with heavy strutting.

Knocking the body gives a dull thud, implying little natural wood resonance and thus the actual sound is quite "stringy". The overall tone balance is quite acceptable but the inherent gutlessness can be compensated somewhat by fitting medium gauge bronze strings.

So, a guitar of some paradox — sound not so good, but playability quite fantastic. It would probably make a good electro-acoustic if fitted with a bug type of pickup. However, in spite of the reservations on sound it can represent amazing value for money, the type of guitar that can be picked up secondhand for around £150. So there are still bargains to be found in the acoustic guitar market.

Price: £600

Body materials: Mahogany/spruce

Neck materials: Mahogany/maple/rosewood

Fingerboard materials: Ebony

Machine heads: Japanese "Schaller" type

Pickups:

Construction:	★ ★ ★
Finish:	★ ★ ★
Sound:	★ ★
Playability:	★ ★ ★ ★ ★
Value For Money:	★ ★ ★ ★ ★

Distributed by: Chris Eccleshall Guitars, 17c Station Parade, Ealing Common, London W5. Tel: 01-992-4741.

Eko Acoustic Bass

Although it might seem a bizarre (not to say rampantly lunatic) idea to make an acoustic bass guitar, the idea behind it is one of pure common sense. Few bass players these days begin their careers on double basses and find them almost impossibly difficult if they are ever called upon to play one. So what do they do when they're playing in an all acoustic band, or on a number where it is felt that electric bass just wouldn't sound right? Furthermore, what do they do if a folk gig appears where there is no amplification and/or no electrical power? The answer is usually for a band to either use a double bass player, an electric bassist playing quietly or, if they are walking around, say at an open air gig, to use no bass at all.

To the rescue two makers, Guild and Eko. Guild actually offer a four string acoustic bass guitar but theirs retails (currently) at a staggering £855, making it a model for the dedicated or the vastly wealthy only — not the sort of guitar you'd buy for the occasional gig!

The Eko acoustic bass on the other hand costs only £155 and is rather similar in looks to the basic Eko Rangers in that it features the familiar almost yellow coloured spruce top with the mahogany back and sides. Of course the body is considerably bigger than that of the Ranger 6 or 12 but it is by no means uncomfortable.

The neck is the usual Eko mahogany type with a rosewood fingerboard. With this maker's excellent reputation for ruggedness and reliability the obvious worry of warped necks due to the extra tension of bass strings should not be a problem, nor should the body peel apart due to pressure. The guitar looks strongly made.

The machine heads are cheap looking closed back types which as far as one could tell worked well, but is *was* hard to tell, as shall be explained shortly. The bridge is a solid wood type, simply held in place by string tension, the strings themselves terminating in a traditional trapeze tailpiece. Fretting on the sample was fine.

Tuning the Eko, however, was an immensely difficult task; the black nylon clad strings being of rather dubious quality, both from a stretching and tonal point of view. I don't know who made these strings, nor whether the Eko would take, say, Rotosound Jazz Bass (smooth wound) strings but one hopes it would. The nylon strings gave a tone some way between a string bass and a fretless but they were very hard to keep in tune on the sample and were very muffled in sound. In fact the bass was very quiet too and one would rather doubt that it would be heard above two acoustic guitars and a handful of vocalists in a folk ensemble without amplification.

Too quiet, hard to hold in tune, muffled in tone and with a rather dead E string on this sample, the Eko acoustic bass was so desperately calling for new strings of better quality that reviewing it was a difficult task. This is a great pity as it's a nicely made instrument with the appearance of ruggedness and a price which makes it accessible to most players.

Price: £155

Body materials: Spruce top/mahogany back & sides

Neck materials: Mahogany

Fingerboard materials: Rosewood

Machine heads: Unidentified

Pickups:

Construction:	★★★★★
Finish:	★★★★
Sound:	★★*
Playability:	★★★★
Value For Money:	★★★★ or ★★*

*See text

Distributed by: Rose-Morris & Co. Ltd., 32-34 Gordon House Road, London NW5 1NE. Tel: 01-267-5151.

Eko Ranger 6 Jumbo

Some instruments (just a very few) have been on the market for so long that they feel as much a part of the business of making music as old "standard" songs which everyone knows. The Eko series of Italian made acoustics has a couple of these in their Eko Ranger 6 and (12 string version) the Ranger 12. It might be tempting to think that the reason an instrument hangs around so is because of its inherent quality compared with the opposition, but in this market nothing can be taken for granted and so a look at a new sample seems to make sense.

The Ranger 6 is a similar guitar to the 12. It has that odd looking large body with a very odd grained mahogany back and sides, all of which are finished in a high gloss varnish. The mahogany neck sports a rosewood fingerboard, but it's as well to remember that this is an *Italian* guitar, not a Japanese one and so the woods used, although they may be broadly the same type do tend to look confusingly different from one another. Don't be fooled by this.

Fretting on this sample followed time honoured Eko principle by using a zero fret, not a unique idea but an old one with a very respectable pedigree, however much the Japanese makers may have made it unfashionable. A zero fret guarantees accurate intonation regardless of the nut (in this case a rather average quality plastic type) and it is a feature of those superbly accurate guitars from Shergold too — so don't assume that it's just a cheap way around intonation problems, it works well enough when it's properly used, as it has been here.

Another distinctive feature of the Ranger is an adjustable bridge. On this sample the action was set too low to accommodate the poor quality strings it came with and a new set would have been called for, probably with a raising of the action to cater for most players' tastes.

Finally, regarding the mechancial bits and pieces, the machines are those open backed types which seem to be beloved of most Italian guitar makers. One cannot think why but personal experience with an ancient Eko 12 tells me that, despite appearances, they are fairly reliable and reasonably well made for the price. A better standard could be achieved, however, with sealed Schaller copies of Japanese origin.

Overall the Eko doesn't play too badly although the neck profile, whilst rather pleasingly shallow, is over-wide for small hands. Young players might find other acoustics on the market at similar prices with easier necks to play but a fully grown player wouldn't find this neck too difficult.

With a raised action and better strings this Eko isn't a bad guitar — in fact at the asking price it's rather good value for money. Possibly the reason the Eko has stood the test of time is that it is precisely that; a reliable instrument which will take a hard life in the hands of beginners without suffering through being too delicate.

Price: £79.50

Body materials: Spruce top/mahogany back & sides

Neck materials: Mahogany

Fingerboard materials: Rosewood

Machine heads: Unidentified

Pickups:

Construction:	★★★★★
Finish:	★★★★
Sound:	★★★★
Playability:	★★★½
Value For Money:	★★★½

Distributed by: Rose-Morris & Co. Ltd., 32-34 Gordon House Road, London NW5 1NE. Tel: 01-267-5151.

Guild D40/NT

Since the virtual departure from the scene of Gibson's acoustic guitars the market for quality American-built acoustic guitars has roughly fallen into two very different camps: those who like and can use Ovations, with their odd body materials and untraditional sounds, and those traditionalists who, preferring a solid wood guitar, opt for a model from the Guild range.

Although they do not have a company history which stretches back as far as that of either Gibson or Martin, Guild have an immense wealth of skill in both design and manufacturing, inherited from ex-Epiphone builders who started Guild rather than go over to Gibson when it bought the Epiphone company. Since then a Guild guitar has been something to reckon with, although their strength has lain in jazz semi-acoustic guitars and pure acoustic guitars, rather than in their solid-bodied rock guitars which are far better than people seem to realise.

The Guild D40 is, in many ways, the basic Guild Dreadnought, a large, extremely well made instrument suitable for many types of playing from Country and Western through Blues to strumming along or folk fingerstyle. The guitar comes in several finishes, our sample, the NT, featuring a spruce top with mahogany back and sides, rosewood fingerboard and rosewood bridge.

Constructional standards are extremely high, and the whole guitar looks as if it were handmade (which, in fact, it probably was). It has an excellent feel of quality about it with a nice weight and balance and gives the impression that a lot of care and attention had been given to both the making and the setting up of it.

The quality extends right to the fretting and cutting of the nut which are both very accurate, assuring the player of perfect intonation.

Having seen how well it is made, playing the Guild was just a shade disappointing. The guitar handles well and the neck is very comfortable, but there was a strangely muffled quality to the tone without the projection and top of some other acoustics that are available these days. It may be, of course, that this is a good quality for some players and that what we have called "muffled" they would call "soft" or "balanced" — and it's true that there is nothing harsh about the sound of this Guild.

Pricewise the Guild is very good value in that it costs considerably less than the equivalent Martin, but it's also a very different sounding instrument from any Martin that this reviewer has tried in recent years.

It's impossible to fault this instrument in terms of its construction and may be unfair to castigate its sound. Some acoustic players might welcome its mellowness — this reviewer found it on the dull side, but then I favour bright and generally livelier sounding acoustics.

Price: £482.71	
Body materials: Spruce top/Mahogany back, 2 sides	
Neck materials: Mahogany	
Fingerboard materials: Rosewood	
Machine heads:	
Pickups:	
Construction:	★★★★★
Finish:	★★★★★
Sound:	★★★
Playability:	★★★½
Value For Money:	★★★★

Distributed by: C. Summerfield Ltd, Saltmeadows Rd, Gateshead, Tyne & Wear NE3 4UX. Tel: 0632-770431.

Harmony Sovereign

Although we have tended to concentrate on the acoustic guitar market from the point of view of buying new models, many people, of course, begin playing on a secondhand instrument. In looking at the secondhand market, generalisations are not the order of the day.

Acoustic guitars, in particular, have many subjective factors to them. As you get into high price brackets, the law of diminishing returns steps up. Instruments become worth whatever the buyer is prepared to pay, conversely at the lower end of the market, the guitar as an investment is not usually recommended.

Yet certain guitars always tend to crop up in the "For Sale" columns, and not only hold their value, but in some cases increase substantially. One such model is the Harmony Sovereign. The Harmony company folded about seven years ago; a Sovereign would then cost around £70 but nowadays you will find them fetching double that price. The fact that there are still a lot of these guitars in circulation, prompts us to include it in our reviews.

The body is the same basic size as a Dreadnought but is much thicker in the waist with the larger bowl (ie behind the bridge) looking positively pregnant. The fingerboard is wide at the body join, tapering just slightly to a wide nut. The head shape echoes the body's coarse lines.

Surprisingly, the decorative inlay on the head stock proves to be pearl. The machine heads are ancient, the original "three in a row" plastic button heads are uneven and temperamental, and really need replacing. However, one thing that was done was the setting up of the optimum action.

With a wide fingerboard of rosewood fitted with classically thin frets, it was set for a low action, high strings and a considerate left hand. The plastic position inlays and neck binding are "made to a price" features, but do their job well enough on a well varnished mahogany neck.

As already stated, the body is a little odd. The woods used are of standard rosewood and spruce with a very deep finish, so the response is very lively. It is this writer's theory that the finish deadens the treble overtones, while the body punches out the attack. The body, you see, is only about three inches wide.

Whatever the law of Physics may be on such matters, the Sovereign pushes out a lot of volume with quite a distinctive bell-like tone. It almost has a hybrid jazz sound in its grains!

The notes speak equally well from the bottom E to the harmonics, but with a sound which would suggest a boost to the mid range it can make for a perfect picking or soloing acoustic guitar. I don't think Isaac Guillory uses one, but he could. The one fault is when strumming full chords, a fineness is lacking with little separation. For all that, an interesting guitar, somewhat eccentric but with a definite character of its own. Judged on individual merit, the Harmony Sovereign can still be a bargain.

Photo of model unavailable.

Price: £80-£150	
Body materials: Rosewood/spruce	
Neck materials: Mahogany	
Fingerboard materials: Rosewood	
Machine heads:	
Pickups:	
Construction:	★★
Finish:	★★
Sound:	★★★★★
Playability:	★★★★
Value For Money:	★★★½

Distributed by: Only available secondhand.

JHS Encore 12 String

Many players whose prime (indeed their *only*) instrument is a solid electric guitar would like to own a reasonable quality 12 string acoustic. Twelve string guitars have a peculiarly full and resonant sound and lend themselves very well indeed to recording, where they can be effectively mixed into the rhythm tracks to provide a fullness of sound which you can feel more than hear. For all that, good 12 string acoustics are difficult to make, especially to retail at a price level which would attract a player who doesn't really need one *that* much. Those who desperately yearn for one usually end up with either a Japanese laminated-topped type or, if the money for it is there, one of the lyre-backed American made Ovations. Folk players would possibly make straight for a Guild and be happy ever after.

All of which is well and good if you happen to be satisfied with the run-of-the-mill Japanese laminated 12. Many are not, and so the Encore 12 exists to approach the Ovation design at a very cheap price.

The JHS follows Ovation principle by having a lyre back moulded from Fibreglass. The neck is mahogany and the nut, oddly, is aluminium, but the makers very sensibly use a zero fret (12 strings can be hard to cut a nut for to achieve perfect string length and thus intonation). Regrettably the machine heads could have been far better than the open Spanish type fitted to this sample. Given that this is a cheap guitar and that having 12 of them must double the manufacturing costs, they could have been better.

The Encore, however, goes one-up on many other more expensive instruments by having an adjustable bridge which is something for which the makers should be applauded wholeheartedly.

The fretting on this sample Encore was on the thin side but it was, thankfully, very accurate; inaccurate frets are the kiss of death for an instrument which is hard enough to keep in tune at the best of times. The neck is also easy to play; a factor which should endear the Encore even more to the player who usually plays an electric.

Soundwise the tone is a little thin compared with an equivalent 100 per cent wood bodied guitar, but it never booms, which is a major disadvantage when 12 string guitars are amplified on stage. The natural dryness and lack of resonance of the Fibreglass actually *improves* this instrument's chances of sounding good on stage — exactly as they do with Ovations. For all that, this is a very nice sounding instrument (particularly when you look at the price) with a good volume and tonal balance across the strings which should satisfy most users who are not enthusiastic about such instruments. Used, as one suspects it was designed to be used, the JHS is a very nice guitar indeed retailing at a very fair price.

Price: £129	
Body materials: Fibreglass	
Neck materials: Mahogany	
Fingerboard materials: Rosewood	
Machine heads: Open "Spanish" type	
Pickups:	
Construction:	★★★★
Finish:	★★★★
Sound:	★★★★
Playability:	★★★★
Value For Money:	★★★★½

Distributed by: John Hornby Skewes & Co. Ltd., Salem House, Garforth, Leeds LS25 1PX. Tel: 0532-865381.

Manson Sandpiper

Acoustic guitars are a matter of taste perhaps even more than electrics. If you happen to find yourself owning and playing an electric which sounds wrong for one number, or a new band, you can at least modify the sound of your electric through the amp. With an acoustic you are stuck with the sound which the guitar will produce on its own — all the more reason for not just rushing out and buying the first one which you vaguely happen to like the sound of.

This is something which most custom guitar makers are well aware of and a great deal of thought must have gone into the subject under review here: the Manson Sandpiper acoustic. This guitar is very, very good indeed, and congratulations must go to the brothers Manson, who yet again, seem to have catered for most tastes.

The Sandpiper's top is of Swiss pine, the back and sides of Indian rosewood (as is the superb quality binding) and the bridge is fashioned from rosewood too, but this time the expensive Brazilian kind.

The fingerboard on this sample is of super quality ebony and the hardware shows equal care over materials evinced by the makers, although one could well deplore on moral grounds, the use of ivory for the half ivory, half brass nut and the ivory bridge pieces.

The Schaller machines work as well as one has come to expect from this German brand, which is to a degree of perfection arguably unattainable elsewhere, and the staggered Manson bridge is both logical and effective in that it offers a sensible perfection of intonation usually impossible on acoustics.

The neck profile is similar to a Strat in that it offers the famous vintage "V" profile. This makes the Manson easily the fastest playing acoustic that this reviewer has encountered, and thus ideal for electric players who normally find an acoustic just too much hard work after a lifetime spent playing Strats or Les Pauls. Put simply, this is certainly the best acoustic guitar neck that the reviewer has ever encountered at any price!

Soundwise the Sandpiper is very nicely balanced but devoid of that boom which is the curse of normal acoustics when used on stage through a PA system. Of course it doesn't lack bass, but the sound isn't overburdened by it, there's plenty of cutting top there too, ideal for a good snap of the strings if your style leads you in that direction.

In terms of design, sheer manufacturing and acoustical quality, the Manson Sandpiper is easily the equal of anything else currently on the market, and particularly recommended for the player who is used to an electric guitar.

Price: £395	
Body materials: Pine/rosewood	
Neck materials:	
Fingerboard materials: Ebony	
Machine heads: Schaller	
Pickups:	
Construction:	★ ★ ★ ★ ★
Finish:	★ ★ ★ ★ ★
Sound:	★ ★ ★ ★ ★
Playability:	★ ★ ★ ★ ★
Value For Money:	★ ★ ★ ★ ★

Distributed by: Stentor Music Co. Ltd, Blackborough Road, Reigate, Surrey RH2 7EZ. Tel: 07372-40226.

Martin 00028

It is positively amazing how many guitarists who have never played a Martin know of and revere these acoustic guitars. For players these days, Martin is as much part of their heritage as Gibson and Fender, maybe more so as there have been Martin guitars made and sold since the 19th Century.

For all that legendary prowess, the company's recent history in the UK has been very chequered indeed. Martin guitars have come and gone; sometimes you've been able to find them in shops, sometimes not. After a period of very unpleasant industrial action and resulting commercial regrouping, let us hope that the new set-up whereby the company has a full-time representative in the UK will resolve the old problems of supply.

The 00028 under review is made with a spruce top, mahogany back and sides and neck with an ebony fingerboard. Constructional sandards are as high as any and the guitar looks and smells (yes, we're being serious about this) like a handmade guitar. This is one of the last remaining examples of American handcrafted instruments from a mass name and that, apart from any other factor, must account for the extremely high price.

Rumour has it that Martins are not easy guitars to play. It is certainly true that this 000 is not as fast as a Manson or even an Ovation. Some also hold that Fender Strats are more difficult to play than Les Pauls, but that does not make them bad guitars, and a certain amount of "fight" can actually help your sound, thus the move during the past two or three years back to higher actions and heavier strings (a factor reported by several string makers). If pressed, you'd have to admit that there are easier acoustics to play than this 000, but none with its quality of sound. The hardware used is of the first order, as is the fretting and nut cutting. For this price they certainly should have been of a high standard!

The sound of the Martin is totally different to that of the standard Dreadnought. Without losing any bass response, the 000 shape with its narrow waistline and small rounded body has considerably more top and projection than a jumbo type — and yet there is a near perfect balance across the strings too; a sound which will cut through the noise of an acoustic-only gig and make itself heard above the shuffling feet and muttering voices.

Despite the very high price, the Martin 00028 represents near perfection in acoustic guitars. Blues players and finger pickers will find it offers a tone far more suited to them than Dreadnought shaped instruments and that it is well worth assessing before looking elsewhere. This guitar may not suit strummers nor the habitual electric guitar player, but the sound is unique and no guitarist should pass up the chance to try one.

Price: £929

Body materials: Spruce/mahogany

Neck materials: Mahogany

Fingerboard materials: Ebony

Machine heads: Chrome enclosed

Pickups:

Construction:	★★★★★
Finish:	★★★★★
Sound:	★★★★★
Playability:	★★★★
Value For Money:	★★★★

Distributed by: The C.F. Martin Organisation (Europe), "Kinchyle", Church Lane, Great Holland, Frinton, Essex. Tel: 02556-2249.

Melody 800

It's very tempting for the modern guitar player to assume that cheap guitars only come from the Far East but, in point of fact, Italy is capable of producing instruments of quite surprising quality for the money, especially in the acoustic guitar market. Such an example is the Melody 800 which currently retails around the £66 mark.

To look at, the Melody isn't very different from the average acoustic guitar. The instrument sports a spruce top with mahogany back and sides. The neck too is mahogany and the fingerboard is cheap rosewood. There is nothing in either constructional terms nor in the guitar's appearance to suggest that it is any different from a hundred other instruments in this price range.

But a closer examination reveals that the Melody has been rather well put together for the money. The joints are well made and the neck on the sample was true enough for the guitar to be played up high with no serious intonation problems at all.

As with many Italian made guitars, the Melody is let down by its machines which are a type of design usually found on cheap classical guitars, an open backed type of only average quality, fitted with plastic buttons. For the price they aren't too bad in their function but it is hard not to escape the conclusion that a similar guitar from the Far East would have had better quality machines altogether. However, the Melody scores by having an adjustable bridge, not something which many acoustics boast (regardless of price) but well worth having all the same.

Generally speaking, the Melody 800 is a very nice guitar to play. The intonation is good for the price and the neck shape and standard of fretting would make it an ideal instrument for the beginner whose budget would not stretch to a more expensive instrument. Frankly, until one was sure that the guitar is the right instrument, one would not recommend spending in excess of £200 and for this sum the Melody 600 is a good investment.

It would be unrealistic to expect the quality of sound of that of a Martin or Manson from this instrument but it sounds remarkably good for the price. It is a well made and reliable instrument whose ease of playing makes it an ideal guitar for a beginner.

Price: £66	
Body materials: Spruce/mahogany	
Neck materials: Mahogany	
Fingerboard materials: Rosewood	
Machine heads: Unidentified	
Pickups:	
Construction:	★★★★
Finish:	★★★★
Sound:	★★★★
Playability:	★★★★
Value For Money:	★★★★★

Distributed by: Richard Brown Distribution, The Minster, Harbidges Lane, Long Buckley, Northants. Tel: 0327-842677.

Ovation Legend

After a burst of publicity, some raised eyebrows and accusations of gimmickry when they first appeared in the Sixties, Ovation guitars have settled into a respectable niche in the guitar market. Their major impact has been in the electrified acoustic field, and they are the acknowledged leaders, but the company claim that their guitars stand as fine acoustics in their own right. So we have decided to put the purely acoustic Legend through its paces.

No guitarist will be unaware of the Ovation Lyrachord back. Made of a super new glass fibre construction which was a spin off of the space programme, you either love it or hate it. Many purists will argue that you can't improve on natural wood for a guitar, but you cannot argue with the performance of the Legend.

A distinctive shape and beautifully designed cosmetics make this a very attractive guitar. There is no scratchplate, which many seem to like, and the head is a beauty of ergonomics. The machine heads are gold plated and are Ovation's own brand, probably made by Schaller, and perform well.

An ivory nut pulls the strings down a 25 scale length. The superbly finished if rather bulky neck is constructed from mahogany with two maple stripes for additional strength. The fingerboard is ebony which is very smooth and close grained, in spite of a few brown splashes in the wood colouration. Apparently, this is not undesirable in ebony, the blue/black colour cited as "perfect" is unfortunately now mostly a function of staining. The ivory binding and pearl inlays are beautifully made if slightly dressy.

The 20 fret neck joins the body at the 14th fret, leading onto a top of solid sirka spruce. As already stated, it is this, together with the strutting which gives most of the quality to an acoustic sound. The strutting is Ovation's own "A" shaped design and with the high reflectivity of the Lyrachord back, it makes for a very bright jangly sound.

The rather stiff action could tend to be a bit off-putting, but along with most fine guitars, both these factors will undoubtedly improve with age.

The review of this guitar may have been jaundiced by the mediocre set-up of this particular model, but even so it proved difficult to handle an instrument which continually tried to slip off the lap.

Incidentally, the Legend is available with a terrific glass fibre flight case for about £80 extra, and the electrified version of the Legend is available for about £120 more.

Overall, there is no doubt that this is a quality instrument with a fierce, penetrating sound, and the number of professionals now using Ovations testify to that.

But in spite of great cosmetics and a sound which will undoubtedly mellow, at this price it did not convert this reviewer.

Price: £368	
Body materials: Fibreglass/spruce	
Neck materials: Mahogany	
Fingerboard materials: Ebony	
Machine heads: Ovation	
Pickups:	
Construction:	★★★★
Finish:	★★★★
Sound:	★★★
Playability:	★★
Value For Money:	★★

Distributed by: Rose-Morris and Co., 32-34 Gordon House Road, London NW5 1NE. Tel: 01-267-5151.

Ovation Matrix

These partly synthetic guitars are very much a matter of personal taste. Die-hard acoustic players may well prefer the feel and sound of natural wood.

The body of the Matrix has a laminated top of Sitka spruce, a very respectable wood but rather a strange choice for a £300 + guitar used in its laminated form, a constructional pattern normally reserved for cheap guitars. However its combination with "Lyrachord", a Fibreglass body material, is somewhat special and it cannot be compared with other laminates.

The lyre-backed guitar balances well and comfortably played standing but lamentably on the lap where it is forever slipping off. However, these guitars are really designed to be played on stage when the user would be wearing it with a strap.

The sameple sent had been very well constructed, the joint between the artificial back and the wooden front looked perrfect, as did the neck joint. The neck on the Matrix is pretty odd. This consists of an aluminium T-section, around which a Urelite plastic is moulded and then allowed to assume a grain pattern.

Unlike some export Ovations, this model has a genuine rosewood fingerboard so that it can be re-fretted. A number of foreign marketed Ovations cannot be re-fretted, which is quite disgraceful and rightly not exported into the UK.

In use the Ovation is a fine instrument and one can see why they are so popular among amplified acoustic players. The model comes as either pure acoustic or electro/acoustic, this sample was the latter with a transducer fitted beneath the bridge pieces on the walnut bridge, the only control being a top surface mounted volume pot.

Played acoustically the Ovation is quite remarkably balanced across the strings. Whether played with a pick or fingerstyle, the string balance is naturally more consistent than any pure wooden guitar this reviewer has ever come across, each string resounding no louder than it should and offering an unprecedented tonal volume balance. The tone, however, is quite distinct from that of a £300 pure wood guitar and you should try each to see which you prefer.

Playing-wise the sample was not well endowed with its action and strings. The former was too high for some and the strings too heavy. Furthermore the neck was a little on the thick side for this reviewer's tastes and prospective purchasers may prefer other Ovation models, many of which are thinner in this respect.

Amplified the Matrix is very good indeed and has the basic Ovation of tonal fidelity when purely acoustic. It is hard to find a better acoustic for stage work than the Ovation and this sample shows why that is the case.

Confronted by a rather hard neck to play, a fairly high action and a generally forbidding feel, some users may prefer other Ovation models. This guitar is rather an acquired taste with its synthetic neck and its odd playing feel. Consider it very carefully beside other Ovations before buying it is undoubtedly a fine instrument on its own terms.

Price: £325

Body materials: Lyrachord back, laminated Sitka top

Neck materials: Urelite on aluminium 'T' bar core

Fingerboard materials: Rosewood

Machine heads: "Ovation"

Pickups: "Ovation" transducer

Construction:	★ ★ ★ ★ ★
Finish:	★ ★ ★ ★ ★
Sound:	★ ★ ★ ★ ★
Playability:	★ ★ ★ ½
Value For Money:	★ ★ ★ ★

Distributed by: Rose-Morris & Co. Ltd., 32-34 Gordon House Road, London NW5. Tel: 01-267-5151.

Sigma D35

Although undoubtedly one of the best selling brands of acoustic guitars in the USA, little has been seen of Sigma acoustics in the UK since the brand name's inception some years ago.

This may well change in the next year or so as the line is part of the range offered by the celebrated American guitar makers, C.F. Martin and Co. This company has, at last, established its own representative in the UK who is actively selling both Sigma and Martin instruments. There is now a good chance that you will come across Sigmas in your local music shops in the coming months.

Although a Japanese made acoustic line, all Sigma guitars are made of wood specifically chosen for them by inspectors from Martin in Nazareth, USA. The chosen wood is apparently then shipped across to Japan for conversion into guitars of Martin design and then shipped *back* again to the States for a final setting-up and quality check.

The Sigma sampled was a rather splendid looking acoustic, a D35, Dreadnought (jumbo) sized guitar with a solid (i.e. *not* laminated) spruce top, well mated to a splendid looking rosewood back and sides. The instrument bore a mahogany neck with a very attractive ebony fingerboard and had been put together very well indeed.

Playing wise the Sigma had a very pleasing neck, not too wide, not too narrow, with an action well suited to fingerstyle playing and various features (for instance particularly nice machine heads) which give the impression of it being a very reliable guitar indeed. Regrettably, economies *had* been made, such as providing the Sigma with a plastic nut and plastic bridge piece which does seem a shade on the mean side for the asking price.

The neck shape and the string height (despite deriving the proportions from the reputedly difficult to handle Martin range) were easy to live with and the D35 Sigma played and handled very well indeed. The guitar also sounded fine. Despite the large size of the body, the basic tone wasn't at all the boomy, muffled sound of a Dreadnought, copied tenth hand from the inventors, but instead bore a sound several generations removed from a genuine Martin.

This would represent a very nice buy indeed for a serious acoustic player who wanted a quality Martin-like instrument in this sort of price range. It's hard to fault the Sigma. Admittedly it isn't a hand-built Martin but it doesn't cost hundreds of pounds either! Compare it with most similarly priced Japanese acoustics and it has a feel and sophistication better than most. A very good buy indeed for the player who wants a Dreadnought sound but cannot afford the real thing — yet!

Price: £215

Body materials: Spruce top/Rosewood back + sides

Neck materials: Mahogany

Fingerboard materials: Ebony

Machine heads: Unidentified

Pickups:

Construction:	★★★★
Finish:	★★★
Sound:	★★★★
Playability:	★★★★★
Value For Money:	★★★

Distributed by: C.F. Martin Organisation Europe, "Kinchyle", Church Lane, Great Holland, Frinton, Essex. Tel: 02556-2249.

Takamine 360S

Takamine are a Japanese company whose name may not be as familiar as other Oriental instrument makers, nevertheless they have an interesting range of guitars. Despite the comparatively recent rise of Japanese industry, the Takamine company are quick to point out that they are a "family business with generations of woodworking experience".

They have an interesting range of straightforward acoustics and amplified acoustics, but the 360S is a basic middle of range pure acoustic. At first sight it is similar to any number of Martin-style Dreadnoughts. The Takamine name on the headstock in the style of much more celebrated manufacturers may seem a little gauche, but five minutes' playing dispels any thoughts of just another churned out copy.

The finish and attention to detail is excellent, with the overall look being workmanlike rather than luxurious. The basis for the design (Martin D25) is quite spartan and will hold no great appeal for many players, but it is the sound of the instrument which really scores.

Looking at the guitar in detail, it has the "Grover" type machine heads which work well. The neck is probably a little bulky with a standard D cross section, a more triangular shape as on Martins proper would have been better. The fingerboard is made from nice close grained rosewood which has been stained black to look like ebony. The frets are wide and well polished, while a standard dovetail joins neck and body at the 14th fret.

The back and sides are of Jacaranda, exotically grained, which is the one concession to cosmetics on this model. The table or top of the guitar is really where the 360S excels. The sound of any guitar has more to do with the quality of wood and the strutting used in the top than any other factor. The Takamine has a matched two piece of solid spruce which makes it very good at this price.

The resulting sound is terrific; loud and bright with considerable cutting power. It's the kind of sound you associate with Delta bluesmen, all slapping bass and singing treble. Using nickel strings, the sound is definitely toppy, but one suspects that with the quality of the soundboard it will mellow and improve with age.

Full marks also for supplying the guitar in a shaped hard case. While the overall strength of the guitar is impressive, a good case is essential.

For someone who is more concerned with sounding good than just looking good, and who needs an instrument of solid honesty, robust enough to gig constantly, the Takamine is well worth considering. While economies are apparent on details, it is heartening to know that your money is buying you the crucial components of quality.

Photo of model unavailable.

Price: £150	
Body materials: Spruce/Jacaranda	
Neck materials:	
Fingerboard materials: Rosewood	
Machine heads: "Grover" type	
Pickups:	
Construction:	★★★
Finish:	★★★★
Sound:	★★★★★
Playability:	★★★
Value For Money:	★★★★

Distributed by: Woods of Bolton, 15/17 Manchester Road, Bolton. Tel: 0204-27171.

Washburn Prairie Song Custom

There was a time, not so long ago, when the Japanese guitar makers were so diffident about their standing in the British market that to have offered an acoustic guitar at the sort of retail price which this one now asks would have seemed impossible. The fact that Washburn nowadays feel that they can ask over £400 for a guitar of this sort shows just how far they reckon that their market reputation has come. Mind you, they are not alone, as you can pay far more than this for some Yamaha guitars.

The specifications of the Washburn are good, much the same as those of many top American acoustics, in fact, which is perhaps as it should be as the Washburn name is still owned by an American company and it is apparently they, who design all Washburns, those designs being sent across to Japan for eventual manufacture.

The Prairie Song is a pretty amazing looking guitar. The spruce top on this sample being almost exactly bookmatched (it wasn't *quite* perfect) and the back and sides of rosewood which is possibly one of the most elegant looking woods that can be used by a guitar maker for this job. The sample we had was obviously well made and finished.

The neck on the Prairie Song is mahogany and, we are glad to report, the makers have run to ebony for the fingerboard woods as well they should for a guitar in this price bracket! The inlays are abalone and maple. Overall, the Washburn is an attractive guitar especially when held up against a rough and tumble basic Guild or similar.

The neck on the Washburn handles well, the action is low and fast and it feels more suitable for a player whose basic instrument is an electric solid, than many of the other acoustics tried, some of which would present great difficulties to a player more used to lighter strings and lower actions.

The sound is also particularly attractive — the Washburn doesn't have the cumbersome "snap" and "bang" of a Martin nor the immense projection of, say, a large bodied Guild. It is certainly a pleasant and balanced sound and would undoubtedly stand up to the rigours of recording. Whether it would hold its own in a folk club amongst beer swilling hearties is another matter, although, in this respect, it is certainly no worse than many other guitars of this type.

Value for money is rather hard to assess with this instrument. One has to consider that, were it made in America, it would compete pricewise with the average instruments from that country but, being a Japanese instrument, whatever the source of its design, makes it comparable in value only with other Japanese guitars, which may be taken as saying that most American guitars tend to be considerably over-priced in comparison. As things stand this Washburn is probably over-priced when held against the Japanese competition. One feels obliged to point out that for not a great deal more a Guild becomes a possibility and that would, surely, have a better re-sale value, a factor which is certainly important.

Price: Approx £411

Body materials: Spruce/rosewood

Neck materials: Mahogany

Fingerboard materials: Ebony

Machine heads:

Pickups:

Construction:	★★★★★
Finish:	★★★★★
Sound:	★★★½
Playability:	★★★★★
Value For Money:	★★★

Distributed by: Roland (UK) Ltd, Great West Trading Estate, 983 Great West Road, Brentford, Middlesex TW8 9DN. Tel: 01-568-4578.

Yamaha FG 612S

The far-reaching fingers of the Yamaha empire have a firm grasp on the musical instrument business, and their guitar range is comprehensive both in quantity and quality. It may be tempting to date the rise of this company to the Sixties, but as far as making instruments is concerned, the tuning fork logo is testimony to roots of a hundred years.

They have worked in wood for a long time, and with the Yamaha FG 612S we can see how they tackle the 12 string acoustic guitar field. Visually, it has the definitive Dreadnought size 12 string design. Some may say that Yamaha now define that image: the headstock shape has reverted to the older design with edges converging at the nut end, but there are no snagging strings on adjacent pins.

The machine heads are, of course, Yamaha brand "middleweight" Schaller types, and hold the strings in tune nicely, but with varying degrees of stiffness, it may be a different story in a year's time. Twelve strings can be a bit tricky, especially the high octave G which when fretted below the third or fourth fret, often tends to go sharp — but this one didn't. In fact tuning right up to the tenth fret was well up to scratch (using light Bronze strings).

The fingerboard is ebony with diamond shaped pearl position markers. The standard width frets stand quite high and feel slightly rough at the edges. Nevertheless it is responsive to touch, and has little of the stiffness inherent in many "top line" 12 string guitars. The mahogany neck joins the body at the 14th fret, and an ebony bridge of pure elegance complements the fingerboard.

The box is neatly constructed around an X strutting design — rosewood back and sides and (which this reviewer was surprised to find) a solid spruce top with a good straight grain that looks just right.

What does it sound like? One always thinks that a solid wood top (as opposed to a laminate) is a pre-requisite of a top "quality" ego boosting, ethnically correct and uninsurable guitar — important to the sound anyway. So at this price one is well impressed with the design criteria of this Yamaha. However, the performance didn't quite match the promise.

Of course one accepts that new guitars need playing in to mellow down, yet with everything right about it, the feel, tuning, construction and finish, there seemed to be something lacking in spirit. It was not loud, but with the inevitable stringiness common to all new instruments, it became somewhat crashy to this reviewer's ears.

Despite this shortcoming I can still recommend this guitar. For £200 or so, it is great value. It is simple and pleasing to look at and made up of all the right ingredients. I'm sure Yamaha will sell thousands — and they deserve to.

Price: Approx £180

Body materials: Spruce/rosewood

Neck materials: Nato

Fingerboard materials: Rosewood

Machine heads: Yamaha

Pickups:

Construction:	★★★★
Finish:	★★★
Sound:	★★
Playability:	★★★★
Value For Money:	★★★★

Distributed by: Kemble/Yamaha, Mount Avenue, Bletchley, Milton Keynes, Bucks. Tel: 0908-71771.

Yamaha FG 365S II

Yamaha have done more than any other company to dispel the notion that when it came to musical instrument manufacture, the Japanese could only contribute cheap mass-produced copies. Not only did Yamaha evolve their own designs and innovations, but they also introduced manufacturing standards which were incredibly high, resulting in products which were exceptionally well built and durable.

So highly organised is their production, that they can offer wide ranges of instruments, from beginners' models, through to professional guitars. However, even near the bottom of the price range, you will find a very well made product, which offers great value for money.

The Yamaha acoustic guitar range offers something to suit just about every pocket, style and level of playing. The FG 365S steel string represents the lower end of the price range, but nevertheless is the type of guitar which is popular with many people.

Of course there is less scope for original design in the acoustic field, and this one falls into the category which many people will recognise as a typically American style jumbo. The top is made from solid spruce, with the back and sides constructed of three piece Indian rosewood. The fingerboard is also rosewood stained black, with the neck made from nato. The machine heads are Yamaha's own and work well enough, and the overall appearance of the guitar is basic and unfussy.

Soundwise the Yamaha is a little bright and unsubtle, particularly in the treble region, but this is likely to mellow in time, particularly in view of that solid spruce top. There is no reason to expect it to sound like a Martin, because you are not paying Martin prices.

It is not the sort of instrument you would expect to be booming out at a concert, but will probably be an ideal guitar for a songwriter, or for use with friends, working out songs or harmonies. Its appeal will be widespread, because the beginner who may have started on a dubious instrument, will be well pleased with it and you're just as likely to find a working musician carrying one around with him.

Without a doubt it is great value for money, well constructed with a good sound and durable enough to stand up to a lot of playing. It is also worthwhile noting that Yamaha, who were founded in 1887, aren't new to the instrument business. They have considerable experience in woodworking and have combined this with new technology and much research. So really, it's not surprising that their instruments are so well made.

Price: £199	
Body materials: Rosewood/spruce	
Neck materials: Mahogany	
Fingerboard materials: Ebony	
Machine heads: Yamaha	
Pickups:	
Construction:	★ ★ ★ ★
Finish:	★ ★ ★ ★
Sound:	★ ★ ★
Playability:	★ ★ ★
Value For Money:	★ ★ ★ ★

Distributed by: Kemble/Yamaha, Mount Avenue, Bletchley, Milton Keynes, Bucks. Tel: 0908-71771.

Acoustic Profiles

Joan Armatrading

Joan Armatrading is something of an enigma in the female rock stakes. She doesn't use her looks or any kind of manufactured image to help sell her records, and doesn't fall into any stereotyped image of a singer/songwriter.

Yet this immensely talented lady has built up an enviable reputation as a songwriter and musician, which is such that she can summon up a whole host of top players to work on her albums or support her on tour. And her subtle guitar playing complements her creamy soulful voice.

Intensely private and a little introverted, for a long time Joan didn't care too much for interviews. Obviously the long round of interminably banal questions left her unimpressed, but when talk is switched to her music and her guitars, she becomes involved and enthusiastic.

Born on the island of St. Kitts in the West Indies, she later moved to England. Her first musical instrument was the piano, but she found the guitar more interesting and began to play around the age of 14. Jazz guitar chords always fascinated her, and she used to practice them, but it was only when Joan signed to make her first album in 1974, that she really started to work on her playing.

She later changed record companies, but it was her third album entitled simply "Joan Armatrading" which really brought her into the limelight, with the beautiful "Love and Affection" becoming a chart hit from the album. That album was produced by Glyn Johns and featured such top British session men as Jerry Donahue, B.J. Cole and Dave Mattacks, and set a high standard which she has maintained.

Her guitar playing is as sensitive as her songs, and reflects a very intimate style. The legacy of learning all those jazz chords seems to have stayed because the influence is there in her early work, although of late she has become slightly more rock orientated and started employing simpler chords.

On stage she is rarely pictured without an Ovation acoustic, and has several of the instruments which she uses both for studio and live work. In acoustic guitar terms, when compared to the likes of Martin and Guild, the Ovation company are comparative newcomers, but to Joan they have become trusted friends.

Among the models she uses are the Ovation Balladeer which is purely acoustic, but for live work she often uses a Folk Classic with a built in pickup. Not only does the pickup give ample volume for concert work, but Joan likes the overall tone of the instrument. She also has several electric guitars, but never seems to get round to becoming a fully fledged electric player.

Joan forms great attachments to her instruments; they are much more than mere tools of the trade. On one occasion during a European tour, she sent one of her main guitars back to England by plane to be repaired by master luthier Stephen Delft.

Her music has shifted slightly in recent years, with the "Me, Myself, I" album being far rockier than her previous work, and her current recording shows her using synthesizers. But whatever she does still manages to retain that distinct Armatrading style and quality, on which her reputation stands firm.

Mark Knopfler

Acquiring a distinctive guitar sound is something that all guitarists strive for, but few actually achieve. How many guitar players can you positively identify by merely listening to a few bars of their work?

Today, with so many guitar players around, it is probably harder than ever to achieve a personal sound, but one player who has managed to do that remarkably well is Dire Straits' guitarist Mark Knopfler. His beautifully laid back, understated style seemingly echoes another world far removed from the extremes of rock.

Dire Straits came to the fore in the midst of the New Wave explosion of the late Seventies, and their lyrical music seemed a little incongruous among the high energy outpourings of the punk bands. Their immense talent eventually won through, but ironically the first real breakthrough came in America.

Mark began his musical career on the piano, but being a rock and roller, he was always borrowing other peoples' acoustic guitars. Eventually, at the age of 16 he got his first electric guitar which was a red Hofner, and looked similar to a Stratocaster.

Acquiring this electric instrument coincided with his hearing of B.B. King's "Live At The Regal" album and it proved something of a revelation. Later he got into playing a National Steel resonator guitar, and this led to listening to old blues players. However, it was while playing an acoustic guitar that his particular style began to evolve.

Mark found that he could do things with his thumb and fingers that he couldn't do by using a plectrum, and before long he had incorporated this style into his electric playing. This now forms an integral part of that distinctive Knopfler sound.

Prior to joining Dire Straits, Mark had a variety of occupations ranging from journalist to lecturer, but eventually he decided on a full time career in music. When Dire Straits finally broke, a lot of people became excited about his playing, and he even ended up playing on a Bob Dylan album.

Mark's playing reflects a subtlety and taste which seemed to have long disappeared in rock music. His restrained playing fits in perfectly with his songs, and he never tries simply to dominate the tune from the outset. However, although his style can be described as laid back, it doesn't suffer from the indulgence and apathy that seems to grip many American guitarists stuck with the same label.

In concert and on record, Dire Straits can boogie with the best of them, and Mark's guitar often builds up into an intensity that sets the song alight.

Having finally made it with Dire Straits, Mark was able to indulge himself with the instrument of his dreams, a red Stratocaster.

Originally, he had an old Strat which had a selector switch which could be jammed into a middle position to give an out-of-phase sound, but this was eventually replaced by an instrument with a five position selector, which gave him all the options he needs. His favourite instrument at the moment is a Stratocaster put together by the Schecter company, which he feels is more powerful than an original Fender.

As with all great guitar players, the imitators are never very far behind, and already there are scores of young players who want to sound like Mark Knopfler.

John McLaughlin

John McLaughlin represents a very different kind of guitar player to those associated with rock music. He is classed as more of a jazz guitarist anyway, but his whole approach to the instrument is at odds to many of the current self taught players.

With McLaughlin, technique is everything, and hours of complex practice enable him to run over the fretboard with dazzling speed and dexterity, using areas of the guitar which many players rarely touch. Many find him too complex and involved a person, and much of his music remains esoteric. His love of Eastern music and conversion to the philosophy of Indian mystic Sri Chinmoy, served to further alienate many of his fans, but he remains probably the most technically perfect of all modern electric guitarists.

Born in Yorkshire in 1942 he first studied violin and piano before inheriting a guitar in his early teens. This coincided with his first hearing the blues, which was

to have a tremendous impact on a musically disciplined mind. From the blues of Muddy Waters he came through to jazz and Djano Reinhardt, finally getting to grips with the legendary Miles Davis when he was 15.

Jazz became the perfect medium for McLaughlin's fledgling technique, and when he came to London he soon acquired an impressive reputation. In the early Sixties he played with many of the leading lights of the British jazz scene, and this included a spell in the Graham Bond Organisation, who had Jack Bruce on bass.

In 1969 he made his first solo album, "Extrapolation" and that confirmed his status as a prodigious virtuoso guitar player. This attracted the attention of several leading American jazz greats, and led to McLaughlin playing with Miles Davis on two memorable albums "Bitches Brew" and "In A Silent Way".

With his reputation sky high he joined drummer Tony Williams' band Lifetime, which also featured Jack Bruce, in what many consider to have been a band far ahead of its time. Further solo albums followed which enhanced his reputation, and by this time he was firmly resident in America.

Probably his greatest achievement to date was the founding of the Mahavishnu Orchestra which included Billy Cobham on drums, Jan Hammer on keyboards and Rick Laird on bass. The Orchestra proved an innovation producing a blend of electric jazz and rock which was both breathtaking and powerful. It exposed McLaughlin to the rock world and paved the way for a hundred and one jazz/rock crossovers.

After two years of pushing back musical barriers the group was disbanded, and although McLaughlin put together another band under the Mahavishnu Orchestra name, they were never to reach the same heights. For the last few years McLaughlin has had various line-ups playing wildly diverse music from Shakti, which was essentially an acoustic Indian band, to a four piece with Billy Cobham, Jack Bruce and keyboard player Stu Goldberg, which was more about getting back to the roots of jazz rock.

For his electric playing, McLaughlin has of late been using a Gibson 345, which has a humbucking DiMarzio pickup fitted, although during his Mahavishnu Orchestra days, a double necked Gibson became quite a trade mark. He uses Marshall amplification, and very few pedals except for a Roland Jazz Chorus effect.

There is no doubt that many find McLaughlin and his philosophising somewhat overbearing, but few can match his dazzling technique on the guitar. When he's firing on all cylinders, the results are staggering and somewhat awesome. McLaughlin represents the other side of the coin from the self taught guitarists, and there are few players indeed who couldn't learn something from the maestro.

John Williams

One of the greatest classical guitarists in the world, John Williams has become a more accessible figure to rock audiences over the last few years, particularly through his work with the group Sky.

Born in Melbourne, Australia in 1941 he began playing classical guitar at the age of seven. In 1952 he moved to London, and as a young man studied under the great master Segovia. Through his solo concerts and performances with some of the great orchestras, he became a world famous virtuoso.

However, in 1971, John decided to explore other musical directions outside the confines of the classics, and recorded an album called "Changes". For this he recruited a number of famous rock musicians including Rick Wakeman, Chris Spedding and Herbie Flowers. The album also contained a diverse range of material, from the Beatles' "Because" to a Django Reinhardt tune and even a version of the old blues classic "House Of The Rising Sun".

Two years later, ace producer George Martin was brought in for the album "The Height Below" which featured John on electric guitar for the first time. Subsequent albums saw him continuing his experimentation until finally he put together a band in a rock format.

Sky, comprising Kevin Peek on guitar, Herbie Flowers on bass, Francis Monkman on keyboards and Tristan Fry on percussion, evolved a brand of semi-classical music which was to prove very popular. Both on record and in concert, they created something quite unique in the world of rock music. John also managed a solo hit with his version of "Cavetina"

which was the theme tune from the film "The Deer Hunter".

As far as his playing is concerned, his acoustic work is obviously in a class of its own, but the switch to electric was a different matter. Over the years a number of classical performers have expressed their distaste for the amplified instrument, but John had no such attitudes and looked upon the electric guitar as an exciting new challenge.

His first electric was a Gretsch, but near neighbour Steve Howe soon offered him valuable advice. After trying out a number of instruments in the vast Howe collection, John settled for a Gibson Les Paul. However, this did not mean that we were about to see Mr Williams turn into a wailing Heavy Metal axeman.

Because of his strict classical training, John cannot approach the standard rock guitarists' improvisational technique. As he rightly admits, most top rock guitarists have served a long apprenticeship in this aspect, and he could not hope to emulate it. So his electric guitar technique is very much an echo of his classical work.

For stage work, John has used a Gibson RD Artist electric with Sky, and has opted for an amplified Ovation guitar for his acoustic work. The amplifiers tend to be the standard rock guitarists' Marshalls.

His musical tastes reflect the diversity of his playing, apart from the obvious classics and Latin influences he also enjoys jazz, rock and even some country and western. Only someone with such a unique talent could perform classical works at the Albert Hall, jazz at Ronnie Scott's club, and rock with Sky at the Hammersmith Odeon.

Introduction to lead guitars

All reviewing, by its very nature, has to be subjective. No-one can tell you which is the perfect guitar for you. All any reviewer can ever hope to do is state the facts about a guitar: its materials, facilities and constructional details and then attempt to describe the sound of that guitar. Human nature being what it is, he will also pass an opinion on the instrument — but the choice is always yours in the end.

The guitars reviewed here were all assessed on the same basic amplification equipment and under the same circumstances to try and achieve uniformity of opinion. None of them, as far as we can tell, was specially set up for us. In every case we saw these guitars in much the same state that you would find them, hanging on the wall of a guitar shop.

Our scoring system for reviews is based, obviously, on personal taste but we have tried to indicate this where applicable in the text. If you're surprised to see so many guitars getting full marks for construction and finish it is simply because we ourselves were surprised by how many well made, well set up guitars we reviewed. Each instrument was given full marks for these two qualities initially and flaws and faults were subtracted from the total possible marks of five stars. Marks for sound and what we found ourselves calling "playability" are obviously subjective but, hopefully, explained in the review text. Most guitars scored quite highly because few guitars today actually sound bad in a direct sense. Whilst they might not have appealed to the reviewer, it was obvious that others would like them — and so it was near full marks again.

Not every maker or importer is represented equally in these pages, not out of bias in favour of one or against the other. We wanted as many instrument makers represented as possible but a handful were not interested in having their instruments reviewed at all, by anyone. Consequently a few brands are under-represented. This, by the way, is not the case with Yamaha, who were unable to supply us with more than a few samples, as they were in the middle of a complete re-vamp of their range at the time we were compiling these pages and were still waiting for their first major supply of samples from Japan.

To use this guide to the best advantage read through the pages and see which guitars sound like your sort of instrument, then go out and try them and form you own opinions, helped by our comments. After all, it's *your* money and the best we can do is try to help you spend it wisely!

Aria CS 350

The Aria CS 350 is something of a compromise, not that this is to be taken as a criticism. The Aria line as a whole has rocketed since its introduction to these shores to become what is generally recognised as one of the best overall ranges of Japanese instruments, but every maker has his pricing problems and the £200 barrier is one which it must be something of a struggle to satisfy. Below that sort of money people will tolerate design quirks, above it they expect the best, but this barrier is halfway there. Players who spend this sort of money have outgrown cheapies and have their ideal aspirations set on the top line guitars around. How do you satisfy them at this sort of price?

Aria's answer is what can only really be described as a "dinky" little guitar, the CS 350, which sits in their excellent Cardinal range of guitars and basses. The 350, features a bolt-on neck with a very high standard of jointing, two good quality pickups and that usual excellent standard of finish.

The neck offers a full 22 frets but somehow the guitar feels almost a miniature instrument, it's difficult to say why, it may have something to do with the cobalt blue finish of the sample. Whatever the cause, the Aria felt small, light and easy to handle, but possibly just a shade insubstantial.

The body is of ash, the neck maple and the quality of manufacture is little short of excellent, as is the finish. The body is carved away on top for increased comfort giving this guitar a feeling of sheer ease of use.

That ease extends as far as the neck which has a shape not as thin as a Fender but not as fat as a Gibson, a good, typically Aria, sensible compromise that nearly any guitar player, whatever his previous instrument, will swiftly feel at home with it.

It's a very nice guitar to play, this Aria, fitted with good strings and set up to perfection (as all the Arias tend to be) so that a player will feel ideally at home with it within minutes of picking it up in the shop. The pickups are Protomatic Vs, an exposed twin type with one black and one white coil. Running them is a single pickup selector, two volumes, two tones, a coil tap and a phase switch (nice to see such comprehensive specs at this sort of price!).

The sound of the Cardinal does not have a particular character of its own but at this price that's probably asking far too much. What it does have, however, is a tremendous degree of versatility, making it eminently suitable for the player whose work calls upon him to tackle all sorts of gigs.

Basic Fender type sounds are obtainable, ditto those of a humbucking Gibson. The little Aria will do a passable impression of most of them and that confirms it as a potentially hard-working semi-professional guitar.

Aria appreciate that players who can afford this sort of money are probably hard working guitarists on the way up. What they have given them, therefore, is a guitar which will cover them for as many types of work as is possible, all at a fair price. Few players would be unhappy with it. It's just very good value for money!

Price: £194

Body materials: Ash

Neck materials: Maple

Fingerboard materials: Rosewood

Machine heads: Aria chrome plated

Pickups: Protomatic Vs

Construction:	★★★★★
Finish:	★★★★★
Sound:	★★★★
Playability:	★★★★★
Value For Money:	★★★★★

Distributed by: Gigsville Ltd, Phoenix Way, South Drive, Heston, Middlesex. Tel: 01-897-3792.

Aria PE-R80

A particularly handsome looking instrument, the Aria PE-R80 is among the current top priced instruments from Japan, their version (given the vast price differential between Japanese and American instruments) of something like a Gibson Les Paul. The overall looks of the Aria are superb, it possesses that gloss appearance which few other mass produced instruments seem to have and promises some remarkable experiences for the adventurous player.

The choice of woods used in the PE-R80 is excellent. The body is a high quality maple finished in a dark brown stain and well varnished to protect it against life on the road. The neck too is maple, so cunningly welded to the body that it's almost impossible to tell whether it's a straight-through type or a remarkably fine glue jointed design. Either way it's a heel-less joint which facilitates high-up solos with tremendous ease.

The rosewood fingerboard on this Aria is inlaid with a design resembling cloud patterns, making the overall looks of the guitar rather luxurious if somewhat overstated by normal Western standards.

All the hardware is gold plated to an exemplary standard. This mechanical aspect offers the usual superbly smooth Oriental machine heads and a bridge which vaguely resembles a Gibson type in that it features a stop tailpiece preceded by a bridge which is adjustable for intonation individually but not string height, the latter coming from the two screws at either end of the bridge. For the money one would have preferred to have had full adjustment, especially as it's featured on some cheaper Arias. Switchgear on the PE-R80 comprises a top horn mounted selector plus two volume controls, two for tone, and a metal switch for coil tap of the two American-made DiMarzio Dual Sound twin coil pickups.

Some might find the fingerboard profile of this Aria rather strange. It's a well fretted design of extreme comfort but with quite a pronounced camber to it, which takes some getting used to if you're more familiar with flatter types. Still, that experience would give you speed — certainly it should be a fast neck to bend strings on — especially suitable for lead work with that excellent cutaway design where the heel would normally be on a conventionally joined guitar body/neck.

Sound of the Aria is also a shade on the odd side. Even with the single/twin coil possibilities the DiMarzios lend the Aria a bassy tone which is fine for chords but possibly a shade lacking in top frequencies for really trebly solo work. It is a question of taste, however, and many players might find the richness and sustain of this instrument just what they have been hankering after.

This Aria is worth checking out for those who like the warmth of tone and high output power with a well curved profile to the fingerboard. For such a player it would be very good value for money.

Price: £375

Body materials: Maple

Neck materials: Maple

Fingerboard materials: Rosewood

Machine heads: Aria

Pickups: DiMarzio dual sound humbuckers

Construction:	★★★★★
Finish:	★★★★★
Sound:	★★★★½
Playability:	★★★★½
Value For Money:	★★★★★

Distributed by: Gigsville Ltd, Phoenix Way, Heston, Middlesex. Tel: 01-897-3792.

Aria Pro11 TA-60

Semi-acoustics may lack the mobility value of small bodied solids but for a thick blues solo sound or a screaming treble tone there are few solids to touch them. The trouble is that they aren't easy to make to a good standard and the original American professional class instruments (led by the Gibson 335 series) are rather too expensive for younger, poorer players.

It might have been hoped that the Japanese makers would have got the price of this sort of guitar down to manageable proportions but very few have succeeded. One that does come to mind is Aria with their TA-60 — quite an expensive guitar but by no means beyond the reach of a hard-saving semi-pro.

This TA-60 was as immaculately finished as all Aria instruments. In looks the TA-60 is very much like a Gibson double cutaway semi-acoustic. The colour on the sample was a glowing red, complemented by a nice looking cream binding around the rosewood fingerboard which had been fretted very precisely with fat wire. The cream colour is continued as a body binding and on the pickguard too. This would be a very pretty instrument under stage lighting.

Hardware on the TA-60 is excellent. The machines are smooth and feel reliable, the nut is well cut and the bridge features individual adjustment for intonation but, following Brand G's principles, not height. This latter is accomplished by raising or lowering the whole bridge from either side. A gold plated "stop tailpiece" completes a generally pleasing design.

The twin humbucking AL-7 pickups are covered types, controlled by two volumes and two tones plus a sensibly placed selector switch for quick changeovers. In use the pots work progressively and quietly, enabling full use of the wide tonal potential of this guitar to be properly exploited.

Once you've grown used to the odd feeling of carrying a large bodied semi, the Aria soon establishes itself as a very fine guitar indeed. The neck is beautifully profiled and very, very fast to handle; the fret height complementing the light gauge strings supplied with new models. Fret buzz (sometimes a problem with this sort of guitar) was virtually absent and, overall, it played superbly.

The sound is excellent too. Aria's pickups are usually good but these are splendid! The neck pickup can deliver the warmest jazz sound you can imagine which will easily run into blues if you "up" the input gain on your pre-amp, and the bridge pickup will enable long soaring treble sustains to be taken to the edge of feedback — and beyond if you feel like playing that way. Semis can be very versatile instruments when at their best, and this is certainly a good example.

Not a particularly cheap instrument but this Aria's price does include a decent case and it's one of the nicest non-American semi-acoustics that this reviewer has played.

Price: £290	
Body materials: Maple top and back	
Neck materials: Maple	
Fingerboard materials: Rosewood	
Machine heads: Aria	
Pickups: Aria AL-7	
Construction:	★★★★★
Finish:	★★★★★
Sound:	★★★★★
Playability:	★★★★★
Value For Money:	★★★★★

Distributed by: Gigsville Ltd., Phoenix Way, Heston, Middlesex. Tel: 01-897-3792.

Aria YS 300

£170 is not a lot of money to pay for a good guitar these days. There are, of course, instruments of some quality available *below* that price but it's still a good target for an instrument suitable for advanced semi-pro players and affluent amateurs who want a decent instrument with sufficient qualities to take them on to the next stage of their careers. It is the ideal price for the Japanese in some ways too. Their resources seem rarely up to supplying semi-professional instruments significantly cheaper than this and when they eventually work up to the top of their price range they may appear less than perfect value besides British custom made guitars.

In one sense at least, the Aria YS 300 is the epitome of what can be bought for this sort of money. It's an attractive guitar, this sample finished in wine red on its mahogany body which was divided by a central strip of naturally coloured maple. This might give the impression that the YS 300 is a straight-through necked guitar. In fact it features a bolted-on neck and merely masquerades as a straight-through design. The bolt-on joint is, however, a good one, and allows pretty good access to the top frets. The fingerboard is of a good quality rosewood and the fretting on the sample was both accurate and well finished, lending itself to accurate intonation on chords and smooth, comfortable string bending.

Machines were of a generally good average Japanese quality, as was the bridge which features the almost universally found, through-the-body string fastening with full saddle adjustment for height and intonation. Pickup control (there are two Aria Protomatic II's fitted) is via a top horn mounted selector and a single volume plus two tone pot arrangement. At first this might seem a little ungenerous but in practise on stage, single master volume pots can lend themselves to very easy and rapid control, making them ideal for fast changes between solo and rhythm sounds.

Playing the Aria is quite a satisfying experience, especially bearing in mind the retail price. It appears to be a generally good compromise between rhythm and solo sounds with a fine neck and pickups which, if they aren't as powerful as some more expensive types on the market, do at least deliver sufficient whack to drive most modern master volume control equipped amps into a decent lead solo distortion.

The Aria feels a bit light and insubstantial to play, compared to truly professional guitars but the criticism becomes quite invalid when one looks at the price being asked for it.

Price: £170

Body materials: Mahogany/maple strip

Neck materials: Maple

Fingerboard materials: Rosewood

Machine heads: Aria

Pickups: Aria "Protomatic IIs" (plus coil tap)

Construction:	★★★★★
Finish:	★★★★★
Sound:	★★★★
Playability:	★★★★★
Value For Money:	★★★★

Distributed by: Gigsville Ltd, Phoenix Way, Heston, Middlesex. Tel: 01-897-3792.

Ashley Pangborn Warrior

One of the major problems inhibiting British guitar makers is their apparent inability to mass produce their instruments. Even those craftsmen whose guitars follow certain set designs (like Gordon Smith and Peter Cook), as opposed to purely bespoke lines, make so relatively few as to be classed among the "custom" makers. One maker who is offering his instruments on a semi-production basis is Ashley Pangborn whose basses and guitars are available in greater numbers as a result.

The guitar model is the Warrior, which comes in one or two pickup versions. Despite its apparent mass produced label it neither looks nor feels like it. In fact the finish of this guitar makes it look as if it has been the subject of some careful handfinishing — a very nice touch indeed.

The body on the sample was mahogany, with a brown sunburst finish which looked particularly nice over the section of the maple through neck. The fingerboard was luxurious ebony, well fretted and just barely cambered. The rest of the hardware comprised Schaller machines and a Pangborn designed bridge which is a type allowing string-through-body fixing and then brass (untracked) saddles adjustable by spring loaded screws for front to back movements and with two micro-screws per saddle for accurate height. The two twin coil pickups on this guitar are controlled by a standard pickup selector plus two volume and two tone controls and help to give the instrument a very conventional, yet thorough look.

Playing the Pangborn is a pure delight. I personally like ebony fingerboards very much indeed and this one, accompanied by some of the fattest frets (hand polished and rounded at a guess) that I've come across and a slight neck camber make this a very pleasing guitar for soloing. Chord work is fun too and the pickups Pangborn uses are especially good, combining naturally with the density of the wood to produce more raunch and sustain and a curious purity of tone than is usually found on the average Japanese production instrument selling for this sort of price.

Perhaps the only item missing from this instrument is a coil tap — not an unreasonable request at this price. But possibly the maker feels that his instrument is toppy enough without it. Certainly, on the bridge pickup, the Pangborn can screech with the best of them and this, aided by the superbly easy access to the very top frets, courtesy of the through neck makes it an ideal guitar for the hard soloing guitar player.

Pricewise this guitar stands out as being very good value for money. It's a really pleasing instrument to play, has a fabulous sound and looks as if it would be very reliable in use. At the price, there are a couple of British made guitars and possibly a few Japanese instruments which stand comparison. Certainly, there's nothing from the USA — it really is that good.

Price: £319

Body materials: Mahogany

Neck materials: Maple

Fingerboard materials: Ebony

Machine heads: Schaller

Pickups: Schaller

Construction:	★★★★★
Finish:	★★★★★
Sound:	★★★★★
Playability:	★★★★★
Value For Money:	★★★★★

Distributed by: Pangborne Guitars, 12A West Street, Reigate, Surrey. Tel: 07372-44331.

Chandler Guitars/Schecter "Strat"

As well as importing from Schecter Guitar Research in California, Chandler Guitàrs, UK distributors of this line, also assemble and sell whole guitars from Schecter parts. To sample the goods we tried a complete Schecter Strat copy which had been assembled by Chandler for a customer. Frightened of scratching or denting it this reviewer sat down to play. Pretty soon I was standing up — this was *some Strat!*

The guitar in question wasn't exactly a Strat, although its body shape and apparent physical looks might have fooled you. The body is a sunburst ash type, carved very well and finished off (probably in the UK) to virtual perfection by Chandlers. This was fitted with a solid brass high gloss scratchplate and the whole assembly bolted on with four bolts to a solid maple neck. This was a model Chandler had made to special order and so the beautiful maple neck actually had a Gibson radius, as opposed to that of a typical Strat. The fretting on this sample was superb and the guitar overall was perfectly set up for immediate use.

Up on the headstock the brass nut was complemented by a set of gold plated Kluson machines. They worked well enough, more than that I wouldn't care to say. The Schecter Strat also featured a solid brass bridge of truly excellent quality. This was more or less a direct Strat copy, complete with tremolo system but with a short brass arm. In use it was the best new tremolo I've come across; even fairly wild use did not cause the tuning to move much at all.

Departing again from Strat practice, this model also had just two knurled brass pots, one for tone, one for volume. In addition there were three metal flick switches, each of which offered three positions.

Sounds quite beyond the reach of any other Strat or Strat type guitar that I have played poured from this guitar from the moment it was plugged in. I had previously been very impressed with Fender's "The Strat" with its Dan Armstrong development work, but this Schecter model has a superior tone. Each of the three pickups seems to be a single coil unit, tapped by the three way switch for different tones. All the single note lead lines I could think of came ringing out of the Schecter with a strange fire, coupled with a purity and clean top which I have never previously encountered in a guitar of this type. Play around with those three flick switches and all the sounds a Fender lover could ask for are there, from the raunchiest chords imaginable to deafening lead sounds.

The Gibson radius on the neck of the sample didn't feel quite right for me personally but this was just one option which one player had asked for and that's his choice. How useful that the choice *exists!* Without a doubt this is one of the best single coil pickup guitars that I have played. The price may seem steep but wait till you try one!

Price: £500

Body materials: Ash

Neck materials: Maple

Fingerboard materials: Maple integral with neck

Machine heads: Kluson

Pickups: Schecter

Construction:	★★★★★
Finish:	★★★★★
Sound:	★★★★★
Playability:	★★★★★
Value For Money:	★★★★★

Distributed by: Chandler Guitars Ltd, 199 Sandycombe, Kew, Richmond, Surrey. Tel: 01-940-5874.

DiMarzio "Strat"

In an attempt to help players make up their minds about new bridges, pickups, bodies or necks, DiMarzio's UK distributor, Rose Morris and Co., have put together a complete Strat replica from DiMarzio parts, to demonstrate what can be done if a player decides to build his own guitar from an assembly of what are, otherwise, add-on bits and pieces.

The "exercise" Strat features a well made body with a deep brown sunburst on it, looking and feeling (due to the comfortable contouring on the body) like a fine quality Stratocaster of some impressive vintage.

The neck is a maple type with a nice rosewood fingerboard and good quality fat frets which are of uniform height and positioning and thus call for no after purchase wheeling and dealing to bring the guitar up to scratch. The machines are regular Klusons — alright for authenticities' sake but definitely lacking in quality when compared to many Japanese guitars of recent years.

The pickups and bridge, however, are superb. The bridge is a chromed job, fitted with the usual DiMarzio tremolo system (like a Fender) and offering full adjustment potential. The pickups are, of course, three single coil types, run by one volume and two tone pots plus the latest type of five-way selector.

In terms of its sound, the DiMarzio's screaming single coil pickups lend themselves to just the sort of material for which you'd normally use a Strat. The sound is as close as you'll get to a vintage Strat below £500 — it even has the whang bar, don't forget!

Overall the tone is very Fender-like (as one would have hoped), with plenty of superb, out-of-phase sounds on the five-way selector switch and then flicking into overdrive on the back pickup for a solo sound which the majority of players could not fail to be impressed by.

For guitarists who want a vintage-style Strat and who don't mind buying a guitar without "Fender" on the headstock, this has got to be an object lesson. The quality of construction would be down to you, but if the samples of ready fretted DiMarzio necks and contoured bodies are anything to go by, then a really good guitar could be the result of your labours.

The bridge and the fretting, the shaping and the contouring are all near perfect and the sound is capable of anything that a really good Strat can do. For players with the time and faith to have a go, a build-it-yourself DiMarzio must be a tremendous guitar to own.

Price: Approx £350

Body materials: Ash

Neck materials: Maple

Fingerboard materials: Rosewood

Machine heads: Kluson

Pickups: DiMarzio single coil

Construction:	★★★★★
Finish:	★★★★
Sound:	★★★★★
Playability:	★★★★★
Value For Money:	★★★★★

Distributed by: Rose-Morris and Co. Ltd, 32-34 Gordon House Road, London NW5. Tel: 01-267-5151.

Chris Eccleshall Falcon

The past five years have seen the emergence of a new "super breed" of guitar makers in the UK. Many are superlative craftsmen, turning out instruments of unsurpassed quality — usually at prices significantly below those charged by the mass producers who should, by economic theory, have the advantage of economy of scale. These days that doesn't seem to hold true, as the Chris Eccleshall's Falcon guitar ably demonstrates.

The Falcon has a top of beautiful bird's eye maple, carved to shape in the expensive and luxurious way that was a feature of the best of the old Les Pauls. The main body wood below this arched top is a beautiful sample of mahogany, and glued into that body is a neck also of mahogany with an ebony fingerboard very nicely inlaid with a tiny fleur-de-lys pattern. The fretting, too, was of the highest standard, very well set and polished to ensure both accuracy and comfort.

Chris Eccleshall uses a lot of Japanese hardware in his guitars. It is often said that Japanese machines are of the highest quality, generally more reliable in use than types of greater repute and Chris seems to agree because his Tune-O-Matic design bridge is *not* from Gibson, but is a Japanese copy. The silk-smooth machines are Gotohs and work extremely well also.

The pickups fitted to the sample Falcon were a DiMarzio PAF and a Super Distortion. These pickups sounded very fine indeed, not possessing the slightly "rasping" and overblown quality which this brand of pickups has shown before. That must be due to their combination with Chris's superb body design and woodworking. This is a fine, dense, guitar, guaranteeing an excellent sustain.

Chris Eccleshall's Falcon is a remarkable instrument. In some ways it's a bit like a very hot Les Paul with a wonderfully accurate and fast neck and a sound which is fat and warm, the antithesis, perhaps, of a Strat in that respect.

From a playing point of view this must be one of the best guitars in the book — ideally suited as an alternative, perhaps, to the guitarist who might want a vaguely Gibson-like sound but who wants a more individual instrument with that particular "feel" which you will only get from a custom made guitar.

Imagine a handmade Gibson with prodigious sustain, a little more fire, a unique body shape and a lovely, just slightly curved, fingerboard and you're somewhere near the qualities of this Falcon guitar. If the sample Falcon is anything to go by, Chris Eccleshall is one of Britain's finest makers — and this is one of the best guitars this reviewer has played.

Price: £420

Body materials: Bird's eye maple top, mahogany back

Neck materials: Mahogany

Fingerboard materials: Ebony

Machine heads: Gotoh

Pickups: DiMarzio super distortion/DiMarzio P.A.F.

Construction:	★ ★ ★ ★ ★
Finish:	★ ★ ★ ★ ★
Sound:	★ ★ ★ ★ ★
Playability:	★ ★ ★ ★ ★
Value For Money:	★ ★ ★ ★ ★

Distributed by: Chris Eccleshall Guitars, 17c Station Parade, Ealing Common, London W5. Tel: 01-992-4741.

Eccleshall Junior LP

£165 doesn't buy you much in the way of exciting guitars these days. This sort of money will just about obtain for you the run-of-the-mill Japanese copy guitar or, perhaps, one of the originals which are offered by makers like Westone, Aria, Hondo or Ibanez. Either way, you will not be getting anything less than a mass produced instrument for your money so it may come as something of a shock to learn that for a relatively paltry £165 you can buy a guitar handmade by Chris Eccleshall, one of the finest craftsmen working in the UK. Obviously, expecting anything other than the bare basics from *any* maker for this sort of money will only led to severe disappointment but what Chris seems to be able to deliver by way of value for money for the impoverished guitarist really does seem to set a standard that few, if any, can match.

The Junior LP guitar (as the name suggests) is a bit of a copy of a Les Paul Junior, a very plain looking guitar that would not appeal to the really showy Heavy Metal merchants but, rather, an instrument which would appeal to the player who values playability and sound above looks alone. A bare mahogany guitar, the Eccleshall has a fairly thick body with excellent glued neck joints. The hardware carries on this maker's predilection for Japanese made hardware in that it features Gotoh machine heads and a bridge of a Gibson design type which offers full adjustment for intonation but not for string height. A good design, for all that, and there is no evidence of skimping on quality here, regardless of price, either in parts or workmanship.

The plain mahogany body may not be the most attractive ever made and the way in which it tones in with the basic plain rosewood of the neck with its fat, polished Gibson frets, makes the guitar look sturdy and reliable rather than exciting. The thick bodied Eccleshall balances well when played either seated and standing. It is, frankly, just one of those guitars which feels 100 per cent right from the moment you pick it up and start playing. The sound, too, is totally professional, it is firey, warm, savage — however you want it to be.

I feel that Chris is offering a tremendous bargain here that no other maker seems able to equal, let alone beat. As things stand, the name Chris Eccleshall is probably no more than a legend to some readers but I'd recommend you to try one of these guitars before buying anything else in this price range. With its superlative twin coil pickup sounds and a neck which is fast enough for even the most fastidious of players it is a fine guitar at a remarkable price.

Price: £165

Body materials: Mahogany

Neck materials: Mahogany

Fingerboard materials: Rosewood

Machine heads: Gotoh

Pickups: Double eagle

Construction:	★★★★★
Finish:	★★★★★
Sound:	★★★★★
Playability:	★★★★★
Value For Money:	★★★★★

Distributed by: Chris Eccleshall Guitars, 17c Station Parade, Ealing Common, London W5. Tel: 01-992-4741.

Fender Bullet

Despite the prevailing trends away from guitars made in the USA towards those made in the Far East, and an apparently suicidal desire to continually raise prices, there is some hope for the American guitar makers if they can maintain their prestige reputations, ally them to excellent design quality and make some attempt to align their prices towards the Japanese.

The introduction of the Fender Bullet, may signify the turning of the tide. The Bullet is a plain, simple, effective instrument which offers, at a retail price almost absurdly low compared with other brand F instruments, a start for the younger player who, maybe, aspires to a Telecaster but who cannot, yet, afford one.

It is fairly self-evident that the Tele has provided a model for the Bullet. The traditional maple bolt-on neck fixes to a body whose shape is distinctly familiar. Hardware, too, is typical standard Fender; Kluson machines and a string-through-the-body termination system, two rather cheap looking sealed single coil pickups, a three way pickup selector, two volumes and one tone pot of a very good electrical quality and about the weirdest bridge design seen to date.

In an effort to keep the manufacturing costs down, the makers have decided to fuse the scratchplate material (probably anodised metal from the look of it) into a combined bridge unit. Thus the scratchplate bends up at the back to allow the strings to terminate through it. Before they get that far they've passed over fairly typical Fender saddles offering full intonation and height potential on an individual basis.

In use the Fender is fast and pleasant to play. The neck profile is easy and the fretting on this sample was good and true. There was a bit of fret buzz on the low E string, mind you, but regular Fender players will know that problem of old and will probably be as puzzled by it as this reviewer.

Soundwise, the guitar can give any Japanese instrument of similar price a good run for its money. The Bullet feels like a small guitar but there's nothing small about the sound. These new pickups have bags of poke for what they must cost to make, and have more than enough charge in them to drive the average modern pre-amp into distortion. When that happens the Fender does what all true Fenders should — it sings like a thoroughbred. It's a pure single coil sound which you either love or hate, but it's archetypal enough to appeal to most guitarists who like the basic Fender sound.

Being a genuine Fender, the Bullet will almost certainly have a reasonable re-sale value if you ever grow out of it, but, as it stands, this would make an excellent purchase for the young player who wants that particular fire-breathing Fender sound or an impoverished guitarist whose first guitar was a Tele or a Strat. Congratulations Fender, this is a truly superb guitar for the money!

Price: £140

Body materials: Unidentified

Neck materials: Maple

Fingerboard materials: Rosewood

Machine heads: Kluson

Pickups: Fender

Construction:	★★★★
Finish:	★★★★
Sound:	★★★★★
Playability:	★★★★★
Value For Money:	★★★★★

Distributed by: CBS/Arbiter Ltd, Fender House, Centenary Estate, Jeffreys Road, Brimsdown, Enfield, Middlesex. Tel: 01-805-8555.

Fender "Gold" Stratocaster

This guitar, a fairly recent introduction from a newly enlivened and invigorated Fender company, is a fairly conventional modern Strat. It differs from other Fenders in the very high quality gold plated hardware.

That aside, all the traditional Strat qualities are there. The gold version has the later type five-way pickup selector and the traditional white plastic scratchplate and one volume pot plus two tones. The superb design of floating tremolo is fitted and the heavy duty bridge offers the normal total control of intonation and string height adjustments which made Strats seem so revolutionary when Leo Fender first introduced them. It is still one of the best guitar bridges available, with few peers.

At the back of the Strat (where the tension springs are located beneath a plastic plate) you'll find only three of the five possible springs have been fitted, as with all Strats these days. This is to accommodate the lighter gauge strings fitted as standard — the other two come in an envelope in the excellent moulded case along with the complementary lead, strap, cloth and instruction book.

The neck on the sample was maple, well fretted but with a very strange profile. Not being a regular Strat player, and most recent experience being with the definitive model called "The Strat", this shape surprised me in that it was very flat and, although as thin and fast as any Strat I could remember, seemed actually sharp at the edges. Although it never will, it *feels* as though it could actually cut into a hand which was gripping it too tight — rather odd for a guitar designed and made for rock players who habitually use their thumbs to hold down barre chords! Still, maybe this is acceptable to some players — it wouldn't endear this reviewer to a guitar although the neck profile is otherwise blindingly fast and the fretting standard superb.

Soundwise this Strat was just about everything a Strat should be, capable of those piercing, screaming tones which work so well in the hands of a skilled player and tempting him to play around with all sorts of odd harmonics produced by the right hand, secure in the knowledge that the high frequency purity of the pickups wil carry them right on sustaining, provided a sensible amp overload is there to assist.

Only one fault manifested itself on this sample; the tremolo device was a bit "off" in that the strings were inclined to lose their tuning after even a fairly restrained assault upon the gold plated tremolo arm. However, the sample was a rather early one which had been rushed through to the UK for an exhibition appearance and no conclusions about this guitar in general should be drawn from this one sample.

All in all this is a fine guitar — as every Strat should be. You may find the neck profile easier to live with than this reviewer, and you will have to make your own judgement about whether the value of gold plating is worth the difference to *you* over a normally priced and plainer looking model. It is just a rather nice Strat with rather nice gold plating. The choice is yours.

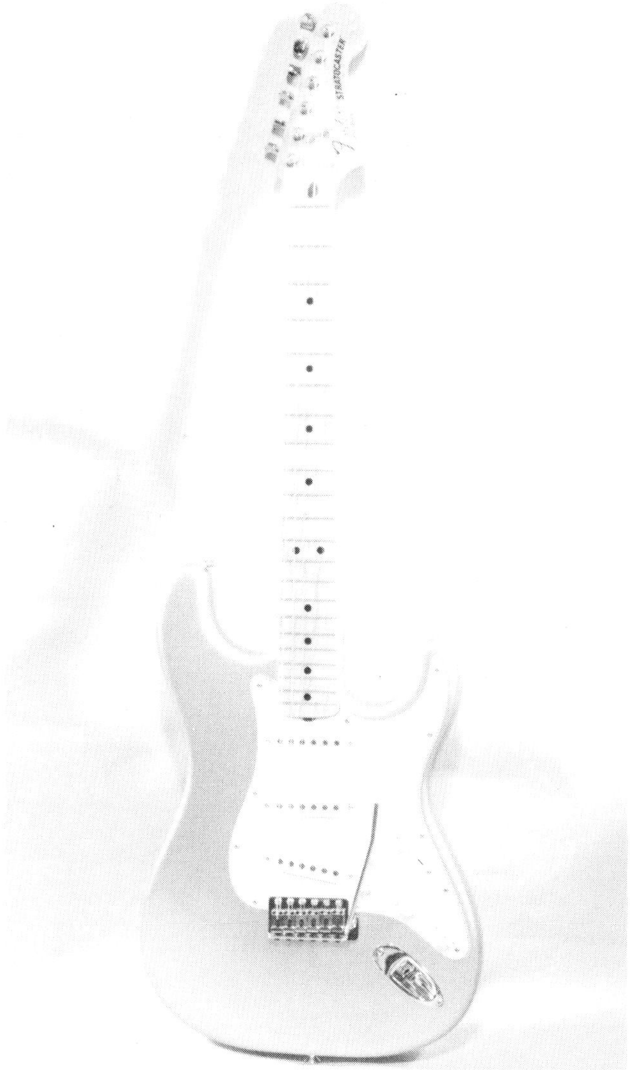

Price: £657

Body materials: Ash

Neck materials: Maple

Fingerboard materials: Maple

Machine heads: Kluson

Pickups: Fender (single coil)

Construction:	★ ★ ★ ★ ★
Finish:	★ ★ ★ ★
Sound:	★ ★ ★ ★ ★
Playability:	★ ★ ★ ★
Value For Money:	★ ★ ★ ½

Distributed by: CBS/Arbiter Ltd, Fender House, Centenary Estate, Jeffrys Road, Brimsdown, Enfield, Middlesex. Tel: 01-805-8555.

Fender Vintage Telecaster

Gibson began the trend of issuing replicas of past designs and now Fender have followed it. A case in point is the Vintage Telecaster, a supremely accurate recreation of a very early Tele which has even been coloured to resemble a well aged guitar. Even the case follows old Fender patterns, coming in a tweed covering, rather than the modern plastic moulding.

As Telecasters have changed surprisingly little since they first appeared, this guitar isn't that much of a stranger. It has brass saddles, domed control knobs, and a black Bakelite pickguard. It still features the rather primitive three-way pickup selector, one pickup set into a screwed-on bridge baseplate with its two strings per saddle arrangement (adjustable for both height and intonation) and a one volume/one tone control arrangement.

It is hard to be certain, but it appears as though the makers have even duplicated the nut material correctly — it's bone, not plastic. The machines are the usual six Klusons and the bolt-on neck will be familiar to all Fender players the world over.

In total, the guitar looks superb. One couldn't say that the yellow contouring of the ash body and maple neck (no applied fingerboard, as it's a 100 per cent pure maple job) looks exactly the same as a real Telecaster from circa 1952 but it does look extremely good nonetheless.

The Vintage Telecaster plays like a dream, too. The neck profile is remarkably comfortable and if you like Fender's scale length and the 21 fret arrangement then this could qualify as one of the best necks you've ever tried. The guitar also sounds very fine. That natural Telecaster bassy boom is there on the neck pickup (not a sound that it's easy to find the right amp setting to make much use of these days) but the bridge pickup gives all the familiar "clang" and "twang" which an amazing span of players from country pickers to hard rockers have used to such great effect over the years.

Of course the guitar doesn't sound like every other '52 Telecaster. Half the reason why old guitars vary is the damage done to the coil windings and the changes, over the years, which take place in the magnetic field of a pickup. It is almost impossible to duplicate this effect but Fender have certainly succeeded in getting as close as possible to the original. The result is a solid instrument constructed with considerable skill and care, playing and looking fine and sounding like the Telecaster of your dreams.

Whether this makes it worth the asking price is debatable. It *is* only a replica and there may well be better instruments for the money with all the latest design improvements, amongst them Fenders. However, this reviewer loved playing it, loved the sound and would like to own one. Once you try one you probably would too!

Price: £620

Body materials: Ash

Neck materials: Maple

Fingerboard materials: Maple

Machine heads: Kluson

Pickups: Fender (single coil)

Construction:	★★★★★
Finish:	★★★★★
Sound:	★★★★★
Playability:	★★★★★
Value For Money:	★★★★½

Distributed by: CBS/Arbiter Ltd, Fender House, Centenary Estate, Jeffrys Road, Brimsdown, Enfield, Middlesex. Tel: 01-805-8555.

Fletcher Coppock and Newman Satellite 90T

Today's beginner can find quite a few instruments on the market selling at around £100 or below which are well worth owning, even if only for the first six months or so of his or her career. Trying to fulfill this need is the Satellite 90T guitar, a humble enough offering but an instrument with some reasonable qualities.

Some of the features of this guitar are almost ludicrously up-market for the asking price. It has a brass nut and a straight-through neck (multi-laminated maple with a rosewood fingerboard) which is reasonably well set into a maple body stained to resemble rosewood. The finish is that deliberately dull, satin effect rather than cheap shiny plastic and overall it doesn't look bad at all.

Hardware on the Satellite isn't too cheap, either. The headstock (vaguely Fender in looks) features a "six in a strip" arrangement of closed back machines. On this sample they seemed reasonably well geared and didn't slip whilst playing.

The bridge is a screw-on plate with what looks like brass alloy saddles riding on it. These are individually lowered by allen screws which are far too sharp and could result in damage to the picking hand if you were playing back at the bridge or clumsily fumbling your way to experiment with damping techniques.

The twin pickups are humbucking types, controlled by the usual two volume, two tone arrangement aided by a flick switch for single or twin coil operation. The neck on this guitar seemed very slim and even qualifies as "well finished" if you take into account the price. It's certainly not hard to play and the fitting of fairly well-finished fat frets helps the younger player too.

Soundwise the Satellite is quite respectable, in fact, for once, what we have here is a guitar at this sort of price which actually sounds better than it looks!

Overall the tone is quite surprisingly full and fat, the coil tap is very useful in that it increases a sound which is already surprisingly versatile due to the pickups themselves. The pots are a bit along "sudden death" lines, they are almost either "on" or "off" without much variability in between. But it's easy to be critical of any instrument retailing around this price level. An experienced guitarist would probably find this instrument distinctly cheap and cheerful but at least he would be able to *play* it — something which would have been very difficult with a beginner's guitar 10 or 20 years ago.

Despite a few faults (the only one of which would be considered serious is that allen screw arrangement on the saddles) the conclusion is that this is a very fair effort indeed for the money. It would make a good choice for players moving on from their first acoustic or possibly a battered old electric hangover from the past. One of the best cheapies that you're likely to come across.

Price: £115

Body materials: Maple

Neck materials: Laminated maple

Fingerboard materials: Rosewood

Machine heads: "Satellite" chrome plated

Pickups: "Satellite" humbuckers

Construction:	★ ★ ★
Finish:	★ ★ ★
Sound:	★ ★ ★
Playability:	★ ★ ★ ½
Value For Money:	★ ★ ★ ★

Distributed by: FCN Music, Morley Road, Tonbridge, Kent. Tel: 0732-365271.

Gibson Firebird II A.S.B.

Possibly one of the best looking guitar shapes ever, the new Firebird resembles the earliest models of this famous name. Its body is probably walnut with a beautiful maple top. The neck is also attractive and is glued in place. To this a rosewood fingerboard has been fixed and fretted with Gibson's usual excellent quality fat fretwire. Like all the Gibsons from their new UK distributor, Rosetti and Co., it had obviously been very carefully set up.

The traditional angled Firebird headstock sports Kluson machines — a symbol of the past, perhaps, but a brand which has no place at all on a guitar costing £925! Down the business end of the new Firebird are the two sealed Gibson pickups, a Tune-O-Matic bridge and another of those innovatory TP6 tailpieces.

Up to now, you will have noticed many similarities between this model and previous Firebirds. But there is one tremendous difference — this Firebird is active, believe it or not. In theory the attractions of an active guitar should be manifold. Active basses are both useful and widely used but, somehow, guitarists have seemed less ready to convert to active instruments, having played the Firebird one can understand why. To start with the Gibson active system is difficult to understand. Guitars like this Firebird, feature four rotary pots, two volumes and two tones which are marked normally for volume (i.e. 0-10) but as -5 to 0 and then +5 on the tones. Zero is presumably supposed to be flat response.

In addition to these, which are top and bass boost, there are also two metal flick switches, one for compression "on" and one for expansion "on". There is also, of course, a pickup selector. Unfortunately the sample came without an instruction manual and this reviewer puzzled for hours over the functions of the various switches and knobs. The volumes were obvious and the active bass boost and treble boost and pickup selector certainly do what they are supposed to do, but the compression either works better on the neck pickup and not at all on the bridge unit or it suits the sound of the bridge unit far better.

Soundwise the Firebird is great when used for chordal work with compression on. A rich, almost Little Feat, chord sound reproduces itself from the guitar, but it doesn't seem to be especially variable so perhaps a variable outboard compression pedal would be a better buy. Either way the guitar works well with the effect, but it is an expensive way of achieving it, especially as its range appears to be fixed. The sound was pleasing, however, on both chords and lead solos on the neck pickup. On the bridge pickup it seemed to have little or no effect.

Playing the Firebird is a good experience, the neck is nice and the sound can be made very expressive (especially with that compressor on) but there are other modern active systems on the market, which are easier to understand and use. Despite this, some players might fall in love with the guitar regardless of the high price.

Price: £925

Body materials: Mahogany

Neck materials: Mahogany

Fingerboard materials: Rosewood

Machine heads: Kluson

Pickups: Gibson

Construction:	★ ★ ★ ★ ★
Finish:	★ ★ ★ ★ ★
Sound:	★ ★ ★ ★ ½
Playability:	★ ★ ★ ★ ★
Value For Money:	★ ★ ★ ★

Distributed by: Rosetti (EMI) Ltd, 138/140 Old Street, London EC1N 9BL. Tel: 01-253-7294.

Gibson Howard Roberts Fusion

Trying to define what is meant by the term "jazz" guitar isn't easy. Often one tends to call any semi-acoustic instrument with an antiquated shape, uncomfortable neck and weak, bassy pickups a "jazz guitar" and, unfortunately, so it would seem do many guitar makers. And yet there is no reason why a guitar suitable for traditional jazzy richness and warmth should not also have a wide range of other tones. Fortunately that's just what Gibson's Howard Robert Fusion is all about.

In terms of its looks it is fabulous. Naturally, it's a semi-acoustic available in two finishes, Fireburst and Antique. The sample was Antique and it was certainly one of the most beautifully coloured instruments this reviewer has ever seen. The top is maple with a well controlled arch to it. The back too is of arched maple as are the sides. The quality of construction was superb and the finish equally good.

Internally there is a solid block of wood (probably maple and spruce) contributing to the sound and sustain of this guitar which is so much better than most semi-acoustics. The machines work reliably and smoothly, as do the two volume and two tone controls which run the two pickups — one standard humbucking type at the front and one "super" model at the back.

The neck on this guitar is also rather impressive. It's a maple job but with a very pleasing ebony fingerboard, fretted to perfection and although possessing dimensional characteristics which aren't exactly wafer-thin, it's fast and very comfortable, aided by Gibson's usual fretting and Peter Cook's setting-up for the UK market.

The bridge is the typical standard Gibson Tune-O-Matic type with no individual height adjustment, followed by the TP6 tuning tailpiece device which works well but I have personally found it hard to get used to. Other players, however, may find this ability to tune strings with the right hand very useful.

The Howard Roberts Fusion is the best sounding jazz guitar that this reviewer has ever played. Its tonal qualities range from extremely clear yet soothingly warm bass to a quite piercing treble. It is a guitar of the most extreme versatility, capable of expressing a delicacy of touch and style that few solids can approach. If "pushed" it *does* feedback, but that internal block helps make it an acceptable feature and the feedback that does come in is both usable and pleasant if you actually play *with* it, rather than fight it.

Even at such a high retail price this remains one of the half dozen or so most pleasing guitars on the market, truly an instrument to break down musical barriers and enable a player to really expand on his style and abilities. By any standards a first rate instrument!

Price: £999

Body materials: Maple

Neck materials: Maple

Fingerboard materials: Ebony

Machine heads: Grover

Pickups: Gibson "Super" humbucker

Construction:	★★★★★
Finish:	★★★★★
Sound:	★★★★★
Playability:	★★★★★
Value For Money:	★★★★★

Distributed by: Rosetti (EMI) Ltd, 138/140 Old Street, London EC1. Tel: 01-253-7294

Gibson Les Paul Custom

On looks alone this Custom Les Paul must be a prince among solid bodied guitars. Its hardware is gold plated, the body of the sample finished in a superb dark sunburst and the whole guitar looks like a good £800 plus worth of wood and metal.

Despite all this glitter and finish, however, many of the same comments apply to the constructional details of this Les Paul as to the other two looked at in these pages. It bears that familiar heavyweight body of mahogany with a carved maple applied top, a neck of maple, a fingerboard of really excellent dark rosewood, fat, typically Gibson frets, good quality Grover machines and all those attributes which have made this such a popular guitar since its inception in the 1950's.

Where this Les Paul differs significantly from the others is in the use of a pair of standard Gibson humbuckers. These deliver a sound which even barely informed listeners would, at once, identify as coming from a Les Paul. This is possibly the archetypal fat sounding Gibson which has been heard on so many records and so many stages over the years. There are numerous other guitars which will approach it these days, but it remains one of the two basic classic sounds of rock guitar, along with that of the single coil Fender Stratocaster.

In many ways this was the Les Paul which appealed to this reviewer most of all. If I wanted a single coil pickup sound with good sustain, there are guitars with far easier necks than those found on Les Pauls. If I wanted a "half-and-half" sound, well, that can be had too. But the sheer warmth and overdrive potential of these pickups seem best suited to the basic qualities of harmonic strength, tonal depth and superlative sustain. Given the choice of any one of the current Les Pauls, I suppose this would be the one I'd opt for — it seems as if all the qualities of the body marry together with those deep voiced pickups to give both a lead and rhythm guitar sound which is almost an archetype. Mind you, it's still all down to taste and your choice may be quite different!

One thing that does stand out is that, with all the historical talk of "fretless wonders" none of them has a thin neck. In fact, by modern standards from both the best UK and Japanese makers (and Gibson's own S.G. to name but one) they all have necks which are positively slow, chunky — dare I commit heresy and suggest clumpy? If you don't mind that, and are one of those guitarists who likes an instrument which puts up a bit of a fight then a Les Paul will suit.

Price: £825

Body materials: Mahogany with maple top

Neck materials: Maple laminate

Fingerboard materials: Rosewood

Machine heads: Grover

Pickups: Gibson "Humbucker"

Construction:	★★★★★
Finish:	★★★★★
Sound:	★★★★★
Playability:	★★★★★
Value For Money:	★★★★

Distributed by: Rosetti (EMI) Ltd, 138/140 Old Street, London EC1. Tel: 01-253 7294.

Gibson Les Paul De Luxe

Like all the Les Paul family of the traditional kind (excluding "bargain basement" versions like "The Paul") the De Luxe shares considerable woodworking and hardware details with the other models in the series. It sports the familiar carved maple top applied to the very thick mahogany body and has a glued neck fitted with a rosewood fingerboard.

This sample came very well set up with a sensible action and string gauge. The fretting was very good and the intonation perfect. Found in a shop like this, you could have taken it straight out that night and played a gig with it without the necessity for any alterations that were not just down to personal taste.

The colouring on the model loaned was "natural" which is exactly what it suggests. Hardware on the De Luxe is just about as standard throughout the range: Grover machines of good quality, a bone nut (or is it plastic — it's hard to tell these days!) with the traditional Les Paul "stop" tailpiece and adjustable bridge. All are well made and finished to a standard which should please even the most critical eyes.

Where this model differs substantially from other Les Pauls is in its use of a type of twin coil pickup designed by the makers to offer a more brilliant sounding output when compared with other humbuckers from the range. These are the small metal types which one can easily mistake for single coil units at a glance. They are, in fact, humbuckers, with that special treble output.

In use the feel of this guitar is virtually identical to that of the Pro model previously reviewed. A blindfolded player would be hard pressed to tell any differences at all — unless, of course, he was plugged into his amp, which is just when the differences would show.

This model has been designed, the makers claim, to give a tonal brilliance which some may want over and above the sheer "screech potential" of the single coil Pro De Luxe model and, certainly, the full sounding humbucking Custom. This reviewer personally found that the sound of this version, whatever its natural merits, just seems to fall between two stools. It doesn't offer the warmth or "bottle" of the full steaming humbucking version, nor does it seem to have the tonal clarity of a single coil model.

However, all the other Les Paul qualities are there from the excellent sustain to the rather fat neck. Whether you'll take to this model of Les Paul or one of the others will be a matter of taste. This might be the one to go for if you feel a Custom is too fat sounding and the Pro is too thin. Whichever you choose you'll be acquiring an equally well made instrument.

Price: £725

Body materials: Mahogany with maple top

Neck materials: Maple laminate

Fingerboard materials: Rosewood

Machine heads: Grover

Pickups: Gibson "brilliant" humbuckers

Construction:	★★★★★
Finish:	★★★★★
Sound:	★★★★
Playability:	★★★★½
Value For Money:	★★★★

Distributed by: Rosetti (EMI) Ltd, 138/140 Old Street, London EC1. Tel: 01-253-7294.

Gibson Les Paul Pro De Luxe

Gibson's Les Paul guitar must be the most famous instrument in this book — and yet so wide is the range these days, so vast the possible permutations of pickups and colours, that each model shares only a few features in common with the next and it's hard to think of any one particular version which epitomises *the* Les Paul.

Nonetheless, the Pro De Luxe model must come pretty close to that description. In common with most of the range, it offers the archetypal Les Paul body, a thick mahogany base with a carved maple top applied. The tremendous thickness of the woods used in all Les Paul models endows each of them, almost regardless of which pickups are fitted, with a legendary sustain characteristic and a richness and depth of tone which instruments made of thinner woods simply cannot offer, however fine their pickups may be.

The neck on the Pro De Luxe is the usual three piece laminated maple job, bearing an ebony fingerboard of truly excellent quality, wearing those wide frets which started the whole trend for fat frets when players really began string bending with a vengeance in the late Sixties.

Like the earliest models, the Pro De Luxe features a pair of plastic enclosed single coil pickups, controlled by a top mounted three-way pickup selector switch and two typically Gibson volume controls plus two more for tone. The machines on the sample were first class, accurate and seemingly reliable, and the bridge was that basic Les Paul type which has a "stop" tailpiece over which the strings fasten before riding up over and across the standard bridge. It has front to back settings for intonation on a saddle by saddle basis, without any provision for setting string height individually.

The Pro De Luxe is a beautiful guitar and the gold colour aplied to the maple top gives it the classic "Les Paul Gold Top" finish.

Playing the Pro De Luxe was a pure delight. The intonation was just about perfect with the action set accurately to height to avoid any fret buzz and yet allowing fast lead lines and smooth, easy string bending. This single coil Les Paul has a basically sharper sound than the humbucker equipped models, as one would expect, but all that density of wood prevents it from sounding like a Fender, despite the similarity, in one sense at least, of pickup winding style. For all that single coil pickup this is a fairly warm sounding, fat chord guitar which flicks over to lead settings with truly excellent sustain. Les Pauls, in general do not offer the thinnest necks on the market and you do have to acclimatise yourself to it and then learn to take advantage of the low action, super-smooth ebony fingerboard and impressive fretting.

For sound this is certainly one of the best Les Pauls of new manufacture that this reviewer has played. Try one for yourself, preferably beside a humbucking equipped model and see which is *your* ideal version. This certainly is close to mine.

Price: £789

Body materials: Mahogany with maple top

Neck materials: Maple laminate

Fingerboard materials: Ebony

Machine heads: Grover

Pickups: Gibson single coil

Construction:	★★★★★
Finish:	★★★★★
Sound:	★★★★★
Playability:	★★★★★
Value For Money:	★★★★

Distributed by: Rosetti (EMI) Ltd, 138/140 Old Street, London EC1. Tel: 01-253-7294.

Gibson SG Firebrand

Ever since the original Gibson SG was launched in the early 1960's, it has been somewhat distinct from the normal run of their instruments, with a well developed following of its own. Trying to withstand the rapidly rising costs of American labour and materials Gibson now offer several versions of this classic and much loved instrument, from the SG Standard (now recommended at over £600) down to this "Firebrand" version which retails below £500.

The SG always was a different sort of Gibson. True, it sports the traditional glued neck joint and the humbucking pickups but the sound was always that much sharper than a Les Paul's and the thin double cutaway body seemed to lend itself to a more extravagant style of playing than the heavier, more staid Les Paul.

The Firebrand version continues that tradition. This sample is 100 per cent mahogany, not the best looking Gibson ever made but very well finished and arriving with an action which was just about perfect, with nice light strings and a feeling that it had been well set up and adjusted. In that area Gibsons seem to be improving all the time since Rosetti and Co. took over the UK distribution of this brand.

The neck joint on the Firebrand is almost heel-less but the strap button does obstruct a little, nevertheless this is a very fast playing Gibson with a very flat and rather wide rosewood fingerboard accommodating even clumsy fingers easily and providing plenty of room for extravagant runs, with notes bent right up high. Lacking the more normal Gibson radius of the fingerboard this sample felt oddly wide and very flat indeed, but this reviewer loved it!

The bridge/tailpiece is the typical Gibson set up whereby the strings terminate in an adjustable stop bar with the bridge itself only adjustable for intonation individually — string height coming from total bridge height adjustment. Intonation on the sample was near perfect. From a hardware point of view the SG Firebrand isn't bad. The Grover machines were a bit stiff but they are a reliable brand and should last for years. The bridge is strong and the twin pickups appear to work very well.

The SG has always been an individualist's Gibson, rather a far cry from the run of the marque's generally thick bodied ultra-sustaining guitars, more functional than decorative, very much the working player's guitar with a sharper sound and bags of rock attack. This "cheap" version of the SG maintains that tradition with its sharper sound and its superb sustain and feedback/overload potential from those two pickups. For some it may lack a finer degree of subtlety which the Les Paul offers — for others it's very much the fire-breathing Gibson lead guitar of their dreams.

Price: £499

Body materials: Mahogany

Neck materials: Mahogany

Fingerboard materials: Rosewood

Machine heads: Grover

Pickups: Gibson

Construction:	★★★★★
Finish:	★★★★★
Sound:	★★★★½
Playability:	★★★★★
Value For Money:	★★★★

Distributed by: Rosetti (EMI) Ltd., 138/140 Old Street, London EC1V 9BL. Tel: 01-253-7294.

Gibson SG Standard

Originally introduced by Gibson in 1961, the SG guitar, and its numerous derivatives, must count alongside the Les Paul as one of the most successful designs the company has ever produced. Essentially today's SG is much the same as it ever was, a guitar which seems incapable of dating, although it comes from that era of Chevrolet Impalas, Rick Nelson records and girls with pony tails.

It is not hard to see why the SG has remained so popular (although it probably is in one of its periodic lulls just now). It's a lightweight guitar with an almost wafer-thin body beside a Les Paul. The neck too is so much slimmer than that of a basic Paul, that it's hard to believe they come from the same maker. But all the same care and attention to detail is there. The rosewood fingerboard is nicely bound and block inlaid, the machine heads are smooth and reliable, the body painted a dense cream and then varnished. Those strangely chamfered sides are stil there too, adding just a shade of comfort to a cradled guitar body and, at the same time, a distinctive look of its own.

The bridge is a typical Gibson design with the strings fastening through a "stop" tailpiece with its height adjustable via two end screws; as is the bridge which also allows for individual intonation adjustment. The twin basic humbuckers have two volume and two tone controls plus a selector switch straight off a Les Paul and still, anachronistically, marked "rhythm" and "solo".

Like all SGs from the past, the sample handled superbly well. The neck is so much easier to play fast on than the fatter, usual Les Paul type and that bound fingerboard with its traditionally broad, polished Gibson frets is perfect for both slow blues soloing (especially with the neck pickup on) and chunky overweight chords.

Trying to describe *any* guitar's sound in words isn't easy and the SG is particularly difficult. The sound is dependant upon the wood on which the pickup is mounted and a dozen other factors besides. This guitar, although it has much of the Les Paul about it, that certain sweetness and warmth, also has a purity and sharpness which even a single coil Les Paul cannot match. The neck is fast and easy to play, especially at the top end where the slimmest of glued joints allows manically fast playing to stretch right up at the top.

The current full asking price of the SG seems modest especially after the discounters have been at work on it. It is not much more than the very top echelons of the Japanese manufacturers charge for their instruments which makes this classic winner a very good buy indeed!

Price: £619

Body materials: Mahogany

Neck materials: Mahogany

Fingerboard materials: Rosewood

Machine heads: Grover

Pickups: Gibson humbuckers

Construction:	★ ★ ★ ★ ★
Finish:	★ ★ ★ ★ ★
Sound:	★ ★ ★ ★ ★
Playability:	★ ★ ★ ★ ★
Value For Money:	★ ★ ★ ★ ★

Distributed by: Rosetti (EMI) Ltd, 138/140 Old Street, London EC1. Tel: 01-253-7294.

Gibson Victory CM MV II

Gibson have made several attempts, over the years, to capture the Fender market in addition to their own. In one sense the latest series of introductions from this maker, the Victory Series, succeeds where previous models have failed.

The Victory MVII is very much a Fender-like guitar to look at, or possibly resembles a typically Japanese guitar. Somehow this instrument *does* have a "Japanese original" look to it — although constructional standards are higher than those found on such guitars, by and large, and it is, of course, American. The sculptured body is comfortable to hold and fashioned from rock maple. It comes in two finishes: Candy Apple Red and Antique Fireburst. The sample was a Candy Apple Red model and was certainly well finished in a glowing red.

The Victory MVII features certain unusual points of design standards, one of the strangest being a bridge which is rather like a Tune-O-Matic but with replaceable bridge pieces in either nylon or brass. Unfortunately these are *still* not readily alterable for individual string height but this optional choice is probably a move towards greater flexibility.

The body is glue jointed to a laminated maple neck, bearing a very well fretted fingerboard and using a gauge of wire which is thinner than that usually found on Gibsons (yet further evidence that this is intended as a challenge to Fender). The machines on the vaguely Firebird-like (but the right way up) headstock are small but of very high quality, as is the one volume (master) control and its tone partner. In addition there is a Strat-like three position sliding pickup selector and a metal flick switch for single/twin coil operation of the two pickups. These latter are a "Velvet Brick" at the fingerboard end and what Gibson call a "special design magnet/iron loaded humbucking pickup" nearer the bridge.

In use the guitar is comfortable to hold and is an instrument which should definitely appeal to the rock player. The sample was well finished in all departments and had a good low action to complement the slight radius of the fingerboard. It is a fast neck, with its typically Gibson 22 frets on a 24¾" scale and runs and licks come off more easily on it than they do on many other guitars. Most players should find this a supremely easy instrument to play.

The "Velvet Brick" pickup is excellent for thick raunchy chords and the bridge end twin coil job will take you into a screaming toppy lead solo with no problems. Unlike some others, the coil tap works well also with a fairly powerful sound as the result; none of the castrated tones which you can get from tapped humbuckers are present here. Altogether a modern player's guitar, the Victory is a very nice instrument indeed, but it is fairly costly and doesn't really sound the same as a Fender — assuming, of course, that this was Gibson's intention. Regard it, rather, as an original with Fender-like qualities in the sound and you won't be far out. Its looks let it down a little, though.

Price: £649

Body materials: Rock maple

Neck materials: Maple laminate

Fingerboard materials: Rosewood

Machine heads: Gibson

Pickups: Gibson "Velvet Brick"/"Special" humbucker

Construction:	★★★★★
Finish:	★★★★★
Sound:	★★★★★
Playability:	★★★★★
Value For Money:	★★★

Distributed by: Rosetti (EMI) Ltd, 138/140 Old Street, London EC1. Tel: 01-253-7294.

Gibson 335 Dot

Known as the "Dot" simply because the makers have used dot position markers rather than the other 335's bar types. This is very much a recreation of Gibson's vintage 335, and is similarly available in a finish known as antique natural (which this sample came in).

There is no doubt that when it comes to manufacturing semi-acoustic guitars, Gibson have most other makers beat hands down. The Japanese have begun to try and penetrate this market in recent years but still many of their guitars tend to feel cheap when compared with the luxurious quality of manufacture of a guitar like this. The deeply arched body is ample, comprising maple back, front and sides with matching maple rims.

The three piece mahogany neck is beautifully made and well fitted to the body as is the rosewood fingerboard with its customary Gibson fat frets which were very well finished on this sample. Hardware is typically Gibson: Grover machine heads, Tune-O-Matic bridge (which offers string height en masse but intonation individually) fitted with a changeable insert on the saddle of either brass or plastic (the choice is yours) and those venerable Gibson pots.

Two immediate quibbles are that the pickup selector on the sample tried clicked through the amp when used (unforgiveable at this price) and that the pots run against a very sharp metal pointer to indicate where they are. This criticism has been made before and labelled "nit picking" but surely at this price, everything should be perfect and this feature and that clicking switch are most certainly not.

However, the guitar is little short of a dream to play. The neck has all the feel and ease of the very best Gibsons. Players who have either never tried or have long forgotten semi-acoustics will probably associate them with wildly uncontrollable feedback, even at fairly low amplification levels. The 335 Dot does feedback easier than a solid guitar will, but it's the sort of feedback which, with a bit of experimentation, a guitar player can learn how to use — if that's the sound he's looking for, of course. The pickups are PAF's and these have more than enough output to drive an amp into overload, a feature, combined with the usable feedback, which could make this far more of a modern rock guitar than some players realise. If that isn't the sound you are looking for, the 335 Dot has plenty of others too, from a wonderful jazz tone to a superb rhythm sound and a lovely country tone and it's far more versatile than most sold guitars.

There's no doubt that this is a very well made guitar indeed, one with a wide range of excellent sounds and a great feeling neck. The only thing seriously mitigating against it is a retail price in the UK which makes it a very expensive instrument. However, its re-sale value should be taken into account when considering it against Japanese competition.

Price: £799

Body materials: Maple

Neck materials: Mahogany

Fingerboard materials: Rosewood

Machine heads: Grover

Pickups: Gibson PAFs

Construction:	★★★★★
Finish:	★★★★★
Sound:	★★★★★
Playability:	★★★★★
Value For Money:	★★★

Distributed by: Rosetti (EMI) Ltd, 138/140 Old Street, London EC1V 9BL. Tel: 01-253-7294.

Gibson 335-S Professional De-Luxe

It is unfortunate that Gibson have chosen to call this guitar a "335" because at least one reviewer has made the mistake of grumbling that it bears little resemblance to the legendary 335 semi-acoustic of so many year's fame.

In common with most Gibsons, the 335-S (the S stands for solid) features the standard Gibson glued neck joint. The body of this sample was a beautiful shade of red mahogany and the neck a stained wood of that type and colour. The rosewood fingerboard does Gibson's reputation credit and the traditional flat neck camber and fat frets prove once and for all that a Gibson is a very special guitar for solo playing where long, slow bends are called for. This sample was finished to perfection with no fret buzz, a sensible action and strings which were heavier than ultra-light but ideal for meaty chords as well as controlled soloing.

The body is small to hold, the balance perfect, and the typically Gibson neck a pure delight to play on. Overall finish is excellent. Gibsons are probably easier to play than most other guitars and this was no exception, the flat-ish fingerboard and the fat frets lending themselves to easy soloing, a function made even easier by the pair of twin coil humbuckers, controlled by two volume and two tone pots plus pickup selector and single/twin coil settings from a metal flick switch.

Hardware is further enhanced by the new TP6 tailpiece, an idea which enables string tuning to be adjusted by the right hand whilst presumably lifting off with the right hand. You turn a knurled screw on the bridge to lengthen or shorten the string and thus alter the pitch. Of course the normal Gibson principles of string length but *not* individual height are applied on the bridge itself.

In the sound department the 335-S is one of the finest Gibsons for years. The new humbuckers are powerful and careful setting will give a vintage Gibson rock sound for soloing. Flick the coil tap and the sound becomes searing and toppy but still powerful enough for a good solo with a decent amp.

The sheer lack of wood in the body, compared to, say, a Les Paul means that sustain isn't endless but the pickups lend themselves to a definitive amp overload sound and feedback is almost incredibly controllable.

The 335-S is one of the best new Gibsons for years, possessing typical manufacturing quality, a wonderfully warm and yet dynamic sound and an unparalleled ease of playing. The only thing against it is the current retail price which marks it very high against Japanese competition. For all that, though, it's an instrument with real character and feel.

Price: £629

Body materials: Mahogany

Neck materials: Mahogany

Fingerboard materials: Rosewood

Machine heads: Grovers

Pickups: Gibson humbuckers (split coil)

Construction:	★★★★★
Finish:	★★★★★
Sound:	★★★★★
Playability:	★★★★★
Value For Money:	★★★½

Distributed by: Rosetti (EMI) Ltd, 138/140 Old Street, London EC1V 9BL. Tel: 01-253-7294.

Gordon Smith Gemini

Northern based guitar makers Gordon Smith have earned themselves something of an enviable reputation during their relatively short career. The Gemini model is right near the top of their range (which starts with some remarkably cheap but high quality instruments) but it still retails below the price of quite a few equivalent instruments imported from the USA.

In terms of its materials, the Gemini is relatively conservative, a mahogany body joined to a mahogany neck sporting a fine ebony fingerboard — the sort of materials which many luxury guitars are made of. The quality of workmanship that had gone into this cherry red sample was obvious, down to the mildly decorative shaped end of the fingerboard and the inlayed bar position markers. Unlike many "luxury" guitars this was not one of those where the money had been spent on decoration; the Gemini is an extremely plain and understated instrument, the legend "Gordon Smith" alone being written in an elegant script on the headstock.

The Gordon Smith features two twin coil pickups made by the manufacturers, and while they work as well as anything currently available, they do let the instrument down in that the top surfaces of them wear a printed "bar" in grey. This isn't in itself a flaw but the printing could have been a little more accurate. One may bė accused here of being over critical, but for this sort of money one has the right to expect even tiny details like this to look right.

The bridge and tailpiece unit are of an unusual design as the bridge base does not marry-up with the dense wood of the body, but rather transmits its sustain through the two vast screws which alter the basic height of the bridge itself. It's interesting to note that despite this perhaps outmoded design feature, the Gemini does not lack sustain — far from it!

Control of the twin pickups is via two tone pots and two volume pots, each of the latter sporting a "pull for single coil" setting. They are well chosen and smooth to use with a good variability of effect on the volume and tone. There's none of the "sudden death" approach here.

Playing the Gemini is delightful. The neck is lightning fast and the fretting of the very highest standard. The guitar also balances in a superior way which makes it doubly delightful to play. Soundwise it's superb. The basic tone of the pickups when set on single tone is powerful and yet not psychotic like some of the worst add-on types. These offer a wonderfully warm and yet tough sounding tonality which can sear away into single coil operation when the volume pots are pulled out. Sustain is also excellent and all the rock guitarist's tricks ring out clean and true.

There's no doubting that this is an expensive instrument, but the makers do offer much cheaper models. However, at this price I can only award it three and half stars because, brilliant as it is, the Gemini isn't a bargain priced guitar.

Price: £696

Body materials: Mahogany

Neck materials: Mahogany

Fingerboard materials: Ebony

Machine heads: Schaller

Pickups: Gordon Smith

Construction:	★★★★★
Finish:	★★★★★
Sound:	★★★★★
Playability:	★★★★★
Value For Money:	★★★½

Distributed by: Keith Hand Musical Supplies, 219 Walmersley Road, Bury, Manchester. Tel: 061-764-1792.

Gordon Smith GS II (Thin Body)

It's no great secret that I'm something of a fan of British guitar makers and their products. One of the most promising makers in the UK is the small Manchester-based group of craftsmen which calls its product Gordon Smith after its founder. Their products are consistently impressive, and receiving a thin bodied GS II to try was something this reviewer looked forward to.

The thin body on the GS II is disconcertingly light at first and it seems impossible that such a thin body could sound good. After the shock of the light body, the width of the neck is the next oddity. It's a tremendously wide, flat, unbound fingerboard with great fat frets on it. Initially it looks as if the Smith will be a distinct chore to play — but in actuality it's quite comfortable once you've adapted to it and the neck is so slim in depth that the width soon ceases to bother you. In fact it's actually rather nice to have enough room for the fingers if you're slightly inaccurate with your fingering!

The machines on the GS are Schallers. The bridge certainly *is* a weird choice — it is off an old Les Paul and looks totally out of place beside modern types. One wonders why they should have chosen it, but it is cheap to buy and works well enough on this axe. It comprises a bar over which the strings virtually wrap to fasten, but the contact area of the string on the bridge is phenomenal by comparison with most normal saddle designs and, additionally there is neither provision for individual height *nor* intonation adjustment! For all that, a very well made instrument which will work acceptably with this type of bridge and the fact that this guitar *does* play well in tune right up the neck with no obvious problems is a considerable tribute to its makers.

Pickups on the Gordon Smith are twin coil secret weapons of theirs. Several makers have expressed a desire to get their hands on these, which is not in the least surprising. Whether it is the pickups or the general standards of construction, this guitar is one of the finest sounding in this whole book — alive, raunchy and warm.

A fine instrument with an amazingly punchy and powerful sound, filled with harmonics and richness and yet capable of overdriving even the meanest amp. Try one, it's one of the best around and is worth every penny of the asking price!

Price: £315

Body materials: Mahogany

Neck materials: Mahogany

Fingerboard materials: Rosewood

Machine heads: Schaller

Pickups: Gordon Smith twin coil

Construction:	★★★★★
Finish:	★★★★½
Sound:	★★★★★
Playability:	★★★★★
Value For Money:	★★★★★

Distributed by: Keith Hand Musical Supplies, 219 Walmersley Road, Bury BL9 5DF. Tel: 061-764-1792.

Guild S-60D

Despite being almost tragically unfashionable, Guild keep soldiering on with their solid electric rock guitars, of which the S-60D is a fine example.

It's disturbing to reflect why some guitars sell and others don't, especially when it affects an instrument as good as this, and one which, to boot, retails at an excellent price for an American "brand name" instrument. One can only assume that the name of Guild is just too closely associated in the public imagination with high quality acoustics and that few people stop to consider their solid bodied models.

The body of the S-60D is an odd shape. From a distance it might be possible to mistake it for a Gibson "one-off", but then it has that distinctive lettering announcing the maker's name. It's a fine looking guitar, the mahogany of the body stained a dark red (in the case of the sample) and bearing all the hallmarks of the legendary Guild production quality. The glued neck is also mahogany and the fingerboard a fine quality rosewood, fretted with 24 fat frets which lend themselves to easy bending and a fine blues/rock style. Access to the top of the neck is easy. The guitar balances extremely well and the neck plays very, very quickly, with a smoothly contoured heel giving good access to the top frets, again, lending the guitar to fast rock solo playing.

Regrettably, one of the obvious economies which Guild appear to have made on this instrument was the fitting of open backed machines on a three-in-a-strip basis, as with a Spanish guitar. Although the machines seemed to work perfectly well, they must put potential customers off this instrument. Even the cheapest Japanese guitars have more attractive looking machines than this.

In the pickup department, however, there has been no scrimping whatsoever as this Guild uses DiMarzio SDSI pickups. There are two of them and, as one might expect, the sound they produce in conjunction with this excellent mahogany body (light though it may be to handle) is quite superb. Control comprises just three rotary pots and one large plastic tipped selector. It may not seem much but it's all you need to take those single coil DiMarzio pickups into a screaming overloaded solo when wired into a good valve amp. Alternatively the Guild will play a role as a rhythm guitar, the pickups not at all as thin as the single coil configuration might suggest their tone would be.

Overall the Guild is a hard instrument to fault and players who fancy something powerful and light, with a feeling of quality without weight — the sort of instrument that you can hardly stand still with whilst playing — should check one of these out. It deserves far more attention that it has had to date and it is hard to believe that the type of machines fitted alone has robbed it of comparative success. Don't overlook it, this Guild is a fine guitar for the money!

Price: £352	
Body materials: Mahogany	
Neck materials: Mahogany	
Fingerboard materials: Rosewood	
Machine heads: Guild chrome plated	
Pickups: DiMarzio SDS-1	
Construction:	★★★★★
Finish:	★★★★★
Sound:	★★★★★
Playability:	★★★★★
Value For Money:	★★★★★

Distributed by: C. Summerfield Ltd, Saltmeadows Road, Gateshead, Tyne & Wear. Tel: 0632-770431.

Hamer Prototype

The movement towards guitars made by small companies is not one that is restricted to Britain. Small guitar makers are very much in vogue in America also, but often their production levels are so low that their instruments rarely reach these shores. One exception is Hamer, a brand created by Paul Hamer, manufactured in Arlington Heights, Illinois and available through just one regular distributor in Britain, Guitar Grapevine in London's West End.

The Prototype is the latest of their guitars, modelled very much in terms of its general appearance and styling on the excellent Special. Broadly speaking, the new Prototype follows the outline pattern of the Special except that it has a slight shaving away of the top of the body to provide more comfortable positioning for the right forearm and similarly on the back where it accommodates the rib cage with greater ease. Constructional standards and general finishing were of the very highest order on this model, and the shade of rich, luxurious conker brown the makers have chosen for the sample tried was among the best finishes encountered; it has an almost antique stain effect.

Hardware details for this model are almost identical to those of the Special: Schaller machines, the "up and under" string fastening and the fully manoeuvrable bridge design. The fretting is polished to a high degree of accuracy and the whole guitar looks to be strong and workmanlike, yet not without grace and subtlety.

Control gear comprises one tone pot and another for volume. This might sound a little meagre until one realises that the DiMarzio pickup fitted in the bridge position actually has three coils, rather than the universal single or twin designs of all others. A quick examination reveals that you've got a twin coil unit as one part and a separate single coil unit as a second. The thoughtfully positioned selector switch provides you with twin coil in the full back position, triple coil in the centre and humbucking when full over. In addition the tone control has been set so as to give "normal" when on around five and then swings back to zero to provide a remarkably fierce treble. One flick the other way on the pickup switch and using the little finger to pull the pot up to 10 gives you a tremendously fat sound with real wailing lead solo potential.

This guitar is thoughtfully made and designed, with a tremendous range of sounds and would be ideal for the experienced rock player who had outgrown the inadequacies and failings of more conventional instruments. One would have to admit that this isn't exactly a cheap guitar but it must be stood beside a Gibson to find its true peer. A player who would prefer a Hamer to a Les Paul would be quite justified and this prototype could well be the classic vintage of the year 2000!

Price: £425

Body materials: Honduras mahogany

Neck materials: Honduras mahogany

Fingerboard materials: Rosewood

Machine heads: Schaller

Pickups: DiMarzio triple coil

Construction:	★★★★★
Finish:	★★★★★
Sound:	★★★★★
Playability:	★★★★★
Value For Money:	★★★★★

Distributed by: Guitar Grapevine, 16 Denmark Place, London WC2. Tel: 01-836-3300.

Hamer Special

This Hamer scores over the other Hamer models reviewed in that it has a unique body shape, albeit not one which is visually as exciting as those of the Vector or the Standard. To counter that, however, some of the wildest colour schemes imaginable are on offer, including black with white models which look disconcertingly like a true "pop art" design from the early/mid Sixties. Under stage lights, though, these models (the Graphics) could look pretty impressive!

The physical details of the Special are fairly unremarkable, but the instrument is a very controlled exercise in standard design techniques, manufactured to a quality which few volume producers seem to be able to reach.

The Special has a surprisingly thick body for such a conventional looking guitar and this, as we know, means that the high quality mahogany will resonate and thus sustain notes far longer than a thinner version. For all that extra wood in the body, the Special is not over-heavy, nor is the neck (which does feel a shade fatter than those on either the Vector or the Standard) anything less than supremely comfortable. However, those who like a bit more to hang onto, should not reject Hamer just on the strength of the other two thinner models — try one of these as well.

The Special's hardware is of a very high standard, the bridge being the same as that on the Vector, offering full adjustment potential and string fastening through the body. The machines too are the same make — Schallers, and the pickups are a pair of DiMarzio humbuckers. Control is Hamer's simple-to-operate but tremendously effective single tone and twin volume arrangement. Yet again the ergonomics of the control placings are fine, with the selector switch at the back of the guitar, easily in reach for fast changes.

Like all Hamers a very nice touch is in the form of a bone nut, far better than the ultra-fashionable brass or the fake bone nylon or plastic types which some other makers use. This is the sort of area where Hamer score continually, care and attention to fine, but vital, detail.

Sound from the twin pickups is very variable indeed — and that means variable from good to even better! The volume control circuit on Hamer guitars is deceptive. You may only have the one pot but it is a compensated type so that the tone doesn't change as you throttle back on the power. It is touches like that which make this such a professional instrument. The tonal range varies between extremely fat and bluesy to a very thin, screaming treble attack which will wail on seemingly indefinitely due to the excellent resonance of the body wood. This is a really raunchy sounding guitar, with a tremendously versatile tonal range which defies the apparent lack of a coil tap.

On balance this is very much an experienced player's guitar, and requires someone with skill to realise the guitar's potential. I found it impossible to fault, especially at such an excellent price.

Price: £345	
Body materials: Honduras mahogany	
Neck materials: Honduras mahogany	
Fingerboard materials: Rosewood	
Machine heads: Schaller	
Pickups: DiMarzio twin coil	
Construction:	★★★★★
Finish:	★★★★★
Sound:	★★★★★
Playability:	★★★★★
Value For Money:	★★★★★

Distributed by: Guitar Grapevine, 16 Denmark Place, London WC2. Tel: 01-836-3300.

Hamer Standard

The Standard is a finely made instrument — that much is apparent from the moment you handle it. The neck fits the hand so well that it almost feels as if it had been crafted with you in mind — it's thin and yet not ridiculously so, made from Honduras mahogany and is one of the fastest necks this reviewer has played.

The fingerboard is good rosewood, fretted to an impressive standard with fat, polished frets — a very well made neck indeed and one which is glue jointed into the body. According to the written data, the Standard has a mahogany body, but my sample had a maple top applied to a mahogany back. The maple bore a deep glowing orange fireburst finish and was lacquered, not finished in polyester. This may account for it having that distinctively "genuine American" look when so many British luxury guitars are polyestered and feel a little plastic accordingly.

Machines on the Standard are six small Schallers carried on a headstock which juts off at an angle rather like that on the Washburn Stage guitar and, hence, causing similar fumbling until you learn to feel your way to each one after some practice.

The bound body wears two DiMarzio pickups which are run via two volume pots, a single tone and a large selector switch. Simple, neat and easy to reach. The chromed bridge is a basic device featuring a "stop" tailpiece and a saddle per string design, adjustable for intonation individually, but not for height.

Tonally the Standard sounds as good as it both looks and feels. It's quite an aggressive instrument with remarkably long sustain for such a relatively thin body and the pickups sound really firey, ideal for an extravagant player who enjoys stretching out into breakneck speed solos.

There's no doubting that this instrument is of the highest possible standard in all its aspects and would suit any rock guitarist who liked the look of it, could afford the asking price and could make good use of that tremendous sound.

Price: £675

Body materials: Honduras mahogany, maple top

Neck materials: Honduras mahogany

Fingerboard materials: Rosewood

Machine heads: Schaller

Pickups: DiMarzio twin coil

Construction:	★★★★★
Finish:	★★★★★
Sound:	★★★★★
Playability:	★★★★★
Value For Money:	★★★★

Distributed by: Guitar Grapevine, 16 Denmark Place, London WC2. Tel: 01-836-3300.

Hamer Vector

The Hamer Vector is based on the Gibson Flying V but it is difficult to call an instrument as well made and as fine sounding as this one a "copy" guitar. Hamer's own attitude seems to be that the shape is "traditional" and they have sought to improve some basic design flaws in the original.

The Hamer is a nice looking machine. It is mahogany with a hand carved mahogany neck, glued very expertly into the familiar V-shaped body. The fingerboard is of good rosewood and the fretting standard on the sample (just picked at random off the wall, not specially set-up) was tremendously impressive. Also worthy of some attention are the Hamer strings which this and the other Hamers come fitted with. They are 9s, perhaps of too light a gauge for normal tastes, but among the very best strings this reviewer has ever played with a tremendously smooth feel on the wound bottoms and a nice stretchy quality on the tops.

Strings fasten through the back of the Vector's body and then ride up over a heavy duty chromed bridge with large saddles, each with full adjustment for intonation and two micro screws per saddle to set the string height individually.

Machines are Schallers and the pickups DiMarzio humbuckers, run from three small plastic knobs and a very conveniently placed selector switch. This latter feature, by the way, seems to be a general plus point with Hamer guitars who have obviously thought their ergonomics out very carefully before going into production. Another significant improvement is the neck to body joint. The 22 fret (on a 24¾" scale) neck is carefully applied so that the common problem on V-bodied guitars of access to the top frets is virtually overcome. It isn't quite as easy as on a straight-through necked V like a Manson, but it is an improvement on most other glued Vs.

Sound from the DiMarzio humbuckers is very wild and it is more at home in the hands of a heavy rock player. For that sort of rock guitarist this fabulously easy neck to play coupled with a fine visual appearance, high quality construction, and very rewarding tonal punch should make this a guitar well worth checking out. Mind you, compare its price with that of an exotic Manson Custom V and you'll see why we haven't been able to award it equally high marks for value rating. A very good guitar, all the same.

Price: £425

Body materials: Honduras mahogany

Neck materials: Honduras mahogany

Fingerboard materials: Rosewood

Machine heads: Schaller

Pickups: DiMarzio twin coil

Construction:	★★★★★
Finish:	★★★★★
Sound:	★★★★★
Playability:	★★★★★
Value For Money:	★★★★

Distributed by: Guitar Grapevine, 16 Denmark Place, London WC2.
Tel: 01-836-3300.

Hondo H-1010WA

Providing playable instruments for guitarists who are either beginning their careers or who are just plain old-fashioned broke is never easy. The difficulties faced by distributors of imported guitars are manifold in this area — do they go for cheap production in one of the countries specialising in cheap guitars (Italy or Taiwan or Korea) and take the risks of sometimes poor quality instruments, or do they better their own margins by going for a superior but costlier instrument from Japan? The answers are as various as the distributors themselves but Hondo have got as close as anyone by going for their "professional" range to Japan and for their "non-professional" instruments to Korea. How long it will be, incidentally, before the enterprising Koreans rival the Japanese is anybody's guess.

The cheapest "pro" designated instrument in the "Hondo Pro" range is a guitar dubbed the H-1010WA, an instrument which retails at about the lowest price possible while still remaining a playable instrument worth serious consideration beyond the first six months of your playing career.

The sample came in a pleasant looking walnut finish applied to a hardwood body. The neck (unidentifiable as far as wood was concerned) was joined to the body by a bolt-on fixing which was rather well accomplished for the price. Overall finish of the Hondo was very good, the fretting accurate and the general action and setting-up very pleasing indeed. Machines look a little cheap on this guitar but they do work well enough and the electrical department is equally well catered for at the price, by offering two twin coil pickups with one volume control, one tone, a single/twin coil tap and a pickup selector.

Neck width on this sample was very pleasing, the type of profile which would be easy for any beginner but not unfamiliar to a professional who happened to stumble on one of these guitars by accident. Certainly no young guitarist is going to be put off by the H-1010WA.

In practice the Hondo performs very well indeed for the asking price. Played through a variety of amps this guitar generally performed far better than we have any right to expect for the price. Even set on single coil there is enough power in these pickups to drive most modern guitar amps into some sort of overload and that is very much the ability which is seriously missing in many cheap instruments currently on the market in this price range.

It would be silly in the extreme to overstate the virtues of this guitar. It is, of course, a cheap instrument and *isn't* a Gibson in disguise, but it does represent excellent value for money for the impoverished beginner who wants a guitar with many of the qualities of a professional instrument.

Price: £119

Body materials: Walnut finish on "hardwood"

Neck materials: Unidentified

Fingerboard materials: Rosewood

Machine heads: "Hondo"

Pickups: "Hondo" twin coil

Construction:	★★★★
Finish:	★★★★
Sound:	★★★★★
Playability:	★★★★★
Value For Money:	★★★★★

Distributed by: John Hornby Skewes & Co. Ltd, Salem House, Garforth, Leeds LS25 1PX. Tel: 0532-865381.

Hondo H-1020WA

This is one of the Japanese-made Pro Series Hondos and, as such, immediately feels a superior kind of beast from those made in Korea the moment you pick it up and hold it. The body is a rather solid and heavy hardwood, very well lacquered and probably mahogany of some sort (or a near relative). The neck is of a similar wood and this is faced with a good quality rosewood fingerboard which has been fretted with those ubiquitous fat frets, rather high in profile but by no means uncomfortable for fast playing.

Although the neck looks as though it has been glued in place (when viewed from the front) it is, actually, a bolt-on type but with a very low profile heel which shouldn't get in the way of fast licks played high up the neck. Mechanically the Hondo 1020 is very much the typical excellent value Japanese guitar. The machines are superbly smooth and rather well gold plated (as is all the hardware) and the bridge is a copy, more or less, of the standard Gibson type.

Two humbucking pickups are fitted to this model, controlled by the usual single selector (not perhaps brilliantly placed, down by the tailpiece) and there are two volumes plus two tones of the typical Gibson design which seems so common on the best Japanese guitars of this type. Body contouring has been well executed on this model to allow for maximum comfort, especially when the guitar is played seated, and overall the conception and execution of the instrument indicates considerable manufacturing expertise and design understanding.

Playing this Hondo is almost as rewarding as holding it. The neck isn't lightning-fast as are some Fender types, but it bears an almost uncanny Gibson-like feel which lends itself to those long, slow, lazy solos and chunky chord patterns which Gibsons are often used for.

From a sound point of view the Hondo isn't, as one would expect, exactly deficient. The pickups could be just a shade more characteristic to give the guitar a real personality of its own and they could also benefit with just a little higher output to drive the cheaper class of transistor amplification into distortion. But, for all that, a decent quality valve amp with master volume or one of the latest series of tranny amps will respond well with this guitar. Its performance, overall, is very good indeed and, like other Japanese Hondo Pro guitars, it seems virtually unbeatable at the price.

Price: £98

Body materials:

Neck materials:

Fingerboard materials: Rosewood

Machine heads: "Hondo"

Pickups: "Hondo" twin coil

Construction:	★★★★★
Finish:	★★★★★
Sound:	★★★★
Playability:	★★★★½
Value For Money:	★★★★★

Distributed by: John Mornby Skewes & Co. Ltd, Salem House, Garforth, Leeds. Tel: 0532-865381.

Hondo Pro Series H-1051

The previous two Hondo Professional Series guitars reviewed in these pages have both stood out for being exceptional value for money. The third model, however, as distinct from the other two, is actually more of a copy guitar, following the lines of one of the Fender Lead Series.

Some instruments have a distinctly professional feel about them, others do not and this is certainly one of the former. The body (made of an unidentifiable hardwood) is quite thick and heavy, qualities which encourage good sustain. The bolt-on neck (perhaps a little on the robust side for some tastes) is maple and the fretting standard very good indeed.

On the machine head front the set supplied with the review sample, whilst being more than adequate for the task, did lack a barely definable "something" compared with those fitted to most better class Japanese instruments. However, with a Fender copy, Klusons are on the originals, so maybe things aren't so bad after all!

The chromed bridge is a respectable design, allowing the strings to fasten through the back of the body and then pass up at a good acute angle to ride over saddles, each of which offers full intonation adjustment plus string height via two micro-screws per saddle. There is *just* the potential there for side slip which is overcome on later series Fender Strats (to name but one model) by "tracking" the saddle screws in grooves to hold them steady. This one should not move much, however, and it seemed more than stable. The pickup on this guitar is an unidentifiable twin coil type placed right up near the bridge, an interesting position in that it promises the normal twin coil bass response countered by the limited string vibration and the placement of it.

Coil gear comprises one clearly marked volume pot, another for tone and two of the clumsiest metal switches this reviewer has ever seen: one for single/twin coil operation, the other for phase. Mind you, the switches work well and they are, of course, copies so one can hardly blame Hondo for this!

Soundwise the Hondo is rather strange as that pickup design and placing combination indicates it would be. There is a certain undeniable twin coil-like quality in the tone but this is matched with a screaming treble response when the guitar is overdriven — in fact overall it's a very loud, rather trebly guitar, the type that many Fender copy players yearn for but rarely get.

This reviewer spent an enjoyable time with the Hondo and finally came to the conclusion that it is best used for rhythm guitar where the twin coil set, naturally phased, pickup sounded really very good indeed for chords. Solo leads were nice too, but it has a fantastic chord sound and would be ideal for a player/singer. Another fine Japanese Hondo Pro guitar and a good bargain at its current retail price.

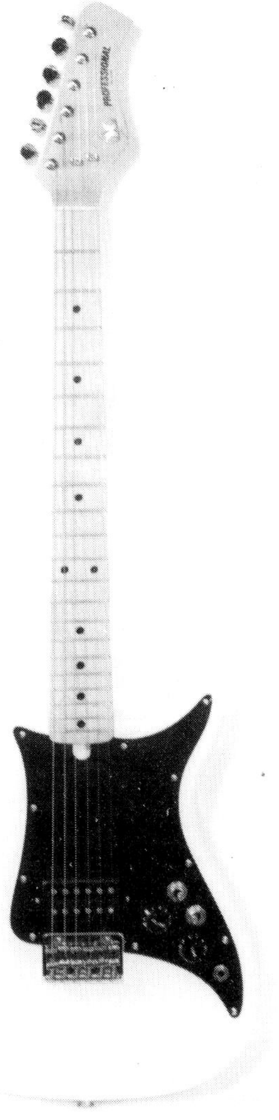

Price: £122

Body materials: Unidentified

Neck materials: Maple

Fingerboard materials: Maple

Machine heads: "Hondo"

Pickups: "Hondo" twin coil

Construction:	★★★★★
Finish:	★★★★★
Sound:	★★★★
Playability:	★★★★
Value For Money:	★★★★★

Distributed by: John Hornby Skewes & Co. Ltd, Salem House, Garforth, Leeds. Tel: 0532-865381.

Ibanez AR 100 CS

So large is the Ibanez range these days that it's impossible to nominate any one instrument as being truly representative of the range. Nevertheless, the AR 100 (part of a new-ish Ibanez sub-species) must be an ideal instrument for the rock player who is moving up from his early guitars and seriously scouting around for something which he can keep for a number of years.

The sample was a beautiful looking instrument, the body face being bookmatched maple (tiger striped) laid over dense mahogany — a combination ideally suited to modern rock guitar playing. The neck was rock maple and the fingerboard, rosewood. Traditional materials well machined and put together with an obvious amount of care and ability.

Hardware on the AR 100 CS was gold plated to a good standard and seemed to be working very satisfactorily. The bridge, following the general pattern on what has been obviously built as a "Gibson type" guitar (maple/mahogany body, humbuckers, glued neck etc.) allows for intonation adjustment but not string height individually. The back of the AR 100 CS is well contoured for increased comfort and the whole guitar balances to perfection. Any player who likes a heavier guitar with a Gibson feel will immediately like it and feel at home with it.

The twin coil pickups deliver a good fat whack into your amp when turned up full, and using the rubber ribbed pots ensure that the flexibility of the controls is at hand even when you're sweating under stage lighting.

Soundwise it is warm and powerful and would certainly suit players who perhaps have their sights set on a top flight Gibson or Yamaha.

It is hard to find any serious grounds on which to criticise this instrument. It does suffer from a slight lack of character, but that would be by way of comparison with another instrument costing two or three times the price of this one. It's a massive tribute to this guitar that one would have to look that far ahead to raise any competition for a guitar of this type.

Nonetheless, no guitar can be perfect for every player and, of course, this wouldn't suit someone who wanted a Fender single coil sound — it's just not that sort of instrument. But if you like Gibsons and just cannot afford one then this has got to be very near the top of your list.

Price: £288

Body materials: Maple and mahogany

Neck materials: Rock maple laminate

Fingerboard materials: Rosewood

Machine heads: Gold Ibanez

Pickups: Ibanez V2

Construction:	★★★★★
Finish:	★★★★★
Sound:	★★★★★
Playability:	★★★★★
Value For Money:	★★★★★

Distributed by: C. Summerfield Ltd, Saltmeadows Road, Gateshead, Tyne & Wear. Tel: 0632-770431.

Manson Flying V

The Manson Flying V is the nearest thing to a work of art in a solid guitar that you are ever likely to see. The body is composed of strip upon strip of exotic woods, each one imperceptibly glued together to form what must be one of the most beautiful-looking instruments ever made for a rock player. Those laminates are of yew, holly, ash, mahogany and paduak and fine strips which could be, at a guess, mahogany. The whole thing is remarkably gloss finished and looks as though it is worth in excess of £2,000.

Like all Manson guitars of the solid type, this one was put together by brother Hugh and fellow craftsman Ian. The acoustics which are of equal quality, are made by brother Andy. The straight-through mahogany neck on the Flying V is faced with a wonderful looking piece of rosewood, fretted to Hugh's usually high standards and with a very fast profile — albeit strung with a gauge of string which proved impossibly light to handle. The action was very low also without a hint of fret buzz.

Machines and bridges on these Manson guitars are both gold plated and come from Schaller, the bridge being the latter's "fine tune" type which is a "right handed tuning" design like the TP6 on many Gibson models these days. The strings fasten into movable clamps which are rotated to move the strings backwards and forwards in a hurry. The strings then pass over rather solid saddles which offer individual adjustment for intonation, but height only via two side screws which move the whole bridge unit and its saddles vertically.

Pickups are from the Rainbow range manufactured in the UK by Kent Armstrong who is probably doing greater things with pickups than any other maker in the world at present. The types fitted to this guitar are enclosed in transparent resin blocks so that the gleaming copper windings of the coils show right through. They sound as good as they look!

Whether you would like to own a Manson Flying V would depend on whether or not you like the basic idea of this design and its Gibson parent. You *cannot* play a guitar of this design sitting down and you will not be getting that fat, warm Les Paul sound from it. This "V" is a bit of a screamer's guitar — a Heavy Metal weapon with ear-splitting top. If that sounds like your sort of instrument then you should definitely try and get hold of one to sample.

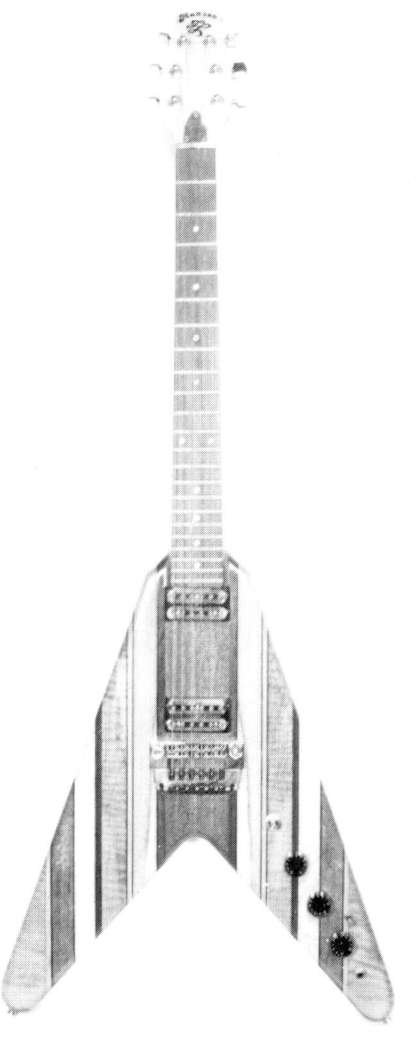

Price: £475

Body materials: "Striped" laminates of yew, holly, ash, mahogany, paduak

Neck materials: Mahogany straight-through

Fingerboard materials: Rosewood

Machine heads: Schaller

Pickups: Rainbow (Kent Armstrong)

Construction:	★★★★★
Finish:	★★★★★
Sound:	★★★★★
Playability:	★★★★★
Value For Money:	★★★★★

Distributed by: Manson Guitars, Windsor Place, Jarvis Brook, Crowborough, East Sussex. Tel: 08926-4266.

Manson Kestrel

The Kestrel is the third of three Manson six string guitars which this reviewer was loaned by the makers and differs considerably in its appearance from the others on account of its being as near to a production instrument as is possible on such a small set up. This too is reflected in the very reasonable price of £268.

Although featuring a body of plain mahogany, the Kestrel, whilst it may be considerably less exotic than Manson's custom guitars, is still very attractive looking. Like the other two Manson guitars, the Kestrel features a straight-through neck, this time of mahogany, cleverly matched to look very much integral with the wood grain on the top.

The fingerboard on the Kestrel is of a very light rosewood; not quite as light as that found on Rickenbackers, but still lighter than most in colour and of excellent quality. Fretwire chosen was a normal fat Gibson type and each fret carefully lapped and polished.

Hardware on the Kestrel is all gold plated, with the exception of the brass nut and brass scratchplate. The machines are Schallers and the bridge an unidentified type which seems sturdy and well designed. Its fixing arrangement wraps and locks the strings around a bar and then channels them over saddles, each of which is adjustable for intonation but not height. Height comes from the two large side screws at either end of the bridge itself.

Pickups are two of those fine sounding Kent Armstrong Rainbow twin coil types. These are controlled by two Gibson type rotary knobs (one tone, one volume), a large brass pickup selector and a small metal flick switch for coil tap.

The Kestrel was immaculately set up and had been strung with those excellent Dean Markley strings of a gauge rather lighter than I might have chosen. Nonetheless, and despite the low action and fine gauge, there was no noticeable fret buzz which indicates how good this neck is.

The feel of the neck is quite slim and very fast indeed, being on the flat side and yet still encouraging the skilled player to attempt some fairly wild string bending. It has a very comfortable profile, well suited for high speed playing of lead lines on long sessions.

The sound from the Kestrel is quite amazing. In an age when many guitars sound very similar (albeit often rather good) the Kestrel is quite unique sounding. The coil tap allows for a very thin, trebly sound and yet a switch over to the neck pickup and back onto twin coil can bring in a quite fat bluesy sound. But the Kestrel is best when it's allowed to employ its own natural voice, which is toppier than most guitars, with excellent sustain and none of the weakness one often finds with tapped twin coil pickups. Like the Merlin Custom reviewed earlier, this is a tremendous sounding guitar which any player who values an individual sound would be well advised to look for and try before buying anything else.

Price: £268

Body materials: Mahogany

Neck materials: Mahogany

Fingerboard materials: Rosewood

Machine heads: Schaller

Pickups: Kent Armstrong "Rainbow"

Construction:	★★★★★
Finish:	★★★★★
Sound:	★★★★★
Playability:	★★★★★
Value For Money:	★★★★★

Distributed by: Stack Music Co. Ltd, Blackborough Road, Reigate, Surrey. Tel: 07372-40226.

Manson Merlin "Custom"

Like the custom Flying V, the Merlin under review here is one of Hugh Manson's experiments with multi-laminates of exotic woods. With a supreme modesty he passes it off as a "joke" guitar. I'm afraid this reviewer can't see the joke as it happens to be one of the best sounding guitars in the book and that retail price of £401 is the real magic!

The Merlin under review was a laminated body model. The woods looked quite superb, comprising strips of carefully laminated ebony, yew, mahogany, rosewood and sycamore. Yet again this is a natural candidate for colour reproduction — especially the back of the guitar which is quite the most beautiful I have seen.

The straight-through neck (typical of Hugh's immaculate workmanship) is of mahogany and this is mated to a fingerboard of rare maccassar ebony, a patterned wood, dark in places, light in others and quite staggering to look at.

The heel-less neck offers virtually uninterrupted access to the top of the luxuriously fretted fingerboard and the profile of the neck with that immaculate fretting job is so fast that I doubt if any guitar player (regardless of his tastes) could criticise it.

Machines on the Merlin guitar are Schallers which work as well as they always do, but the bridge is a custom Manson design, rather strange to look at but effective all the same. The strings terminate at the very end of a brass passageway and then ride up over massive saddles, each of which offers full adjustment potential for height and intonation. They also offer locked saddle movement in the horizontal plane so that, however heavy handed you may be, they *cannot* slip to the side. This is another first rate piece of design and workmanship!

Pickups on the Merlin represent one of those welcome collaborations of two great minds, Hugh Manson and pickup maker Kent Armstrong. The twin coil units fitted to this guitar have a sound which is possibly the best of any guitar reviewed in this book. The two pickups are run by two flick switches (single/twin coil) plus a brass selector switch and three heavy duty brass rotary controls, one volume and two tones.

The Merlin will swing between a deep bass solo blues sound, a middly/treble chord tone and a searing treble lead which somehow manages to epitomise the absolute sound of every rock guitarist's dreams. Perhaps its rather plain shape may not appeal to you. But, for me, the sound it makes, the ease with which it is played makes the Manson just about the perfect rock guitar player's axe.

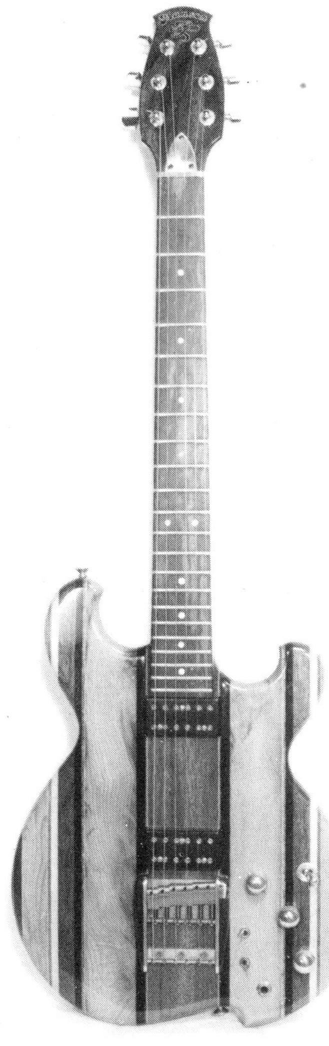

Price:	£401
Body materials:	Ebony/yew/mahogany/rosewood/sycamore
Neck materials:	Mahogany
Fingerboard materials:	Maccassar ebony
Machine heads:	Schaller
Pickups:	Rainbow (Kent Armstrong) twin coil
Construction:	★★★★★
Finish:	★★★★★
Sound:	★★★★★
Playability:	★★★★★
Value For Money:	★★★★★

Distributed by: Stentor Music Co. Ltd, Blackborough Road, Reigate, Surrey. Tel: 07372-40226.

Maya 8012

The Fender Strat has spawned a good number of follow-up ideas down the years and it must be reckoned that some of the most interesting of them, like this Maya, have dispensed with the classic bolt-on neck of the original in favour of a straight-through type. In the Maya 8012's case this is maple with a walnut inset.

The body is a multi-layer construction of walnut, rosewood and ash. Not at all a bad looking guitar, but it could seem a shade garish for some tastes. A brass nut visually complements a heavy cast brass bridge which, combined with the "strings through the body" fixing should ensure a reasonable sustain.

Playability on the well profiled neck with its rosewood fingerboard and fairly fat frets is very good indeed but this sample was set far too low to be playable, the strings rattling against the frets in places. This is not too much to worry about, as any competent dealer or even vaguely knowledgeable guitarist could raise the strings enough to offset this annoying problem. Certainly the bridge has all the adjustment potential necessary for string height as well as intonation setting.

On the pickup side the Maya has three totally enclosed single coil pickups each of which has its own toggle switch to govern on/off and phase. It should have occurred to someone at the makers that this means that the guitar could actually be switched off in mid number (you'd only need to set each flick switch to centre) and this should never be possible as it can lead to embarrassing moments on stage during solos!

Tonally the guitar is thin and sharp, a feature emphasised by setting the pickups onto the out-of-phase effect. In fact the sound is probably far too toppy for most tastes but some players might feel that this is actually a desirable feature. For them (and perhaps them alone) the Maya isn't actually a bad guitar, it just doesn't feel as if it has much character — it's more idiosyncratic than it should be and yet lacks real personality. The sound is more or less unique, but it's a sound which few would probably seek, and the pickup phase switches, though a fairly rare combination, have this important failing in the instant silence potential.

Nonetheless it's a well made instrument and if the sound appealed, then it would almost certainly prove to be reliable in use. There are better Maya guitars around for the player with more typical tastes than this model caters for. In the tonality department its thinness of tone can be positively wearing, and it is difficult to use to wind up an amp into overload with. An odd guitar this one, possibly best regarded as an experiment that just went plain old-fashioned wrong.

Price: £245

Body materials: Walnut/rosewood/ash

Neck materials: Maple/walnut inset

Fingerboard materials: Rosewood

Machine heads: Unidentified

Pickups: Maya

Construction:	★★★★★
Finish:	★★★★
Sound:	★★
Playability:	★★★★
Value For Money:	★★

Distributed by: Stentor Music Co. Ltd, Blackborough Road, Reigate, Surrey. Tel: 07372-40226.

Maya 8085

If the Maya Telecaster copy (the 8097) is a fairly direct "lift" from the Telecaster then this model, the more expensive 8085 is a faithful replica of the good old Strat, right down to a basic nut and bolt system.

There's little that needs to be said about the construction of this instrument to anyone who knows the Fender design. It features a very well contoured, rather lightweight body, with an excellent back and front contoured for playing comfort and a very slim neck, bolted onto the body. This Maya emulates a maple necked Strat and isn't at all bad in its emulation. Taking the neck away it would be very hard indeed to tell that this wasn't a genuine model — it's all there, the three single coil pickups, the latest type of five way pickup selector switch which offers the famous "in between" pickup settings, in addition to the basic job done by the original Fender design.

The hardware on the Maya is generally of fine quality. The machines aren't exact Kluson copies but they work smoothly and seem to hold their tuning well and the bridge follows the basic design ideas perfectly, right down to the through-the-body connection to the springs of the tremolo device which comes as standard on this model. Regrettably this sample came without an arm.

It wouldn't be very easy to tell that you were holding a fake Strat until you started playing it. The body weight and balance aren't too unfamiliar but the neck profile and radius of the fingerboard curve don't seem to resemble those of the latest Fenders and so one can only assume that an older, thicker, Strat neck has been used as the model for this copy. It's not that the neck is a hard one by normal standards, in fact it's a fast and accurate neck, just that it's quite obviously not a wafer-thin as the latest Fender types.

Similar to the Maya Tele, the sound is an approximation of a real Fender. The five way selection of pickup configurations is all there, even the clanky out-of-phase tones and the pickups have enough meat to drive a decently pre-amped circuit into a fairly reasonable distortion. It's a good sounding guitar but it's *not* a Strat — how could it be for this price?

One major quibble, however, is that this sample came with awful heavy gauge strings with a wound third — guaranteed to put any player born after 1950 off right away! If the distributors release their Maya "Strats" like this it's a great pity and must be marked down on "finish" for this alone. For the player who must have a copy this isn't at all a bad guitar. It's well made and sounds pretty good, but it isn't that cheap and there may be those who'd argue that one of the newer "own design" models on the market might offer better value. A good copy, all the same.

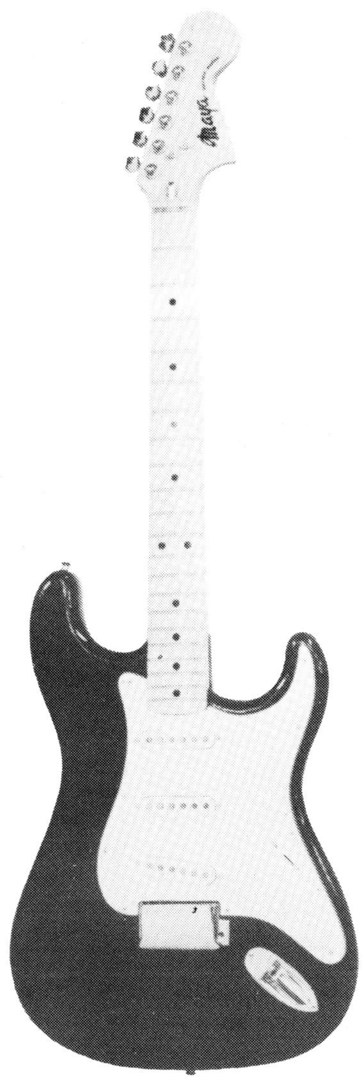

Price: £165

Body materials: Mahogany

Neck materials: Maple

Fingerboard materials: Maple

Machine heads: Unidentified

Pickups: "Maya" single coil

Construction:	★★★★★
Finish:	★★*
Sound:	★★★½
Playability:	★★★½
Value For Money:	★★★

**See text on strings.*

Distributed by: Stentor Music Co. Ltd, Blackborough Road, Reigate, Surrey RH2 7EZ. Tel: 07372-40226.

Maya 8097

This Japanese-made guitar is a copy of the apparently ever-lasting Fender Telecaster. These days most makers from Japan have abandoned copying and tend to offer their own designs partly through fear of possible copyright difficulties, but more through a realisation that copying will never allow them to take over the lead market. A copy is only, even if better than the original, a copy. A guitar which at least *looks* different can command a much higher price.

The Maya 8097 then can be looked upon as one of the last of a dying breed. It is, in fact, a very good copy of a Tele visually, sporting a maple body and bolted on neck, fitted with excellent quality machine heads and a bridge which is no worse, nor any better, than the original — that old faithful design where three fully adjustable saddles carry two pairs of strings each.

Pickups on the Maya resemble some Tele types, in that they are single coil designs but covered in chrome plated casings. The controls feature a rather clumpy three position pickup selector switch and two very good quality metal capped pots, one for volume, one for tone.

Constructionally speaking the sample was very well finished with the neck joint well accomplished and the maple fingerboard accurately fretted with wire which is probably a few gauges thicker than Fender normally use — a good point, as it increases sustain and can assist string bending.

However the Maya does *not* feel like a genuine Telecaster; the body is a shade too thin and the weight just isn't there for any experienced Fender player to make a mistake over. Still, it's a nice handling instrument and seems to have been very well made for the price. Soundwise it's not a genuine article either. What the Maya does is offer qualities *similar* to a Tele's but not identical. The treble pickup is very brittle and sharp (but it isn't the same as the original) and the neck pickup delivers a good fat tone which could come in useful, although most players would probably use either both pickups on, or the bridge on its own. Regrettably, like a real Tele, is the tendency for the bass pickup to drown-out the bridge one so that switching from a bass rhythm to a toppy solo means a loss of power, just what you don't need, of course! Careful setting of the volume control would be needed to overcome this.

All things considered this isn't at all a bad guitar if a copy of a Telecaster is what you want. Presumably it's intended for a beginner and it certainly has a good neck, decent sound and a reliable quality feel to it which would satisfy owners of reasonable skills. Possibly the only thing going against it is that there are currently some Japanese own design guitars which have, frankly, overtaken the tonal range of this model and they sell for about the same sort of money. If you're satisfied with this sound, though, and like the looks then you won't go too far wrong with one of these.

Price: £105

Body materials: Maple

Neck materials: Maple

Fingerboard materials: Maple

Machine heads: Unidentified

Pickups: Maya single coil

Construction:	★★★★★
Finish:	★★★★★
Sound:	★★★
Playability:	★★★★
Value For Money:	★★★★

Distributed by: Stentor Music Co. Ltd, Blackborough Road, Reigate, Surrey RH2 7EZ. Tel: 07372-40226.

Moonstone Eclipse Active

Moonstone guitars and basses are rare in the UK, but there is always the chance that you might come across one either new or secondhand. In common with many of the more interesting guitars currently on the market, they come from a small manufacturer, in this instance based in the USA.

The most striking aspect of the Moonstone is the marble effect due to the redwood burl applied to a body centre of mahogany. This is penetrated by a straight-through neck of maple wearing a beautiful ebony fingerboard. The overall look of the guitar is staggering and the sample tested was exceptionally well made and finished.

Hardware consists of a gold plated stop-type tailpiece with individual adjustment for intonation but, following Gibson principles, it only offers string height adjustment via two screws; one at either end of the bridge. The logic of this is that the relationship between the neck contour and the bridge is fixed so there is no need to adjust string height individually. The machines are Grovers (rather stiff in this case) and the nut is bone — a better choice than brass in most cases.

The ebony fingerboard is inlaid with abalone, as is the headstock, where the name Moonstone is engraved and beneath which is another piece of fine craftsmanship, an abalone crescent moon. Frets are on the fat side, but those on this sample protruded a little outside the width of the neck. Apparently some players appreciate this — either way it is definitely a deliberate move on the part of the makers, and not a fault.

The twin pickups are American Bartolinis: a passive one in the neck position and an active ES1 by the bridge. These are tamed by four heavy brass pots, a three way selector and a three position switch for Eq boost. The neck profile on the guitar is rather strange — disconcertingly wide with a very flat profile. This would be unfamiliar to most players and would, therefore, take some getting used to. The active Eq, thankfully, is relatively straightforward: the pickup selector effectively controls the active in/out by switching between the neck (passive) and the bridge (active) units. Power outputs are similar enough for the passive output not to be drowned when run in conjunction with the active.

This beautifully made and attractive guitar is certainly an individual's model. Worth looking for if you like the sound of it and think you'd like that wide, flat neck.

Price: Unavailable

Body materials: Redwood burl and mahogany

Neck materials: Maple

Fingerboard materials: Ebony

Machine heads: Grovers

Pickups: Bartolini

Construction:	★★★★★
Finish:	★★★★★
Sound:	★★★★★
Playability:	★★★★
Value For Money:	**See price**

Distributed by: No UK distributor at time of going to press.

Ovation UKII

Looking somewhat Gibson-like, the Ovation has a body made of a plastic material Ovation call "Urelite". This is coloured black but a rather pleasing attempt to simulate a grey wood finish had been made on the top and back of the sample. It certainly looks rather distinctive.

The body on the UKII is, as one might expect, rather lightweight but not unpleasantly so and the neck which is wood, is bolted on to a central aluminium frame around which the Urelite body is moulded. A nicely finished rosewood fingerboard, fretted with accurate fat gauge fretwire, had been well fitted onto the Urelite and the neck itself secured to the body with four bolts.

Overall the guitar was well finished although one of the four rotary pickup controls had not been sufficiently secured to the body. More worryingly, the whole assembly itself was loose, however it was a sample guitar and may well have been through the wars before we got to see it.

On the hardware side the Ovation UKII is fitted with extremely luxurious looking gold plated parts. The machines are of a very high quality and were very well plated. The bridge too had been well made but the design of it is a little strange. Basically a cast bridge block is afixed to the Urelite with two heavy duty screws. Each string rides over a saddle. Ovation, like Gibson, have opted for the type which will not rise individually. To alter string height you adjust the two screws. Intonation is altered by screwing the saddles back or forth by screw heads which run from the pickup backwards towards the string end fastening. This is actually virtually impossible because, on the sample, the screw heads were made inaccessible by their proximity to the bridge pickup.

The pickups are twin coil designs with bar type magnets. Each has a small plastic slider switch fitted to give single or twin coil settings. There is also a top horn mounted selector and the previously mentioned four pots. Ovation claim a 20dB improvement in noise levels from these pickups and, certainly, they seemed quiet in the sense intended but they are also high in output — very high it seems and with a strange sound, making this a very individualistic sounding guitar.

Frankly, I can't make up my mind about this one. There's a tremendous bass from the neck pickup and reasonable treble from the bridge pickup (when used single coil) but there's an odd muffled tonality overall which one would need longer to assess.

The neck is also very wide indeed but it's also quite fast and with a very pleasant slight camber to it. Overall I cannot make my mind up about this guitar. I liked the looks of it and the weight and balance of it. The neck was fine for this reviewer but it also flexed too easily for my tastes.

Definitely a guitar to look for and to try, this one, but you'll need to live with it for a while before making up your mind too, I suspect.

Price: £425

Body materials: Urelite

Neck materials: Unidentified wood

Fingerboard materials: Rosewood

Machine heads: Ovation

Pickups: Ovation twin coil

Construction:	★★★★★
Finish:	★★★★★
Sound:	★★★
Playability:	★★★
Value For Money:	★★★

Distributed by: Rose-Morris & Co Ltd, 32/34 Gordon House Road, London NW5. Tel: 01-267-5151.

Peavey T-15

Despite a great deal of speculation about what they actually plan to do to the traditional American guitar market, still only a handful of Peavey models are available in the UK. US demand, apparently, is very high, and much of the talk was the result of an open-hearted honesty about research plans. The latest outcome (at the time this review was written) of that research is the Peavey T-15; an unashamed beginner's guitar which comes either with an "electric" case or a normal one. The electric case is, in fact, a nice moulded plastic type with a built-in mains powered practice amp.

Intended partly for younger players with smaller hands, the T-15 features a scale length of only 23½" — that's 1¼" shorter than a Gibson's standard scale and 2" shorter than a Fender's. It makes for easy access to the chords and faster runs up the scale if you've got small fingers.

In fact there is definitely a touch of the Lilliput about this guitar — it features a small body made of unidentified "hardwood" with a bolt-on maple neck. The neck had been well fretted on the sample and the whole instrument feels, if somewhat small, then also nice and "tight" as well as fast to play, partly on account of its small-ish neck with a fairly flat fingerboard.

Hardware is only average in quality: Kluson machines with plastic buttons, a metal nut (not brass) and a strange bridge design which offers adjustment for string height but not for string length — this latter being achieved by Peavey's own compensating bridge design. Frankly this reviewer is not too happy with this and would rather have sacrificed string height for normal intonation adjustment.

Pickups are twin single coil types with one exposed bar-strip type magnet, run via a single metal pot for tone and ditto for volume. There is also a three way selector switch. Needless to say the diminutive neck is fast — very fast indeed, but it may prove a shock for some players used to more normal sizes. Soundwise the guitar isn't bad at all, rather sharp and harsh, perhaps, but a sound that would appeal to many younger players.

Overall the guitar has a fairly good (but rather "machine made") feel and a sound which matches that impression. It's not over-priced for what it offers the younger player at £166.75 for the guitar alone. The case (which adds about £55 to the price) contains a very good mains operated practice amp with quite a large speaker built in. It offers volume as both pre-and post pre-amp and an equaliser (tone) pot. It's surprisingly loud and offers good potential for overload settings. To be *really* useful, however, it would be better if it offered optional battery powering, perhaps from re-chargeable Ni-Cad cells. Nonetheless it's a loud amp with a good sound at a low price, helping to make the Peavey T-15 much more desirable.

Price: £166 (with electric case £217)

Body materials: Unidentified

Neck materials: Maple

Fingerboard materials: Maple

Machine heads: Kluson

Pickups: Peavey single coil

Construction:	★★★★★
Finish:	★★★★★
Sound:	★★★
Playability:	★★★★★
Value For Money:	★★★½

Distributed by: Peavey Electronics (UK) Ltd, Unit 8, New Road, Ridgewood, Uckfield, East Sussex TN22 5SX. Tel: 0825-5566.

Peavey T-30

Launched in the UK with the T-15, the T30 sits, in some ways, partway between that and the original Peavey guitar, the T60. The Southern ash body of the T30 has a natural finish (similar to that of the first samples of the T60) with a very pronounced grain and what Peavey call a "satin finish". It is not bad looking but it does not look as luxurious as other natural wood guitars this reviewer has come across. Just for the record, the T-30 can be had either with the "Electric Case" (Peavey's clever moulded plastic case with a built-in mains powered practice amp) or in a very good quality plastic case.

The hardware on the T-30 sampled was not particularly heartening. The machine heads fitted were Klusons and one of these rather weak types was already exhibiting a lack of precision which would have been unacceptable on any guitar, even a reasonably priced one like this. Considering that some cheaper Oriental guitars feature better quality machines Peavey would do well to upgrade from Klusons to Japanese made machines — regardless of Hartley Peavey's patriotism!

The bridge too isn't a very inspiring design, similar to that of the T15. It's a cast metal type with a "compensating" design which is supposed to provide perfect intonation under all circumstances. This does not allow for proper intonation setting individually when compared with most bridge types although it is adjustable front to back from either side — a compromise in design which this reviewer dislikes. Pickups are three single coil types with bar magnets, one metal volume pot and a similar one for tone. There is also a five-way selector for pickup configuration.

Constructional standards on this bolt-on necked guitar were high and the neck was fretted to a good standard with an unusual wire which, although fat, was also rather on the high side in its profile.

Playing the T-30 is easy. It has a 20 fret neck with what feels like a fairly short scale, although the bolt-on neck joint is a little obtrusive and the odd fret profile feels strange until one gets used to it. The neck is also on the flat side, but allows for considerable speed and is relatively comfortable to handle.

The best point of the T-30 is its sound — very much like a Fender in some ways (especially with that five-way switching of the three pickups) it offers some very pleasant out of phase capabilities. It will also distort well and lends itself to really good solo sounds plus some nice fat chords.

Overall this T-30 is a distinct case of the curate's egg. Notwithstanding the price, the fittings like the machine heads and the use of such a simple bridge design let this instrument down when compared with the better and similarly priced instruments from the Far East. This is unfortunate as the actual *sound* it makes is very good indeed.

Price: £189

Body materials: Ash

Neck materials: Maple

Fingerboard materials: Maple

Machine heads: Kluson

Pickups: Peavey single coil

Construction:	★★★★
Finish:	★★★★
Sound:	★★★★★
Playability:	★★★★
Value For Money:	★★★½

Distributed by: Peavey Electronics (UK) Ltd, Unit 8, New Road, Ridgewood, Uckfield, East Sussex. Tel: 0825-5566.

Peavey T60NM

The Peavey T60 was Peavey's first tilt at the guitar market and, apart from launching versions with optional rosewood necks and coloured bodies, little has changed with this instrument over the years.

When it was introduced it seemed pretty obvious that Peavey had put a great deal of thought into the T60. The whole instrument has obviously been designed to offer the best of both Gibson and Fender design whilst still being a very cheap and easy guitar to manufacture. The Peavey has two twin coil pickups with a unique tone control arrangement. Four metal pots are fitted; two for volume and two which instead of offering a normal passive top cut facility, actually act as gradual coil taps, turning the twin coils to single as you rotate them. You also have two metal switches, one for pickup selection, one for phase — a very versatile arrangement indeed.

The T60 doesn't actually *look* like an expensive guitar. The rather utilitarian nature of it doesn't justify a price of over £300, especially when there are many other fine guitars which now retail below that figure. On the other hand all those others are from the Far East, making this guitar one of the cheapest American made guitars on the market. The T60 has a scale length of 25½" with 21 frets so there is more reason to compare it with, say, a Stratocaster as a potential purchase.

Mechanically the T60 is good. The machine heads are smooth and seem to be very reliable and the bridge is die cast and solid — well screwed down onto the body and with excellent adjustment potential for both string height and intonation.

Overall the T60 still seems to play rather well (despite all the newer guitars this reviewer has tried since it was first introduced). The fingerboard is rather flat and takes a little getting used to, but the fretting is good and the guitar can soon feel very familiar and quite fast to play. The sample could have had a slightly lower action but it certainly wasn't faulty and would be easy to lower if one wished.

Conceptually, one would have to describe the Peavey T60 as a bit of a machine of a guitar. The sound is very versatile, ranging from a thick twin coil "poke" to a very thin over-the-top treble. But, despite that tonal range the guitar feels, looks and sounds like a machine. A nebulous term but perhaps one you'll appreciate when you see the guitar.

The Peavey T60 is a working man's axe — a guitar with reliability and a good tonal range. That it may lack real personality in both mechanical and sound terms is hardly a criticism of it at the price. If a hardworking career is what lies ahead of you, and if a guitar which will imitate rather than originate appeals then this is a very sensible purchase indeed.

Price: £328

Body materials: Ash

Neck materials: Maple

Fingerboard materials: Rosewood

Machine heads: "Peavey"

Pickups: Peavey twin/single coil, adjustable

Construction:	★★★★★
Finish:	★★★★★
Sound:	★★★
Playability:	★★★★
Value For Money:	★★★★★

Distributed by: Peavey Electronics (UK) Ltd, Unit 8, New Road, Ridgewood, Uckfield, East Sussex TN22 5SX. Tel: 0825-5566.

Peter Cook Axis

Peter Cook currently offers two instruments, the Axis guitar and its bass counterpart. He makes other designs too but these are his staples. The guitar version is a rather substantial looking and feeling instrument, almost old-fashioned in a virtuous way, with a carefully glued neck and a thick body offered in a choice of several woods, the best looking of which is, undoubtedly, the most expensive — rosewood. Like the bass, however, the guitar is an active instrument, run from on-board PP3's.

This sample was a mahogany model, beautifully finished with a slight green stain applied around the edges of the glossy body. The overall level of craftsmanship is superb. The body of the guitar is mahogany, as is the neck, but the fingerboard is a traditional rosewood, although of a lighter colour than is often seen. It has been well fretted with wide gauge wire, each fret having been precisely polished and lapped at the ends for accuracy and comfort.

Pickups on the mahogany version are Schaller and these require no further endorsement. Neither does the Badass bridge which offers excellent sustain and very precise adjustment individually for intonation and string height. After the bridge the strings feed through the back of the body. Nicely contoured, the Axis even has two strap buttons fitted to the body base so that it can be left standing up with more security than most guitars. Used as a passive, the Axis offers one master volume pot and two extra controls, one for each pickup, plus a large selector switch and a small metal phase switch. The active power is switched in by a third switch which has three positions; active on, active off/straight-through or passive with top cut.

Playing this guitar is easy. Peter has a very traditional instrument on offer here, almost chunky in its solidity but which, although it has rather a substantial neck, is fast to handle and possesses excellent natural sustain. Frankly, this reviewer couldn't persuade himself to be very interested in its passive sound but when the active switch is on, the guitar comes alive to offer the phenomenal range of sounds which have made this so successful an instrument. Switched to active the two back rotary pots now become frequency sweep and peak and notch, and careful setting of them offers you a range of sounds possibly unparalleled in anything short of a synthesised guitar or one or two other custom actives. A massive range of sounds is there from weird thin tones which make a Telecaster sound "fat" to a thickened-up Gibson-like warmth.

The only complaint, is that I would never personally be able to remember precisely which setting provides which sound and would fear making silly mistakes pre-solo. I'm sure that many could get used to it with time, however, but guitarists, as a breed, have yet to take to active guitars en masse and this confusion is probably the reason why. A superbly well made, if rather traditionally constructed instrument, with very advanced electronics.

Price: £386 (In mahogany)

Body materials: Optional mahogany/maple/rosewood

Neck materials: Optional mahogany/maple/rosewood

Fingerboard materials: Rosewood or ebony

Machine heads: Schaller or Grover

Pickups: Peter Cook twin coil (active powered)

Construction:	★★★★★
Finish:	★★★★★
Sound:	★★★★★
Playability:	★★★★★
Value For Money:	★★★★★

Distributed by: Peter Cook Guitars, 69 Station Road, Hanwell, London W7. Tel: 01-840-1244.

Rickenbacker 330

Rickenbacker were the first company to produce electric guitars commercially way back in the Thirties, although it was left to Leo Fender to produce the kind of instruments which have spawned today's electric guitar industry.

Nevertheless, Rickenbacker instruments have played an important role in the history of rock music, and the 330 is a part of that history. It is one of the most distinctive looking guitars around today, and remains the same as when it was first introduced in the Sixties. It gained popularity in the hands of John Lennon, Pete Townshend and a whole host of others, but rather faded from view in the late Sixties and early Seventies. It wasn't until Paul Weller of the Jam started using one, that interest was renewed and today a number of young bands can be found using them.

As mentioned earlier, the 330 has one of the most distinctive shapes around. A semi-solid body it has two very distinctive cutaways and a rather odd shaped soundhole. It may look slightly odd in view of many of the modern streamlined instruments, but some people like Paul Weller were actually attracted by its shape.

The body is made of maple and the neck is a three piece laminate of maple and walnut. The machine heads are Klusons and the truss rod system is somewhat special; comprising two rods running underneath the lacquered rosewood fingerboard.

The Rickenbacker has two pickups which are both single coil and mounted on rubber bases. There are five controls altogether, both pickups have tone and volume controls, while the fifth enables you to mix the tone, and finally there is a selector switch for the pickups.

The look of the instrument isn't improved by the slabs of white plastic here and there, but then again it does contribute to that distinctive image. The sound of the instrument is unique and there are many who can distinguish it from any other, it is a strong "jangly" kind of sound which really cuts through. If you have been used to more subtle sounding instruments then you could be in for a shock, and no matter what the volume level or the tonal mix, that unmistakable sound Is always there.

Having said that, the guitar isn't particularly versatile, and is most often used as a good rhythm guitar rather than a lead instrument. It can do one basic job very well.

In real terms it wouldn't be particularly good value for money, because it doesn't possess the kind of features and versatility that many modern guitarists have come to expect from an instrument. However it is certainly a meaty instrument and you know you've got something solid when you've got a Rickenbacker. If your music requires that unique sound, then there is no substitute.

Price: £460

Body materials: Maple

Neck materials: 3 Piece laminate, maple/walnut

Fingerboard materials: Rosewood

Machine heads: Kluson

Pickups: 2, single coil

Construction:	★ ★ ★
Finish:	★ ★ ★
Sound:	★ ★ ★
Playability:	★ ★ ★
Value For Money:	★ ★ ★

Distributed by: Last Known: Wing Amplification Ltd, 15/15a London Road, Bromley, Kent. Tel: 01-464-3190.

Schecter Tele

The Seventies saw the growth of the spare parts side of the guitar industry. A number of companies sprang up catering solely for the bits and bobs which make up an electric guitar. Initially it was mainly replacement pickups, but gradually they went on to offer just about everything you could ever want to replace on your instrument. Finally, these companies reached the point where they could build you a complete guitar from materials and hardware of your own choosing.

One such company was Schecter, and their Telecaster is a prime example of the ultimate in customising. The Schecter Tele has aroused much interest among top players, and recently Pete Townshend has been seen using one.

It should be made clear that Schecter have no connection with CBS Inc. who make Fender Telecasters, and all the parts that go into making these instruments are their own, although the design is obviously based on the Fender Telecaster. What Schecter have produced is a very high class instrument which has a sound and a style all of its own.

The neck and fingerboard of the particular model under review, is made of maple, while the body is mahogany. The machine heads are Klusons with a gold plated finish and the rest of the metal fittings are brass. There are two pickups as on a Telecaster, but they are single coil with coil taps. The coil tap is operated by the push/pull method on the two controls, one of which is for volume and the other for tone. The only other item is the three-way selector switch which enables each pickup or a combination of both to be used.

The sounds produced by this beautiful looking instrument certainly live up to expectations. The rock guitarist's dream of long, even sustain is pretty well met, with the tone having a ringing quality about it which is quite magnificent. The two pickups with the coil tapping give a useful range of sounds, which should cater for everything you're likely to need.

Although sound is undoubtedly of prime importance to a guitarist, looks will probably come a very close second, and here the Schecter scores highly. It looks like a very special instrument, something that once bought will never be parted with.

If you want the best it will cost you. Still if you do buy one you can have it pretty much put together to your own specifications, which is a nice personal touch. Definitely an instrument that will become a collectors' item, and one to aspire to.

Price: Approx £380

Body materials: Mahogany

Neck materials: Maple

Fingerboard materials: Maple

Machine heads: Kluson

Pickups: 2, single coil & coil taps

Construction:	★ ★ ★ ★ ★
Finish:	★ ★ ★ ★
Sound:	★ ★ ★ ★
Playability:	★ ★ ★ ★
Value For Money:	★ ★ ★ ★ ★

Distributed by: Chandler Guitars, 199 Sandycombe Road, Kew, Richmond, Surrey. Tel: 01-940-5874.

Shergold Custom Masquerader

Shergold are Britain's only mass producer of guitars at the present time. Despite having established a generally good reputation, it would be fair to say that they have yet to make the breakthrough into general acceptance, probably due to having some weird cosmetic and styling traits which they appear to be reluctant to change.

In some ways the Custom Masquerader goes partly down the path of overcoming these oddities in that it is available with an ash body in place of the normal Shergold body wood, obechi, which is considered far too light for comfort by many players. The rock maple neck is joined to the body by a method which most people would wrongly identify as plain screw-on or bolt-on. It is a sort of bolt-on job but Shergold's method is a definite improvement on the laxity which that description normally implies. It isn't an easy neck to move.

Hardware is a mixture of the excellent and the appalling. The machines are Schallers which require little further endorsement. The bridge is a good design of Shergold's own, employing rounded brass saddles, each with full adjustment potential for both string height and intonation setting.

The bad news, however, is that Shergold have placed a ridiculous looking moulded black plastic cover over their rather nice bridge. Thankfully, this can be removed and disposed of which is just as well as it fulfills no mechanical purpose and merely serves to make the instrument look ghastly and cheap.

It isn't helped by the controls, either. These are the two pots (black plastic) and three clumpy plastic half slide/half flick switches which act as controllers for the two black plastic cased twin coil pickups. In theory and in practice, these sharp edged switches are a good idea because they offer you a very advanced choice of pickup selection, humbucking or reverse phase or single coil option on each pickup! Certainly a great change from the one pickup selector and two pots principle of most other makers. In fact, despite the clumsiness of these controls' appearance, they actually work rather well.

The neck is as good as Shergold's necks always are. This means that it all comes with the lowest action of any production guitar around — no fret buzz at all and a superbly well profiled shape. Whether you like it will depend on your taste in neck shapes but you will not be able to fault it on its superb constructional quality.

Tonally the instrument isn't bad but overall Shergold's pickups leave quite a lot to be desired. It's amazing that they didn't give these up years ago and bring in Mighty Mites or something similar. These don't have too bad a sound and certainly the optional ways of setting them provides for a good wide range of usable sounds — but you can never make it take off and fly like a good Gibson or Fender — it did get quite close though.

Price: £235

Body materials: Ash

Neck materials: Rock maple

Fingerboard materials: Rock maple

Machine heads: Schaller

Pickups: Shergold

Construction:	★★★★★
Finish:	★★★★★
Sound:	★★★
Playability:	★★★★★
Value For Money:	★★★

Distributed by: Barns and Mullins Ltd, 155 Grays Inn Road, London WC1. Tel: 01-278-4631.

The Strat (Fender)

The Strat is Fender's latest "up-market" version of their ever-popular legend. It features many of the normal Strat qualities but improves on some, for example, taking its hardware from the Fender "Brass Master" add-on parts range. This means that the Strat (which only comes in two colours, Candy Apple Red or Lake Placid Blue) is fitted with very good quality solid brass parts, each treated with epoxy resin to avoid the corrosion problem which has plagued some other makers' early forays into this metal.

The machines are from Schaller and represent a substantial improvement on the old Klusons normally used by Fender, in that they should last and work properly from the start.

The bridge seems stronger than previous Strat's and offers all Fender's usual adjustment potential for both intonation and string height. The Strat comes complete with the normal Fender tremolo system which is possibly *still* the only design which works. This sample was no disappointment at all in that department.

The neck on the Strat doesn't follow current Stratocaster design in that it is somewhat thinner (thus faster?) and is fixed to the body without the later type's adjustment for neck angle but is constructed of four screws through the base plate which is, as you've probably guessed, made of brass.

Fender have finally adopted the five position selector for this guitar — a great boon as it means that Strat users will no longer have to play the stupid hit and miss game of trying to set the original selector "in between" to get those much sought-after phase sounds. Here it's easy to get those sounds, and there are more too, because this model also has one of its three brass rotary pots wired to offer even more series combinations.

The end result is a Strat with more tonal range than ever before. This could also be attributed to the fitting of a new design single coil pickup in the bridge position called the Super XI, which is said to have 9,000 coil windings as opposed to the normal Fender Strat pickup's 7,600.

In use, the Strat is perhaps the definitive Fender to date. All the usual Strat sounds are there from country picking to Hendrix and through to Mark Knopfler. The neck's slight thinness compared with latter day versions make it even faster than normal and the sound range is superb, especially that hotter new pickup which will sing away into solo work better than any Fender previously played.

The sample was very well made and immaculately finished. It was also the most exciting Fender that the reviewer had ever played; full of this design's fundamental single coil attack, yet with more tonal potential than any previous model. Despite carrying a higher price tag than many Fender buyers will be used to, the Strat represents a serious upgrading of the basic model and should find itself a home with many players who might previously have bought a standard model and customised it.

Price: Approx £450

Body materials: Ash

Neck materials: Maple

Fingerboard materials: Rosewood

Machine heads: Schaller

Pickups: Fender

Construction:	★★★★★
Finish:	★★★★★
Sound:	★★★★★
Playability:	★★★★★
Value For Money:	★★★★

Distributed by: CBS/Arbiter Ltd, Fender House, Centenary Estate, Jeffrys Road, Brimsdown, Enfield, Middlesex. Tel: 01-805-8555.

Vantage Phantom

Vantage guitars look like being one of the success stories of recent years in the UK. Sometimes a new brand just seems to get it right in almost every way and takes off like a rocket. Aria and Ibanez are other examples of Japanese-made instruments that have done similarly well in the past.

The Vantage Phantom is very much in that pure Japanese bracket in both looks and sound. Cosmetically it's rather plain, the straight-through maple neck is set into a dark stained ash body and its apparent dullness brightened by two small walnut strips.

Following modern Japanese practice, the Phantom is provided with excellent quality, gold-plated machines — not bad at the current price! The bridge is a particularly well designed sample, inset into the body for increased sustain and harmonic transmission, aided by a "strings through the body" fastening which must contribute to the excellent sustain this instrument offers.

Control gear on the Phantom comprises four Gibson-like pots (two volumes and two tones) plus a coil tap to convert the twin coil pickups to single coil operation. This is well positioned for quick changes in mid number. Another sensible touch is the placement of the jack socket on the front of the guitar which will help to prevent inadvertent disconnection due to over-enthusiastic lead tugging!

Balance on the Phantom isn't quite perfect, the guitar hangs a bit "nose down" although some players may actually like this feature. The odd feeling is compounded, however, by the fact that the guitar is very light for a solid ash bodied instrument.

Playing the Vantage is a pleasant experience, the neck is very comfortably proportioned and this comfort is aided further by the fitting of fat frets which make string bending so much easier. Those on this model were perhaps less than perfectly finished as there was a shade of fret buzz in places but it would be unwise to deduce too much from one sample.

The pickups on the Phantom are very good, the sound being warm and vibrant on twin settings and yet still capable of a sustained treble when set on single coil. There might be a very slight tendency for the single settings to allow the note to die-off a bit too fast but there is enough basic raw power for a decent amp to help overcome this one problem, minor as it is.

The chief drawback of the Phantom is that it does tend to look too much like a thousand others. But if you can live with that then it's a good example of the best among current Japanese solid electric guitars. Priced as it is, the Phantom may not be an exceptional bargain but it's a good instrument at a fair price.

Price: £298

Body materials: Ash and walnut

Neck materials: Maple

Fingerboard materials: Rosewood

Machine heads: Vantage

Pickups: Vantage

Construction:	★★★★
Finish:	★★★★
Sound:	★★★★
Playability:	★★★★
Value For Money:	★★★★

Distributed by: Stack Music, 9 Stapledon, Orton, Southgate, Peterborough, Cambridge. Tel: 0733-232-440.

Vox Custom 25

Despite bearing a solidly British name, the latest series of Vox guitars is made in Japan. However the design of the guitar has largely been undertaken in the UK by the owners of the Vox name, Rose-Morris and Co., one of the largest distributors of instruments in this country. The British influence on the design is worth a mention because several features of this instrument are fairly obviously not Japanese — a fact which becomes more comprehensible when one realises that guitar circuit designer and author, Adrian Legge, is on the staff of this company and has contributed considerably to the design of its products.

The Vox Custom 25 definitely looks ordinary. It has a plain maple neck set into a maple body, the sides of which are stained to a dark finish. You could not honestly claim this to be the best-looking guitar you'd ever seen, in fact it is decidedly plain which comes as a disappointment from such a legendary name.

However, the instrument is very well made and the hardware has been well chosen. The machines are smooth and reliable in use, the nut is brass, as is the bridge which is very much along Fender Strat lines in conception. This is just as well as it offers a tremolo arm device which works well enough to be worth bothering with.

Pickups on the Custom 25 are DiMarzio bar types, designated X2-Ns. These are very good and control their high output via a flick switch for either/or, two volumes, two tones and another flick switch which gives series (i.e. normal twin coil hum-cancelling) in the down position, single coil both (cancelling the coil closest to the bridge) and parallel when set to the straight up position.

The Vox balances well and handles generally finely. The neck profile is very comfortable indeed and the fretting on the sample tried was excellent.

Plugged in and wired up, those DiMarzio pickups have the kick of an angry mule. The basic sound is on the hard side, rather like a fat Strat in tone but the addition of some cleverly placed capacitors enables the Vox to be set in series and adjusted so that an extra tap comes in on the tone control to give a very convincing "Strat in between" sound. The designers have also fitted a bypass capacitor for each pot so that you don't lose treble as you pull back on the volume power. The bias is in favour of the bridge pickup and it can, set in this way, sound very close to a good old Telecaster.

The Vox Custom 25 is one of the most versatile non-active guitars on the market, but it takes some experimenting with to get all these sounds — not at all the sort of thing a ten-minute try in a shop will reveal. If you can overcome your basic objections to its plain looks, the Custom 25 could prove to be one of the most versatile sounding, easy playing guitars currently selling below the £400 mark.

Price: £329

Body materials: Maple

Neck materials: Maple

Fingerboard materials: Maple

Machine heads: Gotoh

Pickups: DiMarzio X2-N

Construction:	★★★★★
Finish:	★★★★★
Sound:	★★★★★
Playability:	★★★★★
Value For Money:	★★★★

Distributed by: Rose-Morris and Co. Ltd, 32/34 Gordon House Road, Kentish Town, London NW5. Tel: 01-267-5151.

Vox Standard 25

This is (quite self-evidently) a Fender-type instrument. The body shape may only be vaguely reminiscent of a Strat, but the rest of the guitar's features all add-up to a pretty convincing attempt to "do for" the ageing Californian wonder-axe.

Like a Fender, the Vox features a bolt-on neck of maple, with a maple fingerboard and single coil pickups (DiMarzio FS-1s), a tremolo unit (which works in much the same way as that on the original Fender principle) and a general feeling which, hard though it is to put into words, immediately brings to the player's mind, recollections of the "real things" which he may have played in the past.

Mind you, it's unwise to make these comparisons without pausing to reflect that they are, actually, a strong compliment, bearing in mind the price differential between this guitar and a Fender.

Picking up the Vox, it feels bigger bodied than perhaps it should, but it's still by no means uncomfortable to handle. All the control gear (one volume, two tones, a five way pickup selector and tremolo arm) all fall easily to hand, making one feel that the Vox's designers have a good grasp of ergonomics as well as electro-acoustics.

The sample was finished in a black gloss look which contrasted nicely with the maple fingerboard. Overall one would say that this was a well made, if somewhat soul-less, instrument; in that respect very much like the average production-line Strat, in fact!

String fixing on the Vox is through the body and then up and over the individually adjustable saddles on the rather nicely made bridge. The tremolo unit (still rather rare on a Japanese guitar) worked almost identically to that on a Fender Strat and must be praised, therefore, for being one of the best on the market.

The Vox, thankfully, departs from the basic brand "F" practise by employing fat frets on a very well finished maple fingerboard. From a sustain and playing (especially string bending) point of view, these frets are to be vastly preferred to thinner types.

In use the neck feels very comfortable indeed and the DiMarzio pickups sound every bit as good as examples of that American brand always seem to. This is quite a wild guitar. The screaming Fender overload sustain is reproduced remarkably faithfully as are those "in and out of phase" tones which so many genuine Strat players seek. The five way selector helps here and makes the Vox seem like very good value for money.

Just as a brand new Fender Strat is usually a rather machine-like instrument, so is this Vox. It's not a guitar for the really subtle player but would be ideal for the adventurous guitarist who could put these ultra-high powered DiMarzio pickups and that accurate returning tremolo to the best possible use. The only fault in it is, put simply, that it doesn't really have one ounce of originality in it. But, at this price, who's quibbling?

Price: £179

Body materials: Unidentified hardwood

Neck materials: Maple

Fingerboard materials: Maple

Machine heads: Gotoh

Pickups: DiMarzio FS-1s

Construction:	★★★★★
Finish:	★★★★★
Sound:	★★★★
Playability:	★★★★½
Value For Money:	★★★★

Distributed by: Rose-Morris & Co. Ltd, 32/34 Gordon House Road, Kentish Town, London NW5. Tel: 01-267-5151.

Washburn Stage A-15

The A-15 sample we had for review was coloured blue, well finished and featured a glued neck joint with a fairly unobtrusive heel for easy access to the top. Balance of this rather unlikely looking shape is excellent when playing with a strap and surprisingly comfortable when held seated. The rosewood fingerboard on the sample had been well finished and fretted to a good standard with Gibson type wire.

The machines are carried on the single sided headstock at a very strange angle, disturbingly so when you first start playing the instrument. I found myself having to stop and look to see which head I was tuning. The A-15 shares its string fixing through-the-body arrangement with the A-20 and they also have their bridges in common, a perfectly sensible design whereby each string has its own brass saddle which adjusts for intonation and height. The sample came set just a shade too low for both this reviewer's tastes and the guitar's own good. A low action is all very fine from a playing point of view but there does come a point when the apparent advantages of it become outweighed by fret buzz and a lack of string vibration which thins out the overall resonance from the tone. Both failings were present here and it would be as well (especially with the single coil pickups of the A-15) to fit a slightly higher gauge of string and matching action than this sample came with, to get the best out of it.

From a playing point of view, however, the low action was very comfortable indeed, but this would be a remarkable neck even with very heavy strings as it's one of those fairly rare instruments using the old V neck shape originally seen on some Fenders. This makes the Washburn a delight to play, assuming, that is, that you're one of those players who likes this type of profile.

Pickups on the A-15 are three single coil Strat copies, controlled in the typical Fender way with one volume, two tones and a five-way selector. Owing to the excessively low action on the sample it is impossible to say how loud these pickups are but the output from them was rather lacking and it took an unusual degree of pre-amp gain on the test amp to make the instrument overload.

Tones from the five-way selector are excellent and overall it is not a bad sounding instrument. It is no Strat, however, and this reviewer would personally save that little bit harder for its twin coiled brother, the Stage A-20. But some readers may well find that the Fender-like sounds combined with the build quality, and exciting shape of the A-15, plus that neck profile, all add up to making it their ideal guitar.

Price: £280

Body materials: Unidentified

Neck materials: Unidentified

Fingerboard materials: Rosewood

Machine heads: "Washburn"

Pickups: "Washburn" single coil

Construction:	★★★★★
Finish:	★★★★
Sound:	★★★½
Playability:	★★★★★
Value For Money:	★★★½

Distributed by: Roland (UK) Ltd, Great West Trading Estate, 983 Great West Road, Brentford, Middlesex. Tel: 01-568-4578.

Washburn Stage A-20

The A-20 is a guitar of some distinction, and is certainly superior to its smaller brother, the A-15. It has particularly beautiful colouring; the top is of maple, coloured in a most appealing form of sunburst finish and the back a splendid red rosewood. It is one of the most attractive pieces of wood this reviewer has seen in a Japanese production model to date.

Standards overall on this model are excellent. An attractive and very well fretted rosewood fingerboard has inlays of brass tubing for position marking and this combines to make the A-20 look a very classy instrument. Machine heads are of the same type and excellent quality as those found on the A-15 but they are similarly difficult to locate when the guitar is new to you. The bridge design on the A-20 is also the same as that on the A-15 — a very sensible type with good adjustment potential.

Being a "Gibson type" guitar the A-20 features four knurled Gibson type pots: two for volume, two for tone, and two cream coloured twin coil pickups plus a single selector switch. Unfortunately there is no coil tap provided which would have been welcome, especially considering the asking price of this guitar.

The sample instrument was set just that shade higher than the A-15 and its higher output was, no doubt, partly due to that. Furthermore, these twin coil units are generally louder than single coil types as used on the A-15. This guitar has plenty of output power and can be wound up into a powerful sustain/distortion with no need for excessive pre-amp boost.

That powerful sound, combined with a very fast V neck profile and high quality fretting help make the A-20 not only a very fast guitar to play but also a very good sounding one. Despite the fact that these pickups are humbuckers, there is a lot of treble to be had out of this guitar and both the basic tone and sustaining potential are very good.

This instrument is, however, just a shade expensive when compared with some other fine Japanese made guitars. But if you want these sonic and physical qualities in this shape, that is the price you will have to pay.

Price: £317

Body materials: Maple top/rosewood back

Neck materials: Unidentified

Fingerboard materials: Rosewood

Machine heads: "Washburn"

Pickups: Washburn twin coil

Construction:	★★★★★
Finish:	★★★★★
Sound:	★★★★★
Playability:	★★★★★
Value For Money:	★★★★

Distributed by: Roland (UK) Ltd, Great West Trading Estate, 983 Great West Road, Brentford, Middlesex. Tel: 01-568-4578.

Westone Concord II

Since their launch on the UK market, Westone guitars and basses have rapidly established themselves as being among the best value around. Although there is little revolutionary about them in terms of either design or construction quality, they epitomise the best value aspects of Japanese instruments as a breed.

A recent introduction, the Concord guitar takes the price range even lower, offering a Fender Strat-like guitar (although by no means a copy) which will probably retail, after discounts, at around £100.
finished. The body (of unidentifiable hardwood) had been sprayed rather an unfortunate royal blue but the quality of spraying was excellent.

The maple neck bolts onto the body with a small heel which shouldn't get in the way, and a good rosewood fingerboard is applied to this. It had been very pleasantly fretted with medium/fat frets with, perhaps, a slightly high profile but not an uncomfortable one.

The machine heads up on the painted headstock are the typical top quality Japanese type which are almost ubiquitous these days — and rightly so, they're excellent. The rest of the hardware comprises a brass nut and bridge assembly. Both are well made, the bridge being based on the Strat's to some extent, with thick saddles riding on twin screws and offering intonation plus height adjustment on an individual basis. Regrettably, though, the makers had not lacquered the brass on the nut (and possibly not on the bridge either) and some corrosion was already present. Whilst this is unlikely to present a mechanical problem it *is* unsightly.

Three single coil pickups are fitted to the Concord II and these are tamed by the typically Fender, three rotary pots plus a five-way selector switch system which offers a multitude of sounds, including those desirable "out-of-phase" tones which later Strats offer via the five-way switch.

Mechanically and electronically there's little else to say about the Westone except that it seems to be a very well made guitar for the price with a good choice of hardware, suitable for the player who wants a Stratocaster but can't afford one. From a playing point of view the neck isn't as fast as a well honed Strat but it is very fast indeed for the price and should encourage younger players to explore their potential for soloing by giving them as good as they can dish out in terms of accuracy and feel.

The sound is rather Fender-like as one would imagine. There is the country potential of the high treble output in some settings, the jazz/funk potential of the out-of-phase approach and, of course, the savage overload used with a good quality amplifier when ringing harmonics and searing high frequencies can be tortured out of the pickups. At this price the guitar is almost impossible to fault and not only did this reviewer enjoy playing it very much indeed, it is also among the best two or three value for money instruments on the market at the time of writing.

Photo of Westone Concord unavailable. Photo shows Westone Series guitar.

Price: £130

Body materials: Unidentified

Neck materials: Maple

Fingerboard materials: Rosewood

Machine heads: "Westone"

Pickups: Westone single coil

Construction:	★★★★★
Finish:	★★★★★
Sound:	★★★★★
Playability:	★★★★★
Value For Money:	★★★★★

Distributed by: FCN Music, Morley Road, Tonbridge, Kent. Tel: 0732-365271.

Westone Paduak

The Westone Paduak is a strange beast of a guitar. Currently it must be the cheapest active electronics guitar on the UK market and that oddity is compounded by an unusual body shape, faced with unvarnished red paduak. The neck is rather more usual in that it's maple with a one sided headstock carrying the usual high quality Japanese machine heads.

In some ways the Paduak has a very Fender-like feel to it, no doubt attributable partly to the looks, the bolt-on neck, the profile of the fingerboard and the knurled brass Telecaster-like pots. But make no mistake, the Paduak is a unique instrument which differs in many ways from a basic Fender copy.

To start with, the body looks and feels small and light. The Paduak is carved away around the face to give an unusual looking "ledge" effect to it. Then there's the use of just one twin coil pickup in the bridge position. This has the usual two pot set up for volume and tone but it also has two small metal flick switches. One gives you single coil or twin coil settings on the pickup, the other brings in the PP3 powered active circuit.

Unlike many other active guitars the Paduak doesn't have a massive tonal range produced by its active circuitry, in fact the circuit doesn't appear to do anything more than just boost the output. Mind you,the word "just" is unfair here. Although the output of the first samples were somewhere around 25dB this was later tamed in production versions because of complaints that the guitar was *too* hot for sensible use. The Westone still punches out its power like little else on the market. Used without the active switch on, the sound is still very, very good for the relatively low price being asked for it. When that small toggle is activated it soars away into some of the most feedback-promoting sounds ever heard! Of course no guitar is perfect, and some may well feel that the placing of these metal switches tends to make them hard to flick on or off for instant solo effects.

Bearing in mind the price it might be felt that any criticisms at all are mere pedantry because this strange looking guitar is priced low enough to be considered in the beginner's market and yet has a sound and constructional quality which could easily take it onto a professional stage. The hardware matches the quality of the woodwork and the sounds, the machines are quite acceptable and the bridge, which allows for both individual height and intonation setting of the strings, is as good as most on the market — better than many at this sort of price.

Price: £123

Body materials: Paduak

Neck materials: Maple

Fingerboard materials: Unidentified

Machine heads: Westone

Pickups: Westone

Construction:	★★★★
Finish:	★★★★
Sound:	★★★★★
Playability:	★★★★★
Value For Money:	★★★★★

Distributed by: FCN Music, Morley Road, Tonbridge, Kent. Tel: 0732-365271.

Westone Rainbow-1

Semi-acoustic guitars are one of the least successful areas of cheap guitar production. All the more surprising, therefore, when a relatively new name like Westone comes up with a reasonably priced guitar which looks very promising indeed. The Westone range has taken off remarkably quickly since its launch in Autumn 1981 and this manufacturer seems to have something special to offer throughout the whole series of guitars, for what is generally the sort of price one normally expects to pay for no more than a below average Oriental copy.

The Rainbow-1 is made of Canadian ash, this sample stained an attractive dark brown, to a standard that belied the low price. The rosewood fingerboard has been fretted with a good quality fretwire, fat frets as on a Gibson, each of the 22 on the sample well finished. The machines are good, modern, Japanese types with an excellent action and reliable tuning. The nut is brass and the bridge a copy of the typical Gibson "stop" type, with the usual adjustment that this type offers.

The pickups are designated Westone A750 humbuckers, which tells us less than nothing, but in use they seem to work very well indeed. Cheap semi-acoustics often suffer from weaknesses in this department but this most certainly does not apply to the Rainbow which has a very good sound, almost regardless of the selling price.

Not only does the Westone Rainbow-1 sound good, but also plays remarkably well for the money. The neck camber is a happy compromise and should appeal to both habitual Gibson and Fender players who are experimenting with this type of guitar for the first time.

Set on the neck pickup, the tone is bassy but usable for jazz and perhaps some cabaret work. Use both pickups, however, and you're immediately into rock and roll with an exemplary rhythm guitar sound. Pull the pickup selector down a stop further and the Westone Rainbow takes off and flies — amp willing, of course! Used with a high pre-amp gain this setting lends itself ideally to a fantastic sustained solo sound, especially if the player's skill enables him or her to employ the natural tendency of a good semi-acoustic to feedback and then hang on to a note.

At the current price the Westone Rainbow-1 represents exceptional value in terms of both construction and sound. Any player who feels able to use a good semi but cannot afford an American original would have to look a long way to find anyting better.

Price: £197

Body materials: Ash

Neck materials: 3 piece Maple

Fingerboard materials: Rosewood

Machine heads: Rotomatic die cast

Pickups: Westone A750 humbuckers

Construction:	★★★★★
Finish:	★★★★★
Sound:	★★★★★
Playability:	★★★★★
Value For Money:	★★★★★

Distributed by: FCN Music, Morley Road, Tonbridge, Kent. Tel: 0732-365271.

Yamaha AE 2000

This instrument comes in the type of quality case which Gibson should definitely copy. It is made of a sturdy lightweight fibre, at least twice as good as those fibre cases which Gibson supply — some of which would not do justice to a £50 copy! Open the box and the Yamaha leaps out at you — a heavy dose of gold plate poisoning must obviously have seemed like a good idea at the time to the guitar's designers. This, in itself, is all well and good but the interwoven complexities of the gold plated tailpiece is sheer visual overkill.

The woodworking on this guitar is, however, up to Yamaha's usual exemplary standards. The AE 2000 comprises a solid carved spruce top with a very nicely made back and sides of birch and beech. The rounded highly shaped back, particularly, being a most impressive sample of this fine maker's craft.

The maple glued neck has a fingerboard of ebony and offers 20 frets on its 25¼" scale. As is always the case, in this reviewer's experience, of Yamaha instruments, the woods used in this guitar are of the finest quality and the general standard of construction as good as that from any mass maker.

Machine heads on this model are also of the highest standard and are torque adjustable as well — a feature this reviewer is very keen on as wear will take place in time with all machines and adjustment should be offered to take account of this. The bridge design, however, seems quite pointless — whatever jazz purists might say. It comprises a plain wooden bridge piece only adjustable for height and with no normal string by string allowance made to adjust intonation whatsoever. No doubt, the makers would claim that a finely made guitar (which this obviously is) will play perfectly in tune without the need for fancy bridge designs. However strings *do* wear out at unfortunate moments and, even when new, their potential to require special bridge adjustment is legendary — here you have no ability to counter that. I part company then with the traditionalists and would suggest that, whatever might be said in its defence, a better bridge design (with normal saddles) than this should have been employed.

Apart from that the AE 2000 is a very nice guitar. The fingerboard is comfortable and the two humbuckers do an excellent job. Tonal potential ranges from the very warm indeed to the ultra-thin — thanks to Yamaha's innovatory push/push single/twin coil volume controls. This is a well made instrument with a strong appeal to lovers of traditional jazz guitars. It sounds very pleasant and has a comfortable, fast neck. I cannot, however, feel happy with the bridge design or the looks of it. If they don't worry you, however, or (better still) you, actually *like* these features, then this might well pose a serious alternative to one of Gibson or Guild's jazz standards.

Price: £699

Body materials: Spruce top/Beech & Birch back & sides

Neck materials: Maple

Fingerboard materials: Ebony

Machine heads: Yamaha

Pickups: Yamaha twin coil

Construction:	★★★★★
Finish:	★★★★★
Sound:	★★★★
Playability:	★★★★
Value For Money:	★★★★½

Distributed by: Kemble/Yamaha, Mount Avenue, Bletchley, Milton Keynes, Bucks. Tel: 0908-71771.

Yamaha SA 2000

Pricing the SA 2000 at a whisker below the £550 mark means that this highly polished (in all senses of the word) Yamaha semi-acoustic guitar is currently selling for considerably less than the Gibson 335 models which it so obviously seeks to topple.

Yet there is nothing cheap about the looks or the materials of this instrument at all. The body is beautifully made from arched beech and birch, the fingerboard is made of a fine, dark ebony, and all the hardware is gold plated. It looks more like a guitar selling at £1,000 than one retailing at £550.

The metalwork on the sample was of an excellent quality; Yamaha machines are used which are as good as any, the bridge was a well made virtual Gibson copy (saddles with no individual movements) and the embossed stop tailpiece looked very nicely finished.

Beneath the stop tailpiece lies a block of laminated spruce and maple to which it is bolted. This is designed to increase the sustain transmission of the strings and get the guitar away from that "plunky" quality which bedevils cheaply made semi-acoustics.

The ebony fingerboard has that tactile quality to it which many players feel justifies its increased cost over rosewood and the frets set into that wood were very well finished rather fat types with a good profile. The neck itself is well shaped too, with a nice camber to facilitate string bending and easy chord work played up the neck. There are few things more rewarding than a well finished instrument and this was certainly one of those. Overall, then, the Yamaha SA 2000 looks like being an excellent buy — but what about the sound?

Here one is, possibly, in for a surprise because it's a good deal more toppy than one had imagined it might be. Somehow the Yamaha's sound was less warm and welcoming to me than that from its Gibson rival.

Still, the Yamaha plays very well indeed and has a very good sound played through an amp set down below distortion levels, quite capable of producing that unmistakable humbucking sound for fat, country style, rhythm guitar work.

Solos, with the pickups turned on full and your amp cranked-up high, are very much that sort of run-away excitement sound which you can balance into and out of controlled feedback (something which can only be done with the very best semis).

Overall there is no doubt that this Yamaha is a very good guitar, yet for some unfathomable reason, it just left me cold, for all its undeniable virtues. Assuming you don't feel the same way as I did about it, this guitar would represent very good value for money for the player who wanted a high class semi-acoustic.

Price: £549

Body materials: Arched beech & birch

Neck materials: Mahogany

Fingerboard materials: Ebony

Machine heads: Yamaha

Pickups: Yamaha twin coil

Construction:	★★★★★
Finish:	★★★★★
Sound:	★★★★★
Playability:	★★★★½
Value For Money:	★★★★½

Distributed by: Kemble/Yamaha, Mount Avenue, Bletchley, Milton Keynes, Bucks. Tel: 0908-71771.

Yamaha SBG 2000

The SBG 2000, is slightly different from the basic Yamaha SG 2000 in a few respects but most of the comments will apply to the latest series of standard SG 2000s as well.

A heavy bodied instrument, it feels very much like a Gibson Les Paul. Quite obviously Yamaha's designers realised that much of the legendary Gibson's sustain was due to the sheer volume and density of its highly resonant wood. Thus the SG too has a heavy body and partakes of a sound and sustain more like that from a Les Paul than almost any other Japanese maker's offering. In the case of the SBG 2000 this body construction is a T-Cross maple design (Yamaha's own terminology) which means that you have two side pieces of solid maple with the bridge screwed down onto a heavy sustain plate which transmitts its vibrations through a "T" shaped insert of mahogany.

This through-necked guitar is fabulously well made. The laminated maple neck is far more comfortable than many Les Pauls I've played but is still not offensively Fender-like for players who like to have something a bit more meaty to handle than a Strat's neck.

The fingerboard is Yamaha's usual first rate quality of ebony, luxuriously bound in "aged" simulated ivory — as is the whole body. It's a fine looking guitar, especially in the jet black version.

Hardware is gold plated to a nice quality and the machines are Yamaha's usual high quality torque adjustable types. The bridge design is based on a Gibson design and offers full intonation adjustment but not individual string height.

Pickups are Yamaha twin coil units, run from two volume controls and two tones. Very cleverly, Yamaha have now introduced a new pot design where single coil use can be tapped by just a single push on the pot. Push again and the spring loading gives you twin coil. Push again, and you are back on single, a very fast system and extremely neatly executed.

SG 2000s are always a joy to play and this version was no exception. The neck was a sheer delight and the fretting on the sample was very good indeed with only a slight trace of fret buzz present on the "A" string — easy enough to get rid of but, arguably, a case for individual height adjustment on that bridge. Sustain from this guitar was everything its reputation suggested. The sound on single coil was one of the best I've ever heard from a production-made basic humbucking instrument.

I can quite sympathise with those players who argue that the Yamaha SG 2000 is the finest rock and roll production guitar currently available. This sample fully deserved that sort of accolade. From all points of view it is a truly superlative instrument and a credit to its makers. In terms of value for money it is very fair and is certainly one of the stars of this book.

Price: £620

Body materials: Maple/Mahogany

Neck materials: Maple/Mahogany

Fingerboard materials: Ebony

Machine heads: Yamaha

Pickups: Yamaha twin coil

Construction:	★★★★★
Finish:	★★★★★
Sound:	★★★★★
Playability:	★★★★★
Value For Money:	★★★★★

Distributed by: Kemble/Yamaha, Mount Avenue, Bletchley, Milton Keynes, Bucks. Tel: 0908-71771.

Yamaha SC 1200

Yamaha have never directly copied anything and yet their instruments are rarely as innovative in either shape or design as those from some other Japanese makers. It may be that timeless quality which has earned Yamaha their reputation, it may be the recognised quality of their instruments. Whatever it is, somehow Yamaha seem to have become the most prestigious of guitar makers from the Far East. It may, of course, be due to clever marketing in the early days!

The SC 1200 is nothing whatsoever like the Gibson type of instrument which Yamaha are most famous for. Shape-wise this is virtually a copy of a Fender Strat, complete with single sided headstock and three pickups. There are, however, some important differences. The Yamaha has a through-neck, of maple, wears a fingerboard of superb quality ebony, inlaid with a tasteful fleur de lys pattern for position marking. The neck runs into a body of maple, spliced with strips of mahogany. Woodworking quality overall is as high on this instrument as that on any mass production guitar and the overall level of finish is superb.

The bridge is a Fender type with the strings fastening through the back of the body before running over saddles, adjustable both ways for height and intonation. The sample came with an immaculate low action and needed no re-setting whatsoever.

Fretting on the SC 1200 was strangely unfashionable in that it was of a thin wire, more Fender than Gibson in profile. This is a good move on Yamaha's part as the vast majority of Japanese makers now fit fretwire of the Gibson type as standard and, although many guitarists prefer it, there are still some who like a thinner gauge.

Pickups are totally enclosed types, bar magnet designs and wired very oddly in that only one of them (the neck pickup) can actually be turned off. Three metal flick switches control them, one covers on/off for the neck pickup, the other two acting as phase switches for the remaining two. In addition you have two rotary controls, one for volume, one for tone.

However, because each of the switches can be used in combination, the total range of sounds from this guitar is very bewildering. This reviewer found himself virtually incapable of working out what did what was not much the wiser by the time the guitars were returned, except for learning how to turn everything off — something which should *never* be possible on any guitar in order to avoid nasty mid-solo silences due to a quick mistake in setting the selectors!

That aside, the Yamaha has a fantastic sound with really high top potential and excellent sustain. In many ways it sounds far better than a basic Strat and certainly plays better than some off the shelf Fenders. Tonally it must be among the best single coil pickup guitars on the market and it plays as well as it looks and sounds. Excellent value for the adventurous Fender lover who wishes to go one stage further.

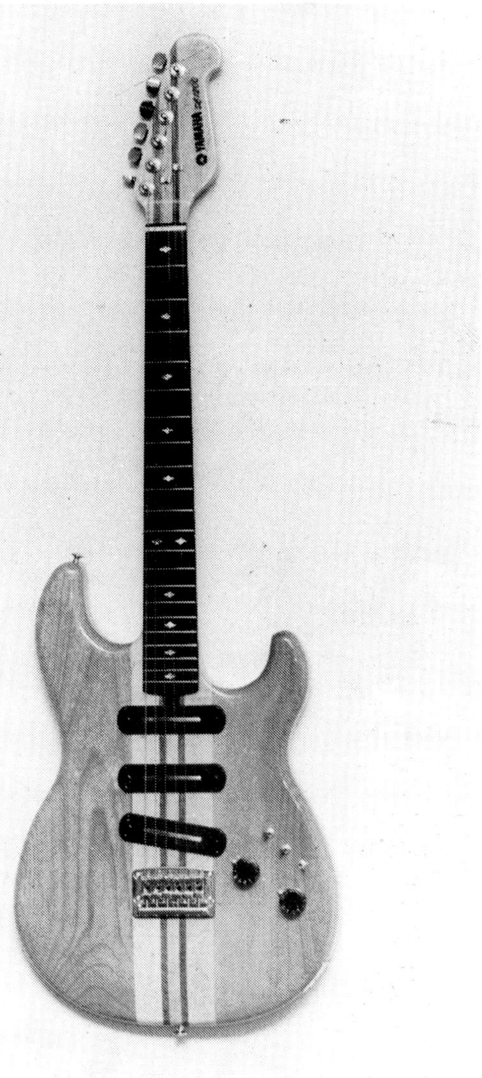

Price: £375

Body materials: Alder/maple/mahogany

Neck materials: Maple/mahogany strips

Fingerboard materials: Ebony

Machine heads: Yamaha

Pickups: Yamaha, single coil

Construction:	★★★★★
Finish:	★★★★★
Sound:	★★★★★
Playability:	★★★★★
Value For Money:	★★★★★

Distributed by: Kemble Yamaha Ltd, Mount Avenue, Bletchley, Milton Keynes, Bucks. MK1 1JE. Tel: 0908-71771.

Lead Profiles

Jeff Beck

Jeff Beck is one of rock's true original performers. A brilliant erratic guitarist, he is one of the few guitar heroes from the Sixties to have emerged with his credibility intact, and his reputation enhanced.

Born in Surrey in 1944, he first attracted attention in a local group known as the Tridents, but his big break came when he replaced Eric Clapton in the Yardbirds in 1965. During the next two years the Yardbirds made some classic singles, and always at the heart of them was Beck's outrageous guitar.

Obviously initially influenced by the blues, he used this as a base for experiments with styles and sounds. For example there's a story from one of the Yardbirds sessions that they needed a sitar sound, but while they were considering hiring the instrument and someone to play it, Beck simply plugged in his guitar through a fuzz box and got the desired effect.

For a brief period towards the end of 1966, both he and Jimmy Page were playing guitar in the group, but then Beck left to pursue other things. Under the direction of producer Mickie Most, he had a brief career as a pop star with singles such as "Hi Ho Silver Lining" and "Tallyman", but soon after formed his own band.

The first Jeff Beck band was a mighty line up comprising Mick Waller on drums, Ron Wood on bass, Rod Stewart on vocals and later Nicky Hopkins on piano. At their best the band was phenomenal and their two albums, "Truth" and "Beck Ola" although inconsistent, produced some magical moments.

In many ways they reflected the erratic genius of their leader, Beck could play great blues guitar, but then he'd suddenly go into things like "Greensleeves" at the drop of a hat. He played some of the most original lead lines around, and you could never be sure where his solos were going to lead because there would always be a few surprises.

The time was right, the band was right and success should have been massive, but it wasn't. In 1971, Beck formed another band which included Cozy Powell among others, but once again the two albums they produced were patchy. Next came a power trio with Tim Bogert and Carmine Appice formerly with Vanilla Fudge, but while they often scaled the heights, they didn't do it quite often enough and split after just one album.

One of the biggest problems for Jeff Beck is finding the right vehicles for his playing. He is not a great writer and so must rely on gathering around him musicians who can write for his highly individual style. In 1975 he got together with former Beatles' producer George Martin and came out with the "Blow By Blow" album, followed a year later by "Wired".

Beck was gradually moving into jazz rock areas which had been opened up by the Mahavishnu Orchestra, and his work began to take on new relevance. Playing with the likes of Stanley Clarke and keyboard player Jan Hammer provided him with a great stimulus which coaxed the best out of his guitar playing.

Beck is very much a musician's musician, the archetypal guitar hero, mean and moody and erratic yet a totally original guitar genius. The Les Paul has been his favourite instrument for many years, but recently he's been sporting a Schecter Telecaster.

When not playing, he indulges in his passion for hot rods and souped up cars.

During the last few years Beck has surrounded imself with good musicians, like ace drummer Simon Philips, spending much of his time touring the world, and after a long absence finally played in England again. His recent albums, thanks to some interesting writing by his fellow musicians, confirm his status as a master guitar player.

Ritchie Blackmore

Ritchie Blackmore belongs to that impressive school of British guitarists who served their apprenticeship in the Sixties, found fame and fortune as guitar heroes in the Seventies, and have become living legends in the Eighties.

He was born in Weston-Super-Mare in 1945, but eventually moved to London where he began to build up a reputation as an exceptional guitarist. The inevitable session work included working with a variety of people, including legendary British producer Joe Meek. With the burgeoning heavy rock scene of the late Sixties developing he formed Deep Purple with Jon Lord and Ian Paice while they were all in Germany.

Initially the group scored a couple of chart successes in the States, but gradually moved towards heavier rock and their 1970 album "Deep Purple In Rock" was a classic which firmly established them as one of the leaders of the genre. In particular, the album highlighted the frantic guitar work of Blackmore which was epitomised on the track "Speed King".

Although a guitarist capable of more subtle and mellow playing, it was the fretboard speed merchant that most people came to see, and they weren't disappointed. The deadly combination of the Fender Stratocaster and Marshall amplification were used to devastating effect to produce the quintessential rock guitar sounds.

However, as time wore on, Ritchie became more and more disenchanted with the band and the direction they were moving in so he got together with the members of an American band, Elf, and cut an album called "Ritchie Blackmore's Rainbow". Soon after he left Deep Purple and settled into his new role.

The history of Rainbow has been marked more than anything by the constantly changing personnel of the band. Ritchie becomes dissatisfied with things very quickly, and his constant search for the right ingredients has meant that no line up of Rainbow has remained constant for long. Personnel has invariably been of the highest calibre and has included the likes of drummer Cosy Powell, keyboards man Don Airey and bass player/producer Roger Glover.

In fact it was former Purple bass player Glover who brought Rainbow from a Heavy Metal cult band to commercial success. Over the last few years, Rainbow have hit the single charts several times, although they have still managed to keep hold of their grass roots fan following. Rainbow live are still a fearsome sight, and have even been known to use explosives on stage.

Blackmore remains something of an enigma. He has lived in the States since 1975 and rarely gives interviews. His playing appears to have mellowed although the audience still seem to want the fast licks and all the guitar showmanship. A definitive Heavy Metal axe hero, his ever changing band remains one of the biggest and loudest rock bands around.

Eric Clapton

Together with Jimi Hendrix, Eric Clapton was one of the leading figures of Sixties music who brought the electric guitar to the prominence which it still enjoys today. Clapton was the arch exponent of "white blues", which blossomed in the Sixties and led to the heavy improvisational aspect of the instrument during the "progressive rock" era.

Born in Ripley, Surrey in 1945 Clapton's interest in the guitar began when he was bought one as a youngster. He soon gave up trying to play it, but returned to the instrument a little later and began to develop an interest in the blues. This interest blossomed when he went to Kingston School of Art, and he was heavily into Robert Johnson, Skip James and Freddie King.

He was eventually kicked out of college, but armed with an old Kay electric guitar, he joined his first real group, the Roosters, at the beginning of 1963. He became part of the West London R&B scene and eventually joined the Yardbirds at the end of 1963. The Yardbirds were a hard blowing R&B band who had taken over the residency of the Crawdaddy Club in Richmond, when the Stones went on to greater things.

During the next 18 months, Eric really got down to learning his craft and quite soon he had a reputation as a hot guitar player. However, when the band started to lean towards mainstream pop, Clapton the blues purist opted out. He played on the first Yardbirds hit, "For You Love" and then left. Having been nicknamed "Slowhand" by Giogio Gomelsky who ran the Crawdaddy, Eric wasn't out of work for long.

John Mayall, himself a blues crusader, recruited him to the Bluesbreakers, and it was here that Clapton turned into a legend and slogans began to appear which declared "Clapton Is God". It was a satisfying time for Eric because he was simply playing the music he loved.

During this time Clapton had a significant effect on the instrument market because his favourite guitar for playing the blues was a Gibson Les Paul. The guitar had gone out of production by then, and wasn't particularly popular, but by the end of the decade they were back in production once more, and became the most sought after electric guitars.

Clapton's Bluesbreakers album is a classic and his playing was truly magnificent. His fluent style burned with an intensity and passion which was really breathtaking. He was to become probably the first star in the pop world to make it solely on his ability as a musician.

However, in those early days Eric was never one to rest on his laurels, and in July 1966 he joined up with bass player Jack Bruce and drummer Ginger Baker to form Cream, one of the most influential bands in rock music. In Cream, Clapton had musicians around him who were his equal on their own particular instruments, and the trio soon began to make their presence felt.

Cream initially started out as a blues band, but gradually their extended solos began to take over until the songs were merely jumping off points for improvisation on a vast scale. They also reckoned that being a three piece they would need to play loud, hence their massive amplification. Add to this the burgeoning psychedelic period and LSD, and you have the mixture which was to produce the phenomenon known as Cream.

Their performances and recording were inconsistent, but when they were hot, they were really hot. Clapton's guitar twisted and turned, and at times his fingers seemed to make time stand still. His live version of "Crossroads" on the "Wheels Of Fire" album is considered by many to be his finest hour, while his use of the wah wah on tracks such as "Tales Of Brave Ulysses" is quite brilliant.

During this period Clapton invariably used banks of Marshall amplification and a whole variety of guitars. One particular favourite was a psychedelically painted Gibson SG, although he was also seen with a Gibson Firebird and a Gibson 335. Cream were undoubtedly one of the pioneers of the musical format which developed into Heavy Metal.

Almost inevitably, Cream burned itself out and Clapton went on to form Blind Faith with Ginger Baker, Stevie Winwood and Rich Grech. Despite a good debut album and an American tour, the "supergroup" tag which had been placed on them, proved too heavy a burden, and after a year they broke up.

The "fastest guitar in the West" image clearly bothered Eric, and the early Seventies saw him trying to become an anonymous guitar player, first behind an American duo, Delaney and Bonnie, and later with his own band Derek and the Dominoes, in which he steadfastly refused to use his own name. The band's initial album had some great moments not least being the beautiful "Layla" which eventually became a Top Ten hit, and Eric's tribute to Jimi Hendrix "Little Wing".

But within a year that band had folded as well, and Eric went into a reclusive period, making few appearances amid trying to overcome a drug problem. In 1974 he bounced back with a new band, a new album "461 Ocean Boulevard" and went out on the road. This was a much mellower Clapton, who was really getting into writing and singing.

Since then he has toured and recorded quite regularly although much more as a writer and singer than trying to out solo everyone. His music shows a great country influence, coming over as a latter day Don Williams.

It may be hard for youngsters who never heard of Clapton in the Sixties to understand what all the fuss is about, but he still commands enormous respect, and every so often a bit of the old magic will shine through.

The Edge

U2 are a young band from Dublin who over the last couple of years have brought a heady breath of excitement into the music scene, and their guitarist, The Edge reflects a new breed of player which suggests that the time may be right to salute a new guitar hero.

Their music is different from any of the categories that currently abound in the music world. They play with the intensity of New Wave and yet their music has a romantic, ethereal quality which is topped off by the soaring guitar of The Edge.

The band were born in the Seventies when all the members attended the same school in Dublin. The school had a liberal attitude to music and encouraged pupils to play. The foursome came together at school and stayed together afterwards, learning as they went along. They soon realised the value of original material, and virtually from the start they were playing their own songs.

After a couple of early singles in 1979, the band were put in the studio with producer Steve Lillywhite and came up with the 1980 album "Boy". Lillywhite was the young producer who'd just recorded Peter Gabriel's highly acclaimed album, and he proved to be ideal for U2, turning out an album of power and beauty.

The Edge's guitar playing was a revelation for many who heard it because it was so new and refreshing. Up until then it seems that guitar players were either New Wave thrashers or Heavy Metal riffers, but here was someone who was neither. His guitar lines weren't about speed but more about choosing the right notes and structuring them, what's more his playing was crystal clear, you could hear every one of those notes ringing out over Bono's falsetto vocals.

For a player who's barely out of his teens, The Edge has already firmly established his own original guitar sound. To get that sound he usually plays a Gibson Explorer and a Marshall 50 watt combo amplifier with echo thrown in, usually by way of an Electro Harmonix unit. He also incorporates a graphic equaliser when he's playing live.

They are the mechanics of the sound, but it is the ideas and the tasteful playing that really make it. Because of the romantic imagery and the ethereal quality of their music, U2 are aware of the dangers of being labelled a kind of latter day hippies' band or psychedelic revivalists, and are determined not to allow self indulgence to creep in.

U2's second album, "October" confirmed the promise of the first, and for a band who are all only just out of their teens, the future seems assured, and with it perhaps the rise of a new and exciting guitar hero.

Scott Gorham

The inclusion of Scott Gorham in the Thin Lizzy line up may have puzzled the band's early fans. After all, here was a hard rocking Irish outfit, who had already recruited a no nonsense Scott Brian Robertson for one guitar berth, and in walks this guy from California wearing tennis shoes to audition for the other place.

Luckily Scott Gorham survived the ordeal and has been an integral part of Thin Lizzy for many years. His guitar playing making up one half of that distinctive Lizzy twin guitar sound. Scott is probably an underrated guitar player, but his work is characterised by a lyrical quality that is uncluttered and simple, but very effective.

His musical career began at the age of 13 in his native Los Angeles. He began playing bass and it wasn't until six years later that he got fed up of lead guitarists stealing all the limelight and decided to switch over himself. He slogged around garage bands and played the usual round of bars and colleges without really getting anywhere.

An initial foray to England ended in disaster, but eventually Scott was persuaded to return by his brother-in-law who was in Supertramp. This time he stuck it out and at one point had his own band in London called Fast Buck. However, when he was recommended for the Thin Lizzy audition by a friend, he went along not knowing about the band or their music.

As it turned out, he really liked the music they were playing and he impressed them with his enthusiasm and the speed with which he picked up the numbers. With Scott in the band, Lizzy had the perfect line up for

their music and they eventually cracked both the British and American markets.

Scott himself puts over a fairly low key image when compared to Phil Lynott or the roster of guitarists who have played with the band, from Brian Robertson through to Gary Moore. He considers that his guitar playing really only began to take off when he came to England.

Clapton and Beck were great influences on his playing, and he certainly has developed a kind of singing tone to his guitar work. Scott describes himself as a "vibrato nut", and it is a technique that has been worked on a lot. He hits the note and then stretches it to give that long slow vibrato, and in his solos, he goes for a lot of melody.

For much of his career in Thin Lizzy, Scott has played a Les Paul, usually a 1959 Standard. Although he liked the sound of a Fender Stratocaster he could never come to terms with the neck on the instrument. However, he has managed to get the best of both worlds by having the Schecter people put a Stratocaster together for him, that is very much his ultimate guitar.

In the studio he often uses a Yamaha SG2000, and while in Japan the company built him a special SG2000 double neck, the only one of its kind.

Scott's proudest moment came when Thin Lizzy played his home town and he stepped out onto the stage where years earlier he used to go and watch bands himself. A great example of a local boy making good.

Jimi Hendrix

Jimi Hendrix is probably the greatest electric guitarist who ever lived. No one had done more since the invention of the instrument to realise its potential and push back the boundaries of electric music. Even today, over a decade after his death, Hendrix recordings sound phenomenal.

Born in Seattle in the state of Washington, USA in 1942, he began his musical career on an old acoustic his father had bought for him. Jimi soon graduated to an electric and began playing in high school bands. He had no formal guitar tuition, but was heavily influenced by the blues, in particular guitarists such as Freddie King and B.B. King.

In the early Sixties he joined the army, but was eventually invalided out after an injury sustained in a parachute jump. Still he had kept up his playing in the army, and when he got out he spent a lot of time on the road playing with a variety of bands, usually as just another guitar player in a backing band.

Even so, Jimi must have been pretty good because he backed such people as Sam Cooke, Jackie Wilson, Wilson Pickett, and Little Richard. Apart from his blues and R&B influences, he was also a big fan of Bob Dylan. Jimi eventually ended up in Greenwich Village, New York, putting little bands together and jamming with other musicians.

In September 1966 he was spotted playing the Cafe Wha by Chas Chandler, ex-bass player with the Animals who wanted to get into record production. Within 20 minutes he had realised the massive potential of Hendrix and persuaded him to come over to England. The deal was clinched when Chas told Jimi that he would introduce him to Eric Clapton.

Once in England, Chas recruited Noel Redding on bass and Mitch Mitchell on drums, and spent all his money recording two songs with Jimi. The first was a Tim Rose number "Hey Joe" and the second "Stone Free" was Hendrix's first attempt at writing. However, the tracks were rejected by every record company who heard them, until one night Kit Lambert of Track Records, heard Jimi jamming in a London club and signed him on the spot.

"Hey Joe" was a hit, to be followed by other classic singles such as "Purple Haze", "The Wind Cries Mary" and "Burning Of The Midnight Lamp", and a couple of inspired albums. Unfortunately this was still an era when pop stars needed an image or a gimmick to get themselves noticed. Jimi earned the tag "the wildman of pop" through his much publicised stunts like smashing his guitar, setting fire to it, and occasionally playing it with his teeth.

Another problem was that many of Jimi's ideas were far in advance of the equipment and recording facilities available at the time. Chas and Jimi, together with various engineers and electronic whizz kids, spent a great deal of time experimenting and dreaming up all kinds of weird things to go with Jimi's music.

His third album, a double entitled "Electric Ladyland" bore the hallmarks of many of these experiments, and is a rock classic. After its release in 1968, Jimi broke up the Experience and worked with a variety of people, seemingly trying to look for a new direction. His appearance at the Woodstock festival in 1969 proved to be something of a high spot, and his version of "The Star Spangled Banner" is another of rock's classic moments.

However, during this period he seemed restless and unsure of which direction he should go. In the summer of 1970 he appeared at the Isle of Wight festival which was to be his last performance. On Friday, September 18 he was found dead in his flat in London, having taken too many sleeping tablets and choked on his own vomit.

There will never be another Jimi Hendrix, his playing was pure inspiration. He translated ideas into sound almost at will and revolutionised guitar playing with a style which ranged from the startling aggression of "Purple Haze" to the beautifully melodic "Wind Cries Mary". He could play fast too, as on "Johnny B Goode", while his magnificent blues playing is often overlooked among all the flash.

The man was pure genius, a true innovator and yet it was not just a question of natural ability. He practiced all the time, and all those years on the road in America backing a variety of artists, obviously served him well. Chas Chandler even recalls Jimi cooking breakfast with a guitar around his neck.

As far as his equipment goes, his main guitar was a Fender Stratocaster, although he sometimes used a Gibson Flying V for playing blues and on one occasion used a Hagstrom eight string bass. Jimi's amplification was invariably four or five Marshall heads with about twice as many speaker cabinets. For effects he used a Vox wah wah, and a Dallas Arbiter Fuzz Face, and later a Univibe to give a Leslie cabinet type of effect.

To many Jimi was the ultimate electric guitar player, and his legacy undoubtedly lives on in countless of today's rock bands.

Steve Howe

Steve Howe strikes you as the kind of musician that many of us would like to emulate. A self taught player, he is a brilliant technician with a tremendous reputation, and his love of guitars is reflected in his staggering guitar collection.

Born in London in 1947, Steve is best known for his work with Yes, although he wasn't part of the original line up. He started playing guitar without the aid of lessons, and set about learning by himself, discovering that he had a great talent for learning by ear. He is convinced that by learning the instrument in this way, his playing has a much greater freedom.

He began playing with numerous bands, one of which, Tomorrow, scored a hit in the late Sixties with the psychedelically influenced "My White Bicycle". When Pete Banks left Yes at the beginning of the Seventies, Steve was recruited to take his place, and from then began to build up a reputation.

Yes were essentially a band of virtuosos who took their music seemingly into the realms of a type of modern classical music. This didn't endear them to everyone and the band was often accused of being pretentious and overblown, but it was hard to deny their musical prowess. Steve Howe was very much a key figure in the development of the band, using a vast range of instruments and an innumerable amount of effects to try and push electric guitar playing to its very limits.

The band were undisputed leaders in the "pomp rock" stakes during the Seventies despite several personnel changes, and solo projects by individual members. For Steve Howe this resulted in the "Beginnings" album in 1975, followed by a further solo project as the Seventies ended.

Howe's solo work has always been ambitious, incorporating a variety of different styles from rock and roll through to country, jazz and classical pieces.

Apart from his ability as a guitarist, one of the things that Steve is most famous for is his guitar collection. Rumour puts it at approaching 150; the value of which one can only speculate on. Steve does not, however, merely buy the guitars and forget about them, as he uses many of them for recording, and playing live.

His favourite guitars are undoubtedly Gibsons, which is reflected in his collection. He is one of the most informed people on the instruments outside Kalamazoo, and will spend hours talking about the various models and developments through the years. Eventually, the Gibson company had a special Steve Howe model made which is based on an old Switchmaster but with a few personal modifications.Following the break up of Yes, Steve Howe went on to form a new "supergroup" Asia.

Mick Jones

The Clash are one of the very few punk bands of 1976 to have survived intact. Although their music has evolved over the years, the essential Clash sound and style remains, an important part of which is Mick Jones' guitar work.

It was a popular cry in 1976/77 that the people in the punk bands weren't real musicians, and certainly much of the playing was rough and ready, but really it was all down to a snobbish attitude on the part of many "established" musicians. The Clash came in for their share of criticism, but to Mick Jones it didn't mean a thing as long as the kids liked it.

What is important to Mick is the spirit of the thing, and communications with your audience. In his case it was all down to his simple but rather anarchic style of playing; great slabs of sound which filled the hall and reflected the venom of the songs and the music. It's not pretty, but then it's not meant to be, and one can't help but draw some comparisons with the early Stones.

Mick started playing guitar when he was 16, having tried his hand at drums and bass without too much success. He blew a week's wages to buy an old F-hole Hofner acoustic which he used to mike up. He eventually graduated onto a Fender Telecaster, but his dream guitar was a Les Paul Junior.

Ever since he'd heard that guitarists Steve Hunter and Dick Wagner used Les Paul Juniors on the "Lou Reed Live" album he'd decided that this was the guitar for him. It took Mick six months of hard saving and a lot of footslogging before he finally managed to track one down in London's Shaftesbury Avenue. It was sitting on a top shelf in a shop gathering dust, but he paid out £190 gladly.

Mick now has a number of guitars including a Les Paul Standard but there's invariably a Les Paul Junior in his collection somewhere. He is another guitarist who's not really hooked on effects, but may use the odd phaser. He remains convinced that it's not what you play, but how you play it that counts.

As far as influences go, he's a great admirer of David Bowie's old guitarist Mick Ronson, and the Stones' Keith Richard also rates pretty highly. He can't stand musicians who just seem to play for themselves, and forget about communicating with the audience.

Since their formation in 1976, Mick and the Clash have gone from strength to strength, and they still

retain a hard core of punk fans. To these fans the Clash have remained true to their punk roots, even declining to appear on Top Of The Pops, which would have certainly guaranteed higher chart placings for them. They are also one of the few punk bands to establish themselves in America, particualrly in New York where they have a large following.

There's no doubt that Mick's playing has improved over the years, and he is now an important influence on young aspiring guitarists. Youngsters who have never heard of Eric Clapton or Jimi Hendrix are now modelling themselves on guitarists like Mick Jones.

B.B. King

B.B. King is probably the most revered name in the world of electric blues guitar. His was the guitar style which most influenced the budding white rock guitarists of the Sixties, and he is already assured of legendary status in music's Hall of Fame.

Now nearing his sixties, he still records and tours regularly and it's a tribute to the greatness of the man, that his records have retained a contemporary feel, and his concerts remain exciting and entertaining. If it hadn't been for the likes of B.B. King and his namesakes Freddie and Albert, the rock guitar of the Sixties might have taken on a different form altogether.

Born Ripley King in Mississippi, in 1925, he later moved to Memphis and earned a spot on a local radio show. A DJ there nicknamed him "Blues Boy", which was later shortened to B.B. and the name has been with him ever since. King had been influenced by the country blues artists, but he was also listening to Charlie Christian, one of the early jazz guitar pioneers. He produced a clean sounding, more accessible form of blues, and in the early Fifties had a string of hits in this idiom.

B.B.'s guitar sound was instantly recognisable for it had acquired a real stinging tone. Probably his greatest innovation was the way he used to push the guitar strings up across the frets; he perfected a slow vibrato following a bend which has been adopted by just about every modern electric guitarist.

The result of this technique with the stinging tone, was a sound which was to become synonymous with the blues, and the emotions which were part and parcel of that music. But King wasn't simply an innovatory guitar player, he was an all round performer, his blues drenched voice is still quite exceptional, and the shows he gives are pure joy and great entertainment.

Although he has worked steadily all his life, B.B.'s career was given an unexpected boost in the Sixties, when many young guitar players suddenly began to cite him as a major influence. He did various sessions in which he used people like Al Kooper, Ringo Starr and Alexis Korner, and while some of his collaborations didn't always work, many of his ideas did. One such idea was the use of a string section on the classic, "The Thrill Has Gone", which worked magnificently.

The late Seventies saw him working with the Crusaders, and producing albums like "Midnight Believer" which successfully blended the man's innate talent into modern songs and arrangements. King is also a professional of the highest calibre, who would never dream of cheating his audiences by merely relying on past glories.

His approach to his instruments and his concerts are as down to earth as his music — no superstar scenes here. Usually the only thing he travels with is his guitar, the rest of the gear like amplifiers and sometimes even his backing musicians, he picks up along the way. King has become famous for naming his guitar Lucille, in fact over the years there have been several Lucilles due to various on-the-road misfortunes.

The guitar he currently plays is a Gibson 355 which was specially made for him by the company. He doesn't worry if he can't get the specific amplification he has asked for, yet still manages to get that distinctive sound.

A true original who has achieved so much, yet despite his many talents it's a well known fact that he can't sing and play the guitar at the same time. But then if you can sing and play the guitar like he does, then it doesn't really matter.

Hank B. Marvin

Hank Marvin was the first British guitar hero. Probably no one before or since has single-handedly been responsible for inspiring more youngsters to pick up a guitar than him. And even now, after over 20 years in the business, his unique guitar sound has survived and is still instantly recognisable.

Born in the North East of England, Hank took piano lessons when he was young, but soon graduated onto a banjo, which he bought for £10. Skiffle was all the rage then in the Fifties, and together with a school-friend, Bruce Welch, he formed a skiffle group playing the local clubs. He soon moved over to guitar, and at 16 was given an old Hofner.

Hank soon found that he was quite good at playing melodies, and found himself listening to the guitarists who backed the big American rock and roll stars such as Gene Vincent and Rick Nelson. He was also a big fan of jazz guitarist Barney Kessel.

In 1958 Hank and Bruce decided to try their luck in London, and ended up in the Two I's coffee bar in Soho, which was a haven for many musicians of the time. Their group, the Drifters, ended up backing a young singer, Cliff Richard. By this time, 1959, Hank was playing an Antoria electric, which was the nearest thing he could get to an American guitar at that time.

The group changed their name to the Shadows and began to make hit records with Cliff Richard. Cliff had always promised Hank that if he ever became successful he would buy the guitarist a really good instrument. He kept his word, and Hank sent off to the Fender company of America for a catalogue of their guitars because at that time Fenders weren't available in this country.

Hank reckoned that all the top American players, like James Burton, would play the top of the range instruments, so he chose the dearest guitar in the catalogue — a Fender Stratocaster. When it arrived from America, Hank was stunned when he opened the case. It was quite the most beautiful thing he'd ever seen, a Flamingo pink Stratocaster, the first one in the country.

Following their success with Cliff, the Shadows began to make records on their own, and in 1960 had a number one with the instrumental "Apache". The tune highlighted Hank's distinctive style, clean, crisp playing with unique use of the tremolo arm and echo. This was the sound which brought the Shadows numerous hits.

In 1961 he changed his original Strat for a red one along with Bruce Welch. However, after a while, both guitarists began to have serious tuning problems with their instruments, and in 1963 turned to a British guitar maker, Jim Burns for help.

Hank worked closely with Jim to produce what he felt was the ultimate guitar, the Burns Marvin. Based on a Stratocaster, it nevertheless had a number of special features suggested by Hank. Soon all the Shadows were playing Burns instruments, and the guitars of this period have become collectors' pieces.

Hank played his Burns throughout the Sixties, but around 1970 he had all his guitars stolen, and ended up having to borrow one, which ironically ended up being the original Flamingo pink Stratocaster which Bruce Welch now owned. Hank liked the sound so much that he ordered himself a new one, which he still uses today.

Many people have tried to imitate Hank's sound, and it is fairly easy to get a close approximation. All you need is a Strat with a tremolo arm and a good echo unit, but the essence of Hank's sound is in the technique and cannot be easily copied.

Over the last few years, it has proved a timeless sound with the Shadows having hits again with instrumental gems like "Cavetina" and "Don't Cry For Me Argentina".

Jimmy Page

When Jimmy Page came to the fore as a guitar hero with Led Zeppelin in the early Seventies, he had already built up a considerable reputation as a session musician, as well as an exiciting live player.

Born in Heston in Middlesex, in common with so many rock stars (and particularly lead guitarists) he went to Art College, but soon found that his guitar playing was taking up much more of his time. Jimmy became one of that small but elite band of session guitarists who played on countless hits in the first half of the Sixties.

The guitar triumvirate comprised Big Jim Sullivan, Vic Flick and Jimmy, and Big Jim apparently helped the young Page a long a bit in those early days. These three played on so many hits that it is the source of much interest to fans as to who actually played on what. One of the fiercest arguments has centred on "You Really Got Me" by the Kinks, but legend has it that the young Page played the lead break in the middle.

So great was his session work, that Jimmy actually declined an invitation to join the Yardbirds after Eric Clapton left in 1965. However, a year later he couldn't resist the chance to come out of the shadows and do live work, so when Paul Samwell-Smith left the Yardbirds, the group was shuffled around and ended up with Jimmy and Jeff Beck both playing guitar and Chris Dreja switching to bass.

The coupling of two guitar giants seems

unbelievable today, and in fact the partnership was quite short lived, Beck leaving to go solo. However, this line-up is featured in Antonioni's film "Blow Up" where the Yardbirds are seen playing in a club.

The band carried on after Beck left but folded in 1968. However, the band still had some dates to fulfill so Jimmy Page got together some new musicians and went out as the New Yardbirds, who eventually metamorphosised into Led Zeppelin.

Zeppelin were the natural successors to Cream and Hendrix, and Page's guitar playing soon elevated him to stardom. He probably more than any other guitarist defined that Heavy Metal guitar sound which still dominates music today. The first album showed the full range of Page's talents, taking in blues, heavy rock and even an acoustic track. Subsequent albums epitomised screaming heavy rock, "Whole Lotta Love" from the second album being one of the definitive rock riffs.

Page blossomed as a virtuoso and a showman on stage, using a wide variety of effects to coax even more outrageous sounds out of his Les Paul. At one point he used a violin bow on the guitar and this led to him being dubbed the "Paganini of the Seventies".

Late albums became more varied and subtle, but that underlying feeling of power was always there, and Jimmy's solo on "Stairway To Heaven" off the fourth album is arguably his best. Throughout the Seventies, Page and the band were among the foremost live performers, but the untimely death of drummer John Bonham has not seen them either on stage or in the studio since.

Michael Schenker

Michael Schenker is something of a rarity in the guitar hero stakes because he is one of the few who doesn't come from either Britain or America. Since the advent of rock and roll, the main impetus has come from these two countries, and quite naturally so have all the guitar stars.

However, with his blonde hair and Gibson Flying V, this German player is one of the few Heavy Metal guitarists around today who really projects a strong image. He also belongs to that breed of rock musicians whose exploits off the stage often rival those on it.

Michael has had quite a long and chequered musical career which began at the beginning of the Seventies in Germany. He and his brother Rudolph formed a band called the Scorpions and in 1971 cut an album in Hamburg called "Lonesome Crow". The band built up quite a reputation in Germany, but in 1973 Michael left to join the English band UFO, replacing Mick Bolton.

Life with UFO had its ups and down for Michael, they began to build up a steady following outside

Britain, notably in the USA, but the young German had his differences with the band. He made two albums with them, before leaving and eventually teamed up with the Scorpions again, being featured on their 1979 album "Lovedrive".

However, this reunion didn't last too long and he underwent several traumas before emerging in 1980 with a new album which featured top British session drummer Simon Philips among others. The following year he toured and made another album, but this time with the mighty Cozy Powell in the drum seat.

As for his penchant for Flying Vs, the story goes that he used to play a Les Paul, but borrowed his brother's Flying V one day and liked the sound so much that he decided to stick with the instrument. He is another player who doesn't bother about too many effects when playing live, and his amplification set up, is the inevitable Marshalls, although he tends to go for the 50 watt versions rather than the 100 or 200 models.

Like many of the modern heavy rock guitarists, the influence of the Sixties guitar heroes is there. Practice has made him proficient in the speed and riffs department, but he does put a lot of thought and imagination into his playing and has generated quite a following among Heavy Metal fans.

Michael also lives up to the image of a hard driving rock and roll star, and this has only served to enhance his reputation with the fans. After years of playing under a band name, he has now realised that he has enough pulling power to go out with his own band, the Michael Schenker Group, and be successful.

Andy Summers

The rise of the Police as a superstar band, is one of the great success stories of the Seventies. Coming out of the new wave scene of 1977, they harnessed the power and energy of that movement to their strong melodic songs and added a spice of reggae rhythm that has so far proved irresistible.

Their success has been the result of a combination of factors not least being the musicianship of the individual members. Even now, it is hard to believe that they are merely a three piece, for their music contains such a variety of sounds.

The importance of the contribution of each individual member of the band cannot be over-emphasised, and Andy Summers has emerged as a master guitarist. It is hard to imagine the Police with any other guitarist but him.

Although the Police only came into existence in 1977 as a result of drummer Stewart Copeland meeting Sting, Andy Summers' credentials stretch way beyond this era. Initially the Police had another guitarist but he proved unsuitable, and when Andy came along he fitted in perfectly.

Prior to the Police, Andy had a long history in the rock business. His first band of note was the one which backed Zoot Money in the Sixties, and he then had a long and chequered career playing in various outfits and backing the likes of Kevin Coyne and Kevin Ayres. Rumour has it that he was also shortlisted for the guitar spot with the Stones at one time.

Andy had learned his trade the hard way, he was a great player who was a thorough professional. Obviously, in order to survive for so long, versatility is an important factor, and it is this accumulated knowledge and technique which was to come bursting forth with the Police.

The story of the Police has been well documented; a hard gigging band from the outset they failed to break through in England and subsequently financed their own tour of the States, and by sheer hard work won through, and returned to England as heroes. Andy Summers would not be amused by any talk of "overnight success".

Being a trio presents obvious difficulties, yet the Police have managed to project a really full sound. Andy's guitar is crucial because he adds various tonal colours which are the essence of the band's music. His sense of dynamics never gives the impression that you are missing anything, and to hear him and the rest of the band in concert, is to see an object lesson in how rock music should be presented.

For much of the early career of the Police, Andy relied on a trusty 1963 custom Fender Telecaster, but more recently he's been seen with a variety of guitars, and has also experimented with the Roland guitar synthesizer.

An important part of the Andy Summers sound concerns the effects he uses, which are vital to giving that full Police sound. He has a pedal board made by Pete Cornish which contains a whole battery of phasers and flangers. Andy tries to play the guitar orchestrally, and he's able to do this only by rapid changing from all these different effects.

Andy Summers is a typical example of a hard working guitarist, and for him the hard work has really paid off.

Pete Townshend

Pete Townshend is one of rock's great intellectuals. An articulate thinker and writer, he has become one of the leading figures in the rock hierarchy, giving immense weight and credibility to a culture which was generally derided by the establishment in its early days.

His pen has been responsible for some of the great moments in rock music in the Sixties and Seventies, from the teenage anthem of "My Generation" to the rock opera "Tommy" and the story of the Mods in "Quadrophenia", while his windmilling guitar arm brought a new dimension to rock guitar playing.

The Who started out as the Detours, and later became the High Numbers before they were spotted playing in pubs in the Shepherds Bush area of West London by Kit Lambert and Chris Stamp. The pair took over their management, pushed their Mod image and changed their name to the Who.

Their music, while inspired by the black R&B so beloved by the Mods, turned into their own aggressive brand of rock and in the middle Sixties they had a stream of hit singles. In those early days, Townshend's reputation was founded on the way he used to smash up his guitars rather than they way he played them.

He used to play Rickenbackers, and very often would end his act by smashing the guitar up. The fans loved it, and there are some great pictures of Townshend standing in front of a wall of broken Rickenbackers. But despite this penchant for destruction he did play the guitar in a unique style.

Never a great lead player, he used to concentrate on sledgehammer chording which can be heard to great effect on early hits like "I Can't Explain" and "Anyway, Anyhow, Anywhere". He also used to whirl his right arm round and round as he played the strings, and developed as an incredibly acrobatic performer. The use of feedback and huge amplifier stacks were also early Townshend trademarks.

However, he soon realised that there was more to music than just three minute songs and in 1969 came out with the classic "Tommy" rock opera. Hailed as a masterpiece it was later turned into a film, although for a long time it seemed to be a milestone around Townshend's neck, the uneasy thought always there, that perhaps he could never better it.

"Live At Leeds" is considered by many to be one of the greatest live albums recorded, and showed the power of the band on stage. In 1973 Townshend again came up with a masterwork in "Quadrophenia" which charted the life of a Mod. Despite mixed reviews, it was turned into a highly successful film.

The band were well respected because they had remained intact and presented a strong united image, despite various solo projects by individual members of the band. Their future was threatened by the death of drummer Keith Moon in 1978, but soon after they recruited Kenny Jones and went out on the road to raptuous acclaim, however the future of the band does now seem to be in some doubt.

Townshend has continued his unique brand of guitar playing, from his early Rickenbackers he moved onto Gibson Les Pauls for much of the Seventies. More recently he's been using a Telecaster put together by the Schecter company, although he still retains faith in HiWatt amps for stage work.

Townshend proved that you didn't need to be an extravagant soloist to be a great guitarist.

Eddie Van Halen

Eddie Van Halen represents one of the new wave of heavy rock guitar heroes. His concerts are all about playing fast licks at ear splitting volume to hordes of denim clad headbangers.

Eddie belongs to a generation who grew up on a diet of Cream, Jimi Hendrix and Jeff Beck and have now developed their own brand of rock/blues for the Eighties. And he is in the forefront of the Heavy Metal revival which followed the punk explosion of 1977.

It may come as quite a surprise to some of his fans to learn that Eddie began his musical career around the age of seven playing classical piano. Soon after

moving to California, he and his brother became interested in pop music and while brother Alex found a guitar, Eddie himself set about the drums.

They soon found that Alex was the better drummer so Eddie took over guitar. This was around the time of the progressive rock era of the late Sixties, when extended guitar solos became the order of the day, and proved such an inspiration to the young Van Halen.

That first guitar was an electric from the Sears chain store, and it had four pickups and a wide variety of switches. Eddie maintains that he never had an acoustic but just went straight on to electric. However he soon discovered that the vast array of hardware on his Sears instrument didn't necessarily make for a better guitar, and he soon went to the other extreme.

Eddie put together a rather crude guitar of his own which had the shape of a Fender Stratocaster but featured just one humbucking pickup, one volume control and a tremolo arm. He formed a band with his brother, called simply Van Halen, and soon began to attract attention. By the time he was 21, their debut album had confirmed his speed and dexterity on the fretboard. From then his reputation has blossomed, and although still in his early twenties, he has become a guitar hero to thousands of young fans.

Influences in his playing are obvious, but although his work echoes the likes of Ritchie Blackmore and Jimmy Page, it is to Eric Clapton that he gives greatest acknowledgement. Although, now he doesn't need to copy anyone, having developed his own distinctive style.

In his playing he uses all the standard guitarists' tricks that he has learned over the years, from note bending and fast high speed picking through to the whole range of harmonics. Huge banks of 4 by 12 speaker cabinets powered by over half a dozen Marshall 100 watt amplifiers form an impressive and somewhat frightening sight at a Van Halen gig. And his no nonsense approach is reflected in his set up — very few effects, every dial on the amplifiers turned full on.

Eddie has received the ultimate accolade as a type of guitar has been named after him. This is not to say that he simply endorses one manufacturer's product, because he plays a variety of makes. What has happened is that the Strat type body with a single humbucking pickup, single volume control and a tremolo arm has become such a popular configuration that a number of manufacturers are using it as a basic design. Hence the name Van Halen may become as famous in guitar circles as Les Paul — you never know!

Paul Weller

Paul Weller is without doubt one of the most talented figures to emerge from the new wave movement of the late Seventies. While many of the bands from that musical explosion have burned themselves out, the Jam just seem to go from strength to strength.

Paul himself would be the first to point out that the Jam and their success is the result of three people, Bruce Foxton on bass, Rick Buckler on drums and himself, but there's no getting away from the massive contribution that this young man has made. Still only in his early twenties he has proved himself a good singer, great guitar player and excellent songwriter.

The story of Paul Weller and the Jam goes back to the mid Seventies in their home town of Woking in Surrey. The band grew out of a school outfit, but they developed their music playing countless local gigs. From the outset Paul saw the guitar as a means to writing songs, and in fact he wrote his first song after learning his first chords. He never saw himself as a great guitar hero, and still doesn't, yet he has evolved a highly individual style.

His first really good guitar was an old short scale Rickenbacker which he bought for £80. Paul maintains that he chose this particular guitar not for its sounds, but for its looks, and it certainly is distinctive. However, one can't help noticing that it suited the Mod image which they were projecting, because in the early days of the Who, the Rickenbacker was Townshend's favourite guitar.

By 1977 the band were gigging in London and the whole new wave thing was happening. Their image and music fitted perfectly and they were signed by Polydor. One of the first things Paul did after this was to go out and buy all the Rickenbackers he could find in London.

Already his talent as a songwriter was shining through because his songs told stories of what it was like to be young — something which the supergroups of the day had long since lost touch with. The harsh sound of the Rickenbacker complemented the songs and the music. Not for him those long fluent guitar solos, it was all down to slashing chords, which once again reflects the great Townshend.

Paul is more interested in guitar sounds than any fretboard wizardry, and cites Wilko Johnson, guitarist in the original Dr Feelgood line up, as the first Seventies guitarist who really impressed him. Like Wilko he likes playing rhythm with as few frills as possible, and little or no effects to get in the way of the sound.

Following the success of their debut single "In The City", the Jam began to build on their success. It would have been easy for them to slip into a rut and simply be labelled a Sixties revivalist band but Mr Weller wasn't gong to let that happen. His writing improved with every song and with "Down In The Tube Station At Midnight" he managed to put a whole story onto a single.

As a live band too, the Jam are impressive. The idea of a trio had always been associated with Cream, and still had a kind of "progressive rock" stigma to it. Nevertheless Paul and the others managed to put over their music well, they were a tight unit, a legacy of all those gigs in Woking, their dynamics were right and they were powerful and exciting.

The Jam albums marked the band's progression particularly "All Mod Cons" and "Setting Sons", the latter containing one of their best ever singles "Eton Rifles". Paul continues his love affair with his Rickenbackers and the band go on, and there really seems no limit to what they can do or in which direction they will go. They seem set to be one of the important outfits of the Eighties.

Angus Young

There can be few stranger sights to the unenlightened onlooker than that of AC/DC's guitarist Angus Young in full flight. How do you explain a guitarist dressed up in schoolboy uniform (complete with short pants) rolling around on the floor, while churning out a gut wrenching riff at ear splitting volume?

Being Australian might have something to do with it, but you have to admire the guts and determination of this band from Down Under who had the nerve to come to Britain and show us how heavy rock should really be played. And the leading light in this "coals to

Newcastle" situation is the aforementioned Angus Young, the mad axeman of the Fourth Form.

When AC/DC first came to these shores in 1976 the British music scene had largely forgotten what real loud rock music was about, so the band set out to change things. That they have certainly done, and guitarist Angus Young has shown many aspiring youngsters just how to play hard uncompromising rock guitar.

Angus comes from a large musical family which included his elder brother Malcolm, who also plays guitar with AC/DC. His first guitar was a Woolworth's type acoustic which kept going out of tune, but Angus persisted and finally inherited an old Hofner from Malcolm. Early influences were Chuck Berry and the Stones, and Angus joined the inevitable succession of school bands.

Competition was fierce between the two guitar playing brothers but when Malcolm decided to form AC/DC in 1974, it was only natural that he should include his brother in the line up. A couple of hard gigging years in Australia, proved once again that there is really no substitute for regular playing if you want to become a tight band.

The schoolboy image was suggested by one of the Young sisters and while Angus at first thought it was a bit daft, he soon got into it. It was certainly original, and went down very well with audiences, and makes his on-stage antics seem even more bizarre.

Angus is one of the few modern guitarists who choose a Gibson SG as their main instrument. He reckons that it is the meanest guitar they make, and has a collection of about half a dozen of them. For amplification, he plumps for the almost inevitable array of Marshalls, which give him the ultimate live rock guitar sound.

As befits this no nonsense Aussie, he doesn't use any gadgets or effects pedals to alter his sound, preferring just the natural sound of his high powered SG through cranked up Marshalls. Angus's one concession to technology is the use of transmitters on his guitars instead of the usual guitar leads to the amplifier. Apart from giving him greater mobility on stage, he also believes that the transmitters take less away from the overall sound than conventional leads.

It will be interesting to see if Angus ever grows out of his short trousers, but you can guarantee he'll never grow out of his love of hard driving rock and roll.

Introduction to bass guitars

The bass guitar story starts with the Fender Company in the early Fifties. The technology that created the first mass produced, solid bodied electric guitars, was being used to develop what was really a new instrument — the electric bass.

The stand up bass had long been a problem in 20th Century music; insufficient volume for dance bands, bulky, expensive and difficult to record and reproduce realistically. However, when Fender introduced their first model, aptly named the Precision, it was the effortless predictability of intonation that made the fretted instrument attractive to guitarists and beginners alike.

Amplification was still a problem, for while guitarists were able to make a great noise through relatively small speakers, the new generation of bass players found they needed something more substantial. Luckily for them, advances were being made in commercial loudspeakers and by 1960 the electric bass guitarist was here to stay.

The decade that followed was dominated by a handful of classic designs that catered for all styles and tastes, and the American companies led the way with their superior sound, feel and standard of finish. The Hofner violin bass was popularised by Beatle Paul, but apart from that German made hollow bodied model, the leaders were the Fender Precision and Jazz, the Gibson EB range, the Epiphone Rivoli and the Rickenbacker 4001.

In the early Seventies the market was flooded by almost unbelievably cheap Japanese copies of famous basses and guitars, killing off modestly priced second division models on both sides of the Atlantic. The attentions of discerning players turned to the original Fenders rather than the new products of the company now owned by CBS.

Meanwhile, smaller American companies continued to innovate; the Alembic had greater tonal power through active electronics inside the body and Ampeg's hollow body scroll neck was an aesthetic success. This bass was also fitted with a vibrational rather than electromagnetic transducer which produced a warm, natural sound.

The bass player's special amplification problems mentioned earlier are related to the high electrical energies needed for lower frequencies and in speaker systems which must be heavy duty enough to move large volumes of air in sympathy with the transient, percussive styles of the musicians.

Popular configurations of speakers have included 8 by 10, 4 by 12, and 1 by 15 or 18 folded horn cabinets. The latter are enormously efficient but can lack clarity without a separate mid-range unit. These problems have been traditionally overcome in studios with the use of fast attack compressors or limiters, and some bass amplifiers now incorporate this control of dynamics.

As far as the instruments themselves are concerned, the dominance of the classics has been ended with the emergence of quality Japanese products from the likes of Aria and Ibanez and more recently the rise of British manufacturers like Wal and Overwater.

Aria CSB 450

This Aria is possibly the most basic design of bass that you can get. It features a well carved body of ash with a glue-jointed neck of maple, sporting a rosewood fingerboard of good quality.

The bridge and machines functioned as well as most modern hardware (it is certainly almost unheard of these days to come across functionally bad machines). The bridge is a professional looking heavy-duty chromed device that carries the terminations of the strings, which previously have ridden over tracked saddles, each of which adjust every way for both intonation and string height.

The CBS has one pickup, an ARia MB III of "split" design which, presumably, follows the normal Precision design but doesn't really sound like one, which shows how bare appearances can be deceptive. Control gear for the solitary pickup could hardly be simpler, just one volume and tone, quite sufficient but hardly offering the potential of some other instruments of similar price.

Playing the CSB (part of Aria's Cardinal series) shows you how this maker won their reputation for really nice quality instruments. Setting-up of this sample was excellent, really first rate, and the neck was fast, comfortable and inviting. The neck profile is fairly straightforward in that most players with normal hands and fairly average tastes could handle it with ease. It's narrower than some but by no means uncomfortably so and ideal for a beginner.

From a tonal point of view the CSB is as plain as one would expect from such a simple looking bass. However, the sound is good, a nice strong bass tone with the sort of versatility which would be positively inoffensive to any player but, it must be said, devoid of any real tonality of its own. Some players might find this a good thing, certainly it would ideally suit the bassist who preferred to rock away at the back of the band without any desire to step up forward and play a leading role in the overall mix.

Pricewise the instrument may seem a bit on the expensive side, but you have to take into account the fact that all Aria prices include a reasonable quality case. With some other brands, cases are extra. As a case is a definite necessity, this can, if you look at things in the right way, knock about £30-£40 off the price (Aria actually price theirs at £37).

How you take to this bass will be very much a matter of your own playing personality. Frankly, it just isn't "up-front" enough for this reviewer, either in terms of looks or sound, but others may feel differently. Notwithstanding what was said about the case, this does seem a bit too expensive to call a five-star bass in the value for money stakes, but it's a good one, make no mistake about that.

Price: £233

Body materials: Ash

Neck materials: Maple

Fingerboard materials: Rosewood

Machine heads: Aria

Pickups: Aria MB111 split

Construction:	★★★★★
Finish:	★★★★★
Sound:	★★★½
Playability:	★★★★★
Value For Money:	★★★★

Distributed by: Gigsville Ltd, Phoenix Way, South Drive, Heston, Middlesex. Tel: 01-897-3792.

Aria SB60

Like all the most successful Aria basses, the SB60 seems to have learned more than a few passing lessons from its bigger and tremendously successful active brother, the SB 1000.

Despite its attractive looks the SB60 is, in fact, a rather simple instrument from a constructional point of view. As with many of the best Aria basses it features a straight-through neck of maple, inset with mahogany strips and well matched with a carefully applied and finished rosewood fingerboard.

The body appears to be ash and this one came finished in a golden yellow colour which is one of the best finishes Aria currently offer.

Hardware is an area in which Aria never seem to skimp and the SB60 is graced with a set of nicely smooth and reliable machines. The bridge too is very good. It's a solid chrome plated job where the strings terminate into slots at the back after riding over heavy saddles which are adjustable in the usual essential directions. Although not tracked exactly as a Fender, Aria have their own effective solution to prevent side slip on string saddles which is to mount each saddle in a channel which has the same stabilising effect whilst, probably, giving more sustain than the much vaunted new Fender style.

The single pickup is a totally enclosed type which one would assume to be a twin coil design. Controls comprise a single volume pot, one for tone and a small metal flick switch which is probably a single/twin coil tap.

The neck on the SB60 seemed just a shade wider than that on the SB1000. However, this feature doesn't make the SB60 difficult to play, far from it. Traditionally Aria basses have excelled in the ease of playing department and this is no exception. The shape encourages one to play up in the high registers and the finish of the fingerboard and frets was as good as it usually is with this marque.

Soundwise the Aria was very pleasing. Run with the flick switch giving the bassier of the two tonal settings it seemed very much the ideal sort of bass for good old heavy rock, and with the switch set the other way, so that the sound was more biased towards the treble tones, it gave a sound which most players would be happy to use with funkier outfits.

Pricewise the SB60 might seem a bit on the high side — unless you've actually played one. It's perfectly true that there are now several actives of redoubtable quality on the market for similar money but, for the player who doesn't like active basses and wants a fairly versatile, beautifully finished, reliable, good sounding axe, this must be a pretty good buy.

Price: £299

Body materials: Ash

Neck materials: Maple/mahogany strips inset

Fingerboard materials: Rosewood

Machine heads: Aria

Pickups: Aria

Construction:	★ ★ ★ ★ ★
Finish:	★ ★ ★ ★ ★
Sound:	★ ★ ★ ★
Playability:	★ ★ ★ ★ ★
Value For Money:	★ ★ ★ ★ ½

Distributed by: Gigsville Ltd, Phoenix Way, South Drive, Heston, Middlesex. Tel: 01-897-3792.

Aria SB 1000

The fact that the Aria SB 1000 was one of the first modern Japanese electric basses to break through from the semi-pro level and appeal directly to some very important professional players doesn't seem to have rendered it out of date by any standards at all. In fact, so successful has been the SB 1000 that many other Aria basses have been visually designed to look somewhat like it.

One of the first attractions for the novice SB 1000 user must be the sheer playability of the instrument. The maple neck is extremely well finished and the sample this reviewer tried had one of the speediest profiles yet encountered, complete with a wonderfully set action and a fretting standard and general shape which encouraged playing far higher up the neck than on the average bass. There's nothing to discourage the adventurous bassist here. That maple neck is faced with a lovely Jacaranda fingerboard which is well fretted with a very good quality fat fretwire.

As with the best of modern Japanese basses, the Aria features a straight through neck, the maple core running through a body made of well finished ash with inlaid strips of what is probably mahogany set in for both visual and, possibly acoustic, effect. The overall impression given is one of a fairly "pretty" instrument, yet one which, paradoxically, is a very functional bass indeed.

The hardware of the Aria is of an excellent quality with a brass nut matched by a very heavy duty brass bridge which must contribute to the overall sustain the bass possesses.

The pickup on the Aria is a single plastic enclosed job which may look rather spartan but, allied with one of the best active circuits on the market, gives a tremendous tonal versatility. This pickup is controlled by one volume, one tone, a small metal flick switch and a six position click stop switch. This latter switches in the twin PP3 powered active circuit. Run passive, the SB 1000 is more impressive than many basses; the single volume control working in a nicely graduated manner and the tone giving a good range between high-ish top and a fairly deep bass. Pull the flick switch to the active setting, however, and the SB 1000 comes alive. I'm still not sure, after some time with the bass, of the function of the various positions of the click switch, but the settings certainly vary the tone remarkably well, giving a range from very high top to very low bass with some very odd "Q filter" sounding positions in between.

Since its introduction the Aria SB 1000 has become one of the standards by which active basses are judged. I am forced to say that time may have by-passed it slightly now as a handful of other makers have come up with equally effective sounding basses for less money. Nevertheless, the Aria will remain the instrument which pioneered active basses for the Japanese makers. It remains a historic instrument with a sound, a style and a fast neck, that should satisfy players for many years to come.

Price: £432

Body materials: Ash/mahogany strips

Neck materials: Maple

Fingerboard materials: Jacaranda

Machine heads: Aria

Pickups: Aria active powered

Construction:	★★★★★
Finish:	★★★★★
Sound:	★★★★
Playability:	★★★★½
Value For Money:	★★★★

Distributed by: Gigsville Ltd, Phoenix Way, South Drive, Heston, Middlesex. Tel: 01-897-3792.

Aria SBR 80

Aria (possibly along with Ibanez) are just about the brand leaders among Japanese instruments in this country, a success partly due to the tremendous efforts of Gigsville, the line's importers, and partly due to the inherent qualities of the guitars and basses themselves. Equally, guitars and basses have proved to be priced just right and to offer what the Great British rock public seem to want. Early among Aria successes were their basses, notably the excellent SB 1000 active which possibly did more than any other active bass to convert British players. So successful has this instrument been that a whole line of SB1000 look-alikes has sprung from this eminent source, including the SBR 80 under review here.

Like many Arias, this sample came with an unusual but very pleasant finish, a glowing golden colour which made a great change from sunburst. The body is ash, the straight-through neck maple, and the whole instrument has that solid and dependable yet strangely elegant feel which seems to characterise this maker's instruments.

The 24 fret neck is well set to the body, the back of which is carved away nicely to accommodate players who like to experiment up high with their runs. The bass is amplified via two Aria MB-11 pickups, twin coil types which are controlled by a large rotary pickup selector plus two flick switches for "dual sound" effects. At a guess this is probably a series/parallel or twin/single coil arrangement. Volume and tone controls are twofold but are "doubled up" pots where one half takes volume and the other tone — nice and easy to use on stage.

The hardware is of Aria's usual standard, small, good quality machines, a brass nut, nicely shaped fat frets and a bridge of the inset solid brass type where the strings terminate through the back rather than passing through the body to fasten. The saddles are "tracked" and offer full adjustment potential.

Playing the bass can be a bit of a surprise if you're used to more typical Arias. This one came with a higher action than the reviewer was used to and with a wider neck. Apparently some players have been asking for this option over the more typical narrow-ish neck of other Aria basses. However, many prefer the older, thinner type for the increased speed it offers.

Soundwise the Aria is quite a long way from many other modern Japanese basses. The tone is fuller and warmer than most, a sound which you'll either like for its individuality or, possibly, feel is a bit out of date. It's the hardest job in the world, trying to describe a sound in words, but don't expect this model to have that sharp, "twang" beloved of modern jazz/rockers, it's more individualistic than that and a matter of personal taste. Please note, however, it's not a bad sound — just different from many other "modern" basses.

Bearing in mind that the competition has been somewhat shaken up in the bass market of late, it's not possible to give this instrument 100 per cent value for money rating. It's just a shade expensive by the latest standards, even with the case thrown in.

Price: £390.50

Body materials: Ash

Neck materials: Maple

Fingerboard materials: Rosewood

Machine heads: Aria

Pickups: Aria MB11

Construction:	★★★★★
Finish:	★★★★★
Sound:	★★★★★
Playability:	★★★★★
Value For Money:	★★★★

Distributed by: Gigsville Ltd, Phoenix Way, South Drive, Heston, Middlesex. Tel: 01-897-3792.

Ashley Pangborn Chieftain I

Similar to a Fender in looks the Pangborn Warrior is a very tasty looking bass indeed. It sports an ash body with a bolt-on maple neck with rosewood fingerboard. The Fender looks are carried over to the neck profile which is vaguely Fender-like in shape and feel, making it quite familiar territory for players who are considering moving up from one of the endless Precision copies and derivatives currently on the market.

The hardware, however, is a good head and shoulders above anything Fender have to offer. The most impressive item of it is the superb Schaller bass bridge which rates as highly as anything else currently on the market. It's hard to say, in purely physical engineering terms, quite why the Schaller bass bridge is so good, all you can say is that, while offering all thc adjustment for string height and length you could ask for, it is also designed to offer a massive solidity and harmonic transfer into the wood.

The Schaller connection goes even further, in that the bass also uses a Schaller pickup wired into an active circuit. This reviewer has to admit that this was his first encounter with this unit and he wasn't expecting miracles. Just because you can make fine bridges doesn't mean that your pickups will be as good.

Playing the Pangborn is a sheer delight. The neck is well fretted and very, very fast. The whole bass feels like the sort of machine that you could take on the road with you and use night after night with no fears, no worries, and a guarantee of reliabilty.

The Schaller runs from a small flick switch (active on/off) and a single tone and volume set-up with an extra pot called "boost". Run passive, the Pangborn is satisfactory but remember that this is not how it's meant to be used. The placement of the active on/off switch by the jack socket shows that the bass is designed to be run battery powered unless the on-board PP3 packs up. So, flick that in and you'll find yourself playing perhaps the best sounding active bass on the market for under £400-£500. That Schaller pickup really kicks the power out and the boost pot gives you all the volume you need to set up one of the best driving dominating bass sounds around. For players who like actives this is about the best value for money currently on the market, even taking on the superb value for money Westone.

The range tonally is high top to low bass with no fancy parametric-induced tones which you can never use either on stage or in the studio. This is a superbly tough bass with a tremendous amount of drive in the sound and a wonderfully chuckable feel to it. It is very much the working player's active bass and it's one with enough guts in the sound to take on a good T'bird any day!

Price: £246

Body materials: Ash

Neck materials: Maple

Fingerboard materials: Rosewood

Machine heads: Schaller

Pickups: Schaller

Construction: ★★★★★

Finish: ★★★★★

Sound: ★★★★★

Playability: ★★★★★

Value For Money: ★★★★★

Distributed by: Music Serve Ltd, 12a West Street, Reigate, Surrey. Tel: 07372-44331.

Ashley Pangborn Warrior I

Recent months have seen the emergence of British handmade instrument craftsmen becoming a serious force in modern guitar construction. Ashley Pangborn, although one of the youngest guitar builders around to have established a reputation, has launched himself into direct competition with other mass guitar builders by introducing a range of guitars and basses to be built and sold on a production basis.

Priced as it is, the Warrior competes head-on with many Japanese imports. From this sample, it would seem as if Ashley has a very strong chance of beating them at their own game. The Warrior looks a mean enough bass to appeal to the baser (pun intended) instincts of the average player. This sample was superbly finished in a very dark blue/black colour. The Warrior is a fairly conventionally designed bass in that it features a solid mahogany straight-through neck joined onto a mahogany body with a piece of maple laid into the body centre. This one was very well finished and looked pretty tough, making it ideal for regular touring use.

The rosewood fingerboard is profiled along with the neck to suit anyone used to a basic Fender type shape, and came very well fretted. Hardware comprises Schaller machines with a bass bridge of Ashley's own design, although it's a single saddle per string type which will be familiar to Precision players. This reviewer prefers the Schaller bass bridge fitted to the more up-market Chieftain model, but it is understood that there's some chance of this change being made in later production samples — although many bassists seem happy enough with the typical Fender bridge.

This very early sample had been fitted (as a prototype) with a good quality Japanese split Precision pickup. Production models would, we are told, feature an improvement on this, as they will be fitted with one of those excellent Schaller bass pickups and should, therefore, sound even better.

Soundwise this sample was pretty good and we would expect production models (fitted with the Schaller) to be better still. Playing this bass for a few hours proved the neck to be superbly comfortable and the sound, the sort of reliable tone which would be ideal for taking on the road, night after night, gig after gig, without any trouble.

Not, perhaps, the most exciting instrument in the Pangborn range, the Warrior is, nonetheless, a very nice bass indeed. Do, however check-out the active Chieftain — now *that's* a veritable killer!

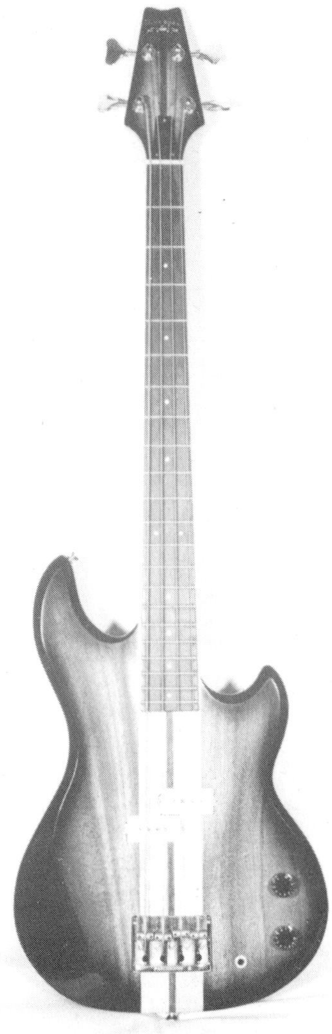

Price: £289

Body materials: Mahogany/maple

Neck materials: Mahogany

Fingerboard materials: Rosewood

Machine heads: Schaller

Pickups: Japanese on prototype/Schaller on production models

Construction:	★ ★ ★ ★ ★
Finish:	★ ★ ★ ★ ★
Sound:	★ ★ ★ ★
Playability:	★ ★ ★ ★ ★
Value For Money:	★ ★ ★ ★ ½

Distributed by: Music Serve Ltd, 12a West Street, Reigate, Surrey. Tel: 07372-44331.

FCN Satellite

Beginners' basses, like beginners' acoustics, are important instruments in that they have the power to put the prospective player off music for life. A badly warped neck and an action which cannot be held down comfortably can really discourage the aspiring musician who attributes these faults to his playing. For this reason one must be particularly careful when assessing a beginner's instrument. The appearance and sound of the instrument are of less importance than whether it is possible to play the instrument comfortably in tune.

So the fact that the Satellite 91 bass looks somewhat weak and cheap should not be weighed too heavily against it. Admittedly there are far nicer looking guitars within a few pounds of this model (amongst them the same importer's range of Westone basses), but those few pounds could conceivably make all the difference.

Despite the low price, the Satellite features a "through neck" with a body made of a wood resembling rosewood. The neck itself is possibly cheap maple or a maple substitute. The sample in question was fairly well finished and had been reasonably constructed. The machines were large open backed types which although not perfect, held tune and were not difficult to set.

The fingerboard had been pretty well fretted and the bridge an obvious choice of a Precision copy with brass adjustable saddles riding on a metal baseplate.

The sound comes from an unidentified split Precision type pickup, controlled by a single tone pot and one for volume.

In use, the neck was found to be rather on the large side, somewhat grosser than many Fender Precisions and could well present an obstacle to ease of playing for a young person or a woman with small hands whose stretch was just not up to the rather intimidatingly shaped and sized neck.

The sound of the Satellite is average but that makes it pretty fair value for the money. Good pickups can be bought fairly cheaply these days and it seems the makers of this bass have allowed for this and fitted this sample with a decent working coil winding and assembly. The sound is quite punchy and wouldn't go amiss in any semi-pro band.

However, the Satellite does face a tremendous challenge from the same distributor's excellent Westone Thunder 1 bass and it would be wise to consider whether you couldn't stretch that little bit further and invest in one of those instead. If you cannot, this Satellite will not disappoint you but you may be ready for a change up market within months rather than years.

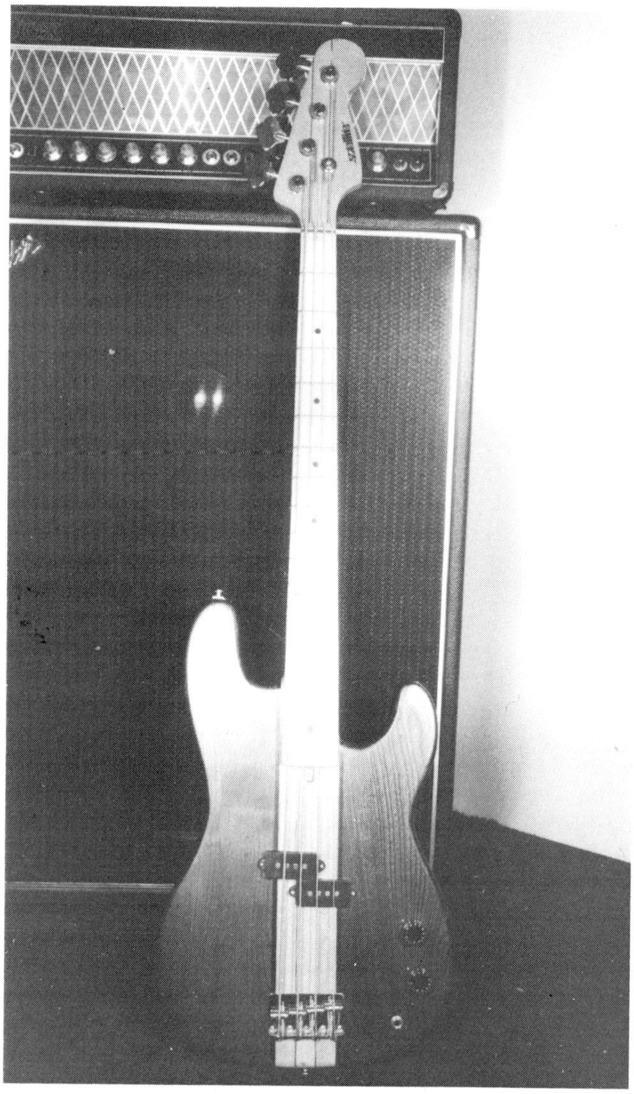

Price: £115

Body materials: Rosewood

Neck materials: Laminate maple

Fingerboard materials: Maple

Machine heads: Satellite chromium plated

Pickups: Satellite "Precision" type

Construction:	★★★
Finish:	★★★
Sound:	★★★
Playability:	★½
Value For Money:	★★★★

Distributed by: Fletcher, Coppock and Newman, Morley Road, Tonbridge, Kent. Tel: 0732-365271.

Fender Jazz

Opinions differ as to the position of the Jazz bass in the market. There are those who regard it as the only suitable bass for playing jazz, some see it as a logical move upwards from the Fender Mustang or the Precision, and many find it the ideal bass guitar for six string guitarists who consider themselves adept at both instruments.

There are two major differences between the Jazz and the Precision (its nearest brother). Firstly, the Jazz has two separate pickups individually adjustable and controllable and of a different design. Secondly, the Jazz has an ultra slim neck, both in width and depth, with a bound-in fingerboard. The body of the Jazz is of slightly different design also — it leans forward a little more.

The pickups are located in the standard positions, one near the neck and one near the bridge. They are rather thin, so they are fairly selective about the string area which they pick up from — this makes for more accurate and individual sounds than the Precision can give. The neck is of hard rock maple with a choice of fingerboards, but there is a white binding strip along both edges. It is also detachable and has a very useful micro adjustment facility for ultra accurate setting up. And being much slimmer, it is also very much faster to play, requiring a degree of accuracy not so necessary in playing the Precision.

Playing the Jazz, therefore , is a relatively easy matter for a capable guitar player. You can move about the scales from bottom to top at considerable speed with good accuracy and there is a quality about this neck that encourages you to attempt feats of speed or stretch, previously only dreamed of.

Ultra low notes, even open E, are nicely firm, not perhaps quite as rock steady as the Precision because the string has less room to resonate in the neck, but perfectly adequate neveriheless. It sings nicely at the top end of the scale, though as with all Fenders, the sustain dies out rather in the upper regions. Tonal separation could be a little better as the chords are still rather muzzy in sound quality (although better than the Precision).

Having two pickups, obviously gives quite a few sound possibilities, you will be very happy whatever your style. Using the treble (bridge) pickup only, with master tone control at half, gives the perfect sound with just the right degree of metal edge. If you prefer to slot your index under the string and make it thrumm, then use the bass (neck) pickup and adjust the master tone to full treble. This gives the deep, slightly anonymous but positive rumble beloved by walkie-bass players, but with a cut on it that projects the sound through the rest of the band — and with careful adjustments, the possibilities are endless.

Price: £340

Body materials: Maple

Neck materials: Hard rock maple

Fingerboard materials: Rosewood or maple

Machine heads: Fender

Pickups: Fender

Construction:	★★★★★
Finish:	★★★★★
Sound:	★★★★
Playability:	★★★★½
Value For Money:	★★★½

Distributed by: CBS/Arbiter Ltd, Fender House, Centenary Estate, Jeffreys Road, Brimsdown, Enfield, Middlesex. Tel: 01-805-8555.

Fender Precision

Nearly everyone has owned a Precision at one time in their career; it is probably the most common bass guitar in the business. Neat and uncomplicated, it represents the standard by which other bass guitars are eventually judged. Like all Fenders they vary in quality, but for many, the acquisition of a Precision is a safe bet.

And safe it is — one split pickup midway between the end of the neck and the bridge, a 20 fret neck in rosewood or maple, detachable in case you drop it, adjustable truss rod and four good solid brass machine heads. One volume control and one tone control, so the guy on the desk can do all the fiddling with the sound.

It is a solid instrument, and one that inspires confidence in playing because there are no frills that you should or should not be experimenting with. All you have to do is get your fingers in the right places at the right time. The neck itself is rather fat, almost crude and you need quite long fingers to be able to handle fast passages on this instrument because the gaps between the strings are really quite wide.

You need to get the action set up absolutely right and keep it that way; fortunately, the simplicity of the bridge design makes this easy. The body is heavy, solid and very well finished in Fender's own "Thick Skin" covering. It also has a nice cutaway where it rests against the body, helping the balance of the instrument. Overall the balance is fairly good, possibly a little neck heavy, but not sufficient to be annoying.

The sounds available are, of course, limited. There are four choices: 1) loud and trebly, 2) soft and trebly, 3) loud and bassy, 4) soft and bassy! The rest is all down to the way you pluck the strings, whether you use a plectrum, and what the man on the sound desk can do for you.

The Precision sound is very recognisable. Fender position their pickups very carefully, so the resonance from each string is equal — this is not one of those instruments where low E blows the cone out of the cabinet, and high G sounds like a mouse whispering in a gale! Roundwound strings definitely sound best on this instrument.

So is the Fender Precision a very ordinary bass? In all the important ways, yes, it is — conventional design, conventional circuitry, conventional bridge and neck designs. But why change (and possibly ruin) a best selling model?

It requires the minimum of looking after, won't scratch easily and therefore represents the ultimate safe buy in bass guitars. Parts and service are cheaply and very easily obtainable, and being mass produced, you can always borrow a friend's without the fear of it feeling like a totally different instrument. The sound is reliable, a no nonsense bass, providing a strong foundation for any band sound.

Price: £295

Body materials: Maple

Neck materials: Hard rock maple

Fingerboard materials: Rosewood or maple

Machine heads: Fender

Pickups: Fender

Construction:	★ ★ ★ ★
Finish:	★ ★ ★ ★
Sound:	★ ★ ★
Playability:	★ ★ ★
Value For Money:	★ ★ ★ ★

Distributed by: CBS/Arbiter Ltd, Fender House, Centenary Estate, Jeffreys Road, Brimsdown, Enfield, Middlesex. Tel:01-805-8555.

Fender Precision Fretless

Bass styles have changed considerably in recent years. When the instrument was first invented by Leo Fender in the 1950's, jokes about the general musical incompetence of bass players were rife. Few guitarists would feel so confident today with the advent of players who are, in their own ways, quite as skilled as the very finest six stringed guitarists.

In addition to this trend to explore the harmonic relationship and counterpoint structures of modern music (be it Heavy Metal or Jazz) one special style has recently emerged as a major force — the expert handling of the fretless bass. Even reputedly "pop" players have taken up this fascinating instrument recently and some very fine work has been recorded with it.

It is only natural that many of the bassists who pioneered this new style started by ripping the frets out of their Fender basses. The Precision is unquestionably the most popular bass yet made and thus it gained something of a reputation as being an ideal instrument for fretless bass also. Now you don't have to desecrate a perfectly good fretted bass, because Fender are offering fretless versions of the Precision.

The sample came with a beautiful ash body, finished in blond, and with the traditional bolt-on neck made of the normal quality of Fender maple with a smooth finished, fine looking fretless fingerboard of rosewood. In the hardware department the Precision didn't differ at all from normal, large open backed machines and that famous bridge, regrettably not "tracked" (a feature of the Fender Brassmaster add-on range of parts). The usual Fender Precision split pickup is fitted and the only two controls are a knurled pot for volume and one for tone.

Does one really need to describe the sound of a Precision? It must be the most frequently recorded bass and the fretless, although differing massively by virtue of the absence of frets, bears all the excellent hallmarks of that basic Fender sound which have ensured a phenomenal run of sales popularity over the years. It's a sharp and yet dry, deep sound, a sound which naturally sits at the bottom of the scale in a band and holds it all down with the drums.

But the Precision does have its flaws as real veterans will know. Something about the basic design allowed a few "dead spots" to creep in, places where the sound goes flat and disappears. Unfortunately one has to report that the fretless version has them too (at least this one did) and one hears that Fender's American engineers are working hard to solve the problem. One wishes them well because the fretless version is basically a fine sounding guitar with all the normal Precision qualities allied to a very nice neck. It would be ideal as a second bass for an existing owner who wanted a fretless too.

Price: £520

Body materials: Ash

Neck materials: Maple

Fingerboard materials: Rosewood

Machine heads: Fender

Pickups: Fender

Construction:	★★★★
Finish:	★★★★
Sound:	★★★★
Playability:	★★★★
Value For Money:	★★★★★

Distributed by: CBS/Arbiter Ltd, Fender House, Centenary Estate, Jeffreys Road, Brimsdown, Enfield, Middlesex. Tel: 01-805-8555.

Gibson RD Artist Active

Despite being one of the earlier active basses on the market, the RD Artist is still very much a part of the Gibson catalogue and has its devotees.

The body of the RD is every inch a Gibson, carrying those stylistic hallmarks which are so characteristic of this American manufacturer. It's a heavy bass, possibly too heavy for some, with a thick solid maple body glued to a heavy duty neck with a maple fingerboard. The neck only offers 20 frets on its 876mm scale and it's a relatively easy instrument to play up high despite having a glued joint as opposed to a straight through or bolt-on neck as have most modern active basses (and, of course, even some Gibsons). The sample was extremely well finished with excellent fat frets and a profile which was not as fat and lumpy on the neck as some of this maker's previous instruments.

Despite an attempt by the designers to contour the thick body for comfort, this body is rather uncomfortable to hold, the neck being thrown out at an angle, leaving it hard to reach. To get the neck in the right position one has to ignore the contouring which made the bass rather hard to hold.

The bridge suffers from that typical Gibson oversight by offering a very substantial construction for excellent sustain (the strings fasten through the back of the body) but with no provision for setting individual string height. True, the bridge design will offer better sustain than the basic Fender Precision design but it doesn't hold a candle to a Schaller, Bad Ass II, Gibson "Victory" Bridge, or even that design fitted to the latest Precision Special which offers decent setting *and* proper sustain. However, string height is changed, albeit all at once, via two rotary knurled screws rather than those old "screwdriver only" types which were quite unsatisfactory to use.

The pickups are twin humbuckers connected to two volume pots, two active tone pots (which centre at zero) to offer cut or boost facilities on bass and treble, a pickup selector and a three position switch, placed at the back which gives you the choice (unique to this bass) of compression or expansion, with the centre setting "off".

The RD's active electronics, combined with the two excellent pickups, give this bass a very acceptable sound indeed, it is by no means the typical old Gibson bass effect which tends towards either the deep bass or the pointless treble, but it is a versatile, modern sounding instrument.

In use the compression is a handy effect to have but, being non variable in this application, would perhaps be better on one's amp where the exact point of compression and its degree could be chosen with greater accuracy. Furthermore, the switch controls tended to crackle and spit somewhat in use which is unforgiveable for this sort of asking price. Some may find this an acceptable instrument but it will remain one for an odd set of tastes. The later Gibson Victory Artist is a far better buy.

Price: £695

Body materials: Maple

Neck materials: Maple

Fingerboard materials: Maple

Machine heads: Grover

Pickups: Gibson RD bass (active)

Construction:	★★★★★
Finish:	★★★★
Sound:	★★★★
Playability:	★★★★
Value For Money:	★★★

Distributed by: Rosetti (EMI) and Co., 138-140 Old Street, London EC1V 9BL.Tel: 01-253-7294.

Gibson Victory Artist

Whatever the prowess of this maker as a fine guitar builder, few would argue with the opinion that their basses, to date, have been disappointing. The introduction of the latest Gibson bass, however, could just see the turning point for this maker, as the Gibson Victory Artist, despite its high retail price, seems to represent the culmination of a series of experiments and consultations.

The immediately striking feature of the bass is its bolt-on neck, possibly the first time this manufacturer has used such a device on its upmarket instruments. However, true to Gibson style, the joint is bolted-on to a very high standard. The sample was immaculately finished with the bolts (not screws) threaded through the bass inserts for extra sustain and reliability. The bass balances well, despite the extra long scale.

The body is constructed of solid maple — the sample was very attractively finished, brightening up that rather plain wood. The neck is also maple with an extra fine quality rosewood fingerboard applied to it. Fretting was rather odd in that these pioneers of the fat fret had chosen to fit a thinner fretwire than might have been expected onto the fingerboard. Machines were good quality open backed types, probably Schallers, and the whole instrument felt supremely taut and well made.

The bridge is excellent and reflects the progress of the Gibson design department. It works by allowing the strings to terminate through the back of a heavy duty block which screws perfectly tightly against the maple body. The strings then travel over very substantial saddles, set on horizontal running screws which adjust for height by very substantial wedges which guarantee superb sustain and harmonic transmission through the wood. Each string is obviously adjustable for intonation and, rarely for any bass, string gap.

Active power is from a single PP3 and this runs three pots; master volume, bass and treble. There are also three "flick" switches, a pickup selector, a switch which gives you active/passive and a deep notch filter (cutting mid and boosting the top and bass end like a loudness control) and, finally, normal active when set fully back.

The treble pots give you 16dB of boost and 18dB cut, as does the bass boost. The rotary pots are full on at plus five and rotating them back to minus five gives maximum tonal cut. The neck is more of a Fender shape and profile than previous Gibson basses, with a 34" scale and a full 24 frets. It is also wider than previous Gibson players may be used to, but by no means uncomfortable.

The new Series 8-B twin coil pickups are excellent in sound and the active controls give a phenomenal range of tonal variations. This is the finest sounding bass that Gibson have ever made. The price may seem a little high but one should equate that with the custom offerings of other companies. For the more affluent perfectionists it's time to give Gibson another try — you're in for a surprise.

Price: £725

Body materials: Maple

Neck materials: Maple

Fingerboard materials: Rosewood

Machine heads: Schaller

Pickups: Gibson Series 8-B Bass

Construction:	★★★★★
Finish:	★★★★★
Sound:	★★★★★
Playability:	★★★★★
Value For Money:	★★★★★

Distributed by: Rosetti & Co. Ltd., 138-140 Old Street, London EC1V. Tel: 01-253-7294.

Gibson Victory Standard Fretless

Whatever may have been said about the general standard of Gibson basses in the past, there can be no doubt at all that the latest models to come from that august maker of electric six string instruments have something very special to recommend them.

The active version of the new Victory bass is reviewed elsewhere and, as has been said, it represents a significant departure in many respects from the standard Gibson basses of recent years. The passive version of the same instrument (reviewed here as a fretless bass) is also a rather special bass.

The sample tried was finished in a glowing red colour; the body is well made and contoured for comfort against the ribs. The bolted neck joint is very well finished indeed and the whole guitar (set-up as are all UK Gibsons by ace guitar man Peter Cook) smacked of perfect finish and quality.

The Victory Standard is a very simple instrument. You either love its vaguely "Thunderbird" design or you don't, but you cannot, in all honesty, fault the constructional quality.

A passive bass, the Victory Standard nevertheless shares many features with the active version. The machines are exceptionally good quality open backed and the bridge (Gibson's own design) must compare with the Schaller Bass and Bad Ass II in terms of massive sustain-inducing quality and excellent adjustment potential (it even allows you to alter the string spacing to your own tastes, a very positive move indeed!). Obviously, unlike the active, the passive Standard bass features far less tonal potential. It is fitted with a solitary twin coil pickup, controlled by one volume pot, one tone pot and a series/parallel switch which effectively allows single or twin coil settings to be used as required.

Guitar and bass necks are, of course, a matter of the player's individual taste but this reviewer maintains that some are quantifiably good and others equally bad. The neck on this bass falls very much into the former category: it's fast, extremely comfortable and the rosewood of the fingerboard is very nice indeed.

The sound of the Gibson is very positive. I tend to prefer the normal twin coil setting for the fatness of tone which it offers, but one has to be cautious here as the sound is dependant upon the amp set-up with which one is reviewing the bass. Obviously, given the money, I'd go for the active version for the phenomenal tonal potential it offers.

Whether active or passive, this fretless version is a very fine instrument indeed. The asking price for what is, after all, a very high quality instrument from a reputable maker is actually not much more than that being asked from some of the more pretentious Japanese models and that implies that this is very good value indeed. The tonal qualities may not be up to those of the active Victory but it is certainly beautifully made, with a good sound and should last a lifetime.

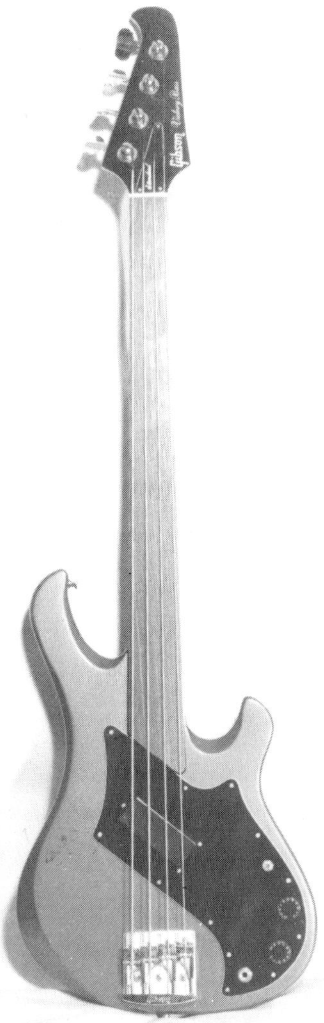

Price: £499

Body materials: Maple

Neck materials: Maple

Fingerboard materials: Rosewood

Machine heads: Grover

Pickups: Gibson

Construction:	★★★★★
Finish:	★★★★★
Sound:	★★★★
Playability:	★★★★★
Value For Money:	★★★★★

Distributed by: Rosetti (EMI) and Co., 138-140 Old Street, London EC1V 9BL. Tel: 01-253-7294.

Hofner S7B

Although still almost exclusively known in the UK for their Fifties and Sixties guitars (which must have been almost ubiquitous beginners' instruments), the West German firm of Hofner is still very much in business on the Continent, having, somehow, survived the onslaught of Japanese makers who have, as Hofner used to, succeeded in making replicas of famous American instruments at a low price. Hofner are nowadays showing a greater originality of design and are trying to make a come-back in this market although they are, no doubt, badly hampered by their old-fashioned reputation.

The S7B is an example of the sort of instrument which they are trying to sell today. It's an odd looking bass with something almost "Thunderbird"-like in the design, reminiscent of some of Gibson's weirder designs.

Like a Gibson the mahogany neck of the S7B is glued to the mahogany body. It's a well made joint, providing a good angle and bearing the hallmarks of a reputable maker in that it's very well contoured at the back to provide easy access up high. The standard of hardware on the sample was very good indeed: the fretting had been well carried out, and the height and positioning accurate. The nut is a well cut brass type and the machines, naturally enough for a German company, are Schallers which are about the best that you can get. The bridge, on the other hand, is less than satisfactory for a modern design in that, although a sustain-inducing heavy duty brass type, adjustment is only provided for intonation, string height being altered en masse as with Gibson types. Furthermore, the action on the sample was a little on the high side and the bridge was pretty well down.

The S7B has only one pickup but this, fitted with Alnico magnets in the coils, has a high output power and is connected to an active circuit — a far cry indeed from Hofners of the past! Control of the pickup is via one tone, one volume, and three flick switches, phase/twin/single, "acoustic filter" and bass boost.

The on-board battery is rather inaccessible but the circuitry does its job well. The bass has a very wide range of sounds, the "acoustic filter" switch giving some very curious (but useful) "Q" filter sounding effects and the tone capable of swinging from a very gutteral Fender-like sound to a deeper bass.

The only fault one found with the sample was that the acoustic filter switch crackled a bit in use but, apart from that, the bass made some very good sounds and the long scale neck was well profiled and fretted for fast playing. The Hofner sounds very promising (although not anywhere near as versatile as some of the latest active basses) and has excellent sustain. It also plays very well indeed. The best thing the maker could do to improve it would be to fit the superb Schaller bass bridge in preference to their own design and perhaps bring the active system in line with some of the more modern types on the market.

Price: £294	
Body materials: Mahogany	
Neck materials: Mahogany	
Fingerboard materials: Rosewood	
Machine heads: Schaller Bass	
Pickups: Hofner (active)	
Construction:	★★★★★
Finish:	★★★★
Sound:	★★★½
Playability:	★★★★
Value For Money:	★★★★

Distributed by: Barrats of Manchester, 652 Chester Road, Old Trafford, Manchester M16 0RX. Tel: 061-872-0713.

Hohner MB-010

It may be (perhaps cynically) assumed that at this sort of price range we're very much "down among the dead men" as far as expecting any sort of quality is concerned, but it must not be forgotten that most guitar pricing for the UK market is a matter of marketing, particularly with regard to Japanese instruments. The actual costs of some of the guitars, which may vary tremendously at a retail level, may not be very great at all in production terms so there is no really valid reason why this sort of retail price level should reflect poor merchandise.

From sight of it alone it's quite obvious that the Hohner MB-010 bass is not poor quality. It's a pure copy bass, of course, but who cares if it is, as long as it's well made and offers a decent sound?

The Hohner consists of an ash body with a maple neck, bolted as on the original and ubiquitous model it copies. It comes with the same cruddy bridge and pickup cover as the original, and these should be thrown away from the start.

Hardware is very good for the price, the bass's headstock sporting large, open-backed machines, the bridge being a bald Fender copy, but without the addition of the latest tracked design which improves lateral stability under heavy-handed styles. Well, what can we *expect* for this sort of money?

The whole instrument, judging by this sample, is very well made and finished indeed, so much so that it's hard to reconcile the selling price. The neck dimensions follow those of a later Precision in that they are not as slim as some of the earlier types, but the neck is by no means fat and was found fast and positive to play, well fretted and generally comfortable for long sessions.

Soundwise the reviewer was a little lost by the fact that the importers had let the sample come with flatwound strings, frankly the only bass he's seen with them for over five years. These strings sound so vastly different from the normal roundwounds of today that it was grossly unfair to make any sort of serious attempt to compare this instrument with its original pattern or, indeed, many other Japanese instruments.

Whilst not being absolutely stunning in tonal range (neither is the original, of course!) this Hohner is very, very good for the price being asked for it. The basic Precision sound is there, one would guess, and even if there might not be *quite* as much poke as on the original at its very best, then this Hohner competes in sound terms with other guitars on the market costing considerably more. If you could live with a copy's looks then this must be an absolute bargain, possibly one of the biggest bargains currently on the UK bass guitar market!

Price: £100	
Body materials: Ash	
Neck materials: Maple	
Fingerboard materials: Maple	
Machine heads: Hohner	
Pickups: Hohner	
Construction:	★ ★ ★ ★ ★
Finish:	★ ★ ★ ★ ★
Sound:	★ ★ *
Playability:	★ ★ ★ ★
Value For Money:	★ ★ ★ ★ ★

**See text.*

Distributed by: M. Hohner Ltd, 39-45 Coldharbour Lane, London SE5. Tel: 01-733-4411.

Hondo Longhorn

It's a bitter irony that a guitar can be launched by a maker only to be greeted by a relatively disinterested response from dealers and public alike and yet, in later years, become sought after as a vintage instrument. Such is the case with one of Dan Armstrong's most famous guitar and bass ideas, the Longhorn, which has just come in for the "treatment" from Japanese/Taiwanese makers Hondo. Japanese/ Taiwanese because some Hondos (those not designated "professionals") are manufactured in Taiwan, whilst those dubbed "professional" are made in Japan.

Finished in a cream colour, the distributors over here were unsure of the identity of the body materials and we refused to scrape away the paintwork to try and find out! Whatever it is, it doesn't seem to be anything special. Regrettably the paintwork extends right up the back of the neck and so that has to remain a mystery too. However, it is possible to identify the fingerboard as rosewood.

Machines are small sealed types which seem proficient in their job and generally speaking the bass, with its unfashionable bolt-on neck, seemed to be very well put together and finished to a good standard.

Unfortunately the setting-up wasn't perfect as there were some false tones and buzzes when playing towards the top of the extra long 24 fret neck.

Other Hondo Professionals that have been tried have been found quite satisfactory in that department so it must be assumed that the reviewers who had this bass before had done their very worst! Quite probably the strings were just on the way out. Still, it would be wise for any prospective purchaser to check this aspect out carefully before buying.

In the bridge department, the Longhorn is a simple-hearted soul. The strings terminate through the back of a standard looking brass bridge and ride over "tracked" saddles which offer the usual full adjustment potential.

Soundwise the Longhorn is on the toppy side with not very much sustain. This, if nothing else, makes it an individual in a time of relatively similar sounding basses dominating the market, but it must limit its appeal.

The sound is generated by a Precision type pickup which is run via a single volume and tone control set-up, although you do have what is called a "bass boost" flick switch. This seems to be some sort of series/parallel switch, all it offers is, at its bassiest, a sound which is still lacking in resonance and when flicked to a sharper sound, the sort of tone which would do well for Question Mark and the Mysterious rip-offs and little else.

Don't be put off by all this gloom, however. It may well be that this sort of sound is just what you're looking for, in which case there's probably nothing at all similar on the market. It's just not very versatile, and seems rather expensive for what it offers.

Price: £225

Body materials: Unidentified

Neck materials: Unidentified

Fingerboard materials: Rosewood

Machine heads: Hondo

Pickups: Hondo "Precision" type

Construction:	★★★★★
Finish:	★★★★
Sound:	★★½
Playability:	★★★
Value For Money:	★★★

Distributed by: John Hornby Skewes & Co. Ltd, Salem House, Garforth, Leeds. Tel: 0532-865381.

Manson Merlin

The brothers Manson (Hugh and Andy) have earned themselves something of a worthwhile reputation over the past few years.

Totally handmade, the Merlin reeks of quality and craftsmanship. The body is dark stained ash with twin strips of red Paduak set into it. The straight-through neck is mahogany and this is laminated with a back strip of maple down the centre. The looks of the bass are fabulous — there's just no other word for it!

Hardware is a mixture of the familiar and the original. The machines are gold plated Schallers, the nut is brass, the bridge a design of their own and the pickups are a pair of those superb Kent Armstrong types which show the coils exposed through a block of impenetrable epoxy resin.

The Manson bass bridge is cleverly conceived. A large lump of brass is taken, shaped and worked to a perfect contour fit of the body. The saddles have two screws, one to raise and lower them, one to lock them firmly in place — this is one bass bridge that *won't* move, however hard you slap at it. Of course, there's intonation adjustment too. It really is one of the best bass bridges encountered to date.

The ebony fingerboard is extremely well shaped, although a little wider than many, and fretted as well as one would have expected from a master craftsman.

Soundwise the Merlin is wonderful. It's an active bass, running from twin PP3's with output matching from an inside fitted adjustment pot. Four flick switches giving pickups on/off, volume boost, treble boost, and active/passive. There are also pots for volume, treble and bass, the bass pot acting as a single tone control when the bass is on active.

In use this is one of the more sensible actives. It doesn't offer you a lot of sounds which can be set (by mistake) on stage, but has a range of extremely fine and powerful tones, from clangy treble to a massive deep bass. Played passive, the Manson is just a good bass but switch in the active and the sound leaps forward and takes off into a very different league, making it one of the most potentially usable stage active bases that is available today.

Overall the Manson Merlin shows just how different a craftsman made bass is from a mass produced bass. There's a sheer joy in playing it (despite that fairly wide neck and the full 24 fret scale) and owning it would be a constant feeling of privilege. The price may seem high but what you'd be buying for this money would be a handmade instrument of inexorable quality and ability.

Price: £535

Body materials: Ash with red paduak

Neck materials: Mahogany/maple

Fingerboard materials: Ebony

Machine heads: Schaller

Pickups: Kent Armstrong

Construction:	★★★★★
Finish:	★★★★★
Sound:	★★★★★
Playability:	★★★★★
Value For Money:	★★★★★

Distributed by: Manson Guitars, Crowborough, Sussex. Tel: 08926-4266.

Maya EB 2000

In an age when just about every bass from the Far East shares the majority of both its components and its ideas on shape and function with every other, the Maya EB 2000 stands out as something pretty unique looking. In fact Maya guitars and basses are generally rather different from run of the mill imports and this EB 2000 is no exception.

This sample came finished in a well applied black which completely hid both the mahogany of the body and the neck. Standards of finish were high and the instrument had a look to it which can best be described as both solid and heavy. Not bad qualities, really, because they help induce sustain and harmonic transmission from the wood to the pickups.

Despite the relatively low asking price, the Maya features gold plated machines, and the whole instrument gives the impression that quite a degree of care had been taken over its design and construction, this carries on to the rosewood fingerboard which was very nicely fretted.

The bridge is a particularly heavy duty one of solid brass (again good for sustain and richness of tone) where the strings, having fastened through the back of the body, pass over tracked saddles, each fully adjustable. In addition to basic tracking, the saddles are also effectively laterally locked by the outer two, pressing against two solid side frames of the bridge base casting. This would make for exceptional stability for players used to wrecking their flimsy bridges by slapping and pulling too hard on the strings (it can be done, you know!).

The same care of design has been taken over the neck dimensions and fretting. The neck is a well made bolt-on type and is a happy compromise of shape and width which hardly any player should take exception to.

The totally enclosed pickups seem also to bear token to a fair amount of design investment in this bass. They are tamed by a pair of volumes, one tone and a pickup selector. Perhaps not the most comprehensive set of controls but the bass has all it needs to deliver a rather impressive sound which, whilst it didn't boast a character of its own did sound basically *right*, neither too far drawn at the top nor too woolly in the bass. A happy compromise in its sound, as in the shape of its neck.

Priced as it is, the EB 2000 is not a bad buy for, possibly, the player moving onto his first new instrument. Probably the only thing against it is the shape, which does make it look rather old fashioned. All you can say is that it looks quite different from most basses which sell in this price range. Ultimately that will either tell for or against it — and only you can decide.

Price: £170

Body materials: Mahogany

Neck materials: Mahogany

Fingerboard materials: Rosewood

Machine heads: Maya

Pickups: Maya

Construction:	★ ★ ★ ★ ★
Finish:	★ ★ ★ ★ ★
Sound:	★ ★ ★ ½
Playability:	★ ★ ★ ½
Value For Money:	★ ★ ★ ★

Distributed by: Stentor Music Co. Ltd, Blackborough Road, Reigate, Surrey. Tel: 07372-40226.

Moonstone Eclipse

In common with the Moonstone active guitar, reviewed elsewhere, the Moonstone Eclipse bass deserves praise for its looks alone. The body materials are, as with the guitar, a clever laminate of a mahogany core with an outer surface of redwood burl, that wood which gives the Moonstone the overall look of a piece of solid beautifully coloured marble.

The neck is maple, running straight through the body in typical modern bass style, but with that maple reinforced with strips of graphite. This reviewer was rather worried by this particular aspect of the Eclipse because British custom bass makers have recently abandoned the use of this type of material due to early problems where the wood wanted to move (as wood will over the years) but was prevented from doing so by the graphite. The consequences hardly bear thinking about so one can only hope that the Moonstone's makers have considered this and, somehow, come up with an answer to this problem before putting this stunning looking bass on the market.

Hardware on the Eclipse is very well chosen. The bridge is a Bad Ass II and amongst the best bass bridges currently available at any price. The Bad Ass rides happily on the redwood body and gives the bass full adjustment potential as well as endowing it with excellent sustain transmission qualities and prodigious mechanical strength.

Machines are from a maker not encountered before, Sperzel, presumably another small American maker, but they worked well. Moving down the Moonstone one finds some of the fattest frets ever come across. They were well polished but protruded slightly over the edge of the fingerboard — a style which, we are told, some players prefer, although it is difficult to see why. The fretting was found to be very accurate but not at all to this reviewer's taste.

The neck on the Moonstone is a full 24 frets, but access to the top, being a straight-through neck is actually pretty good which allies itself, in a way, to the modern American bass sound which the twin Bartolini Bass pickups offer — that 'twang' much beloved of jazz/funk bass players. This neck is a bit on the long side by some standards, but very fast and well suited for that sort of music. The sound of the Bartolini pickups cuts through well and is adequately controlled by the two volumes/two tones arrangement of rotary pots. A metal phase switch is also fitted although one can rarely see the point of these, especially on passive basses, as they tend to emasculate the sound when activated, much as they did in this case.

Overall the Moonstone Eclipse Bass is one of the best looking bass instruments ever seen. It is a rarity (few seem to be available over here) and very much an acquired taste. Well worth trying if you find one for sale and dislike most other basses that you've tried. This one is a real individualist.

Price: Approx £775 (last known)

Body materials: Mahogany core with redwood Burl

Neck materials: Maple reinforced with graphite strips

Fingerboard materials: Ebony

Machine heads: Spiezel

Pickups: Bartolini bass

Construction: ★★★★★

Finish: ★★★★★

Sound: ★★★½

Playability: ★★★½

Value For Money: ★★★★

Distributed by: (Last known) Fordingley Marketing Ltd., Walsall, Staffs.

The Musicman Stingray

The Musicman Stingray was the first bass produced by Leo Fender's new company in 1978, when it quickly earned a reputation as a versatile, general purpose instrument, Comparisons with the products of the old company are inevitable and in two areas there were significant improvements on the classic designs of the Fifties. The active tone circuit was one, while the elimination of so called "dead spots" on the neck was the other.

Live and dead spots are caused by natural resonances in the neck and body resulting in some notes being louder or quieter than others. The Stingray puts out a very even level throughout its range. The headstock has the unique arrangement of three heads along the top in the normal way and one on the bottom. This makes the stock slightly smaller, which looks very neat, but after two years this reviewer occasionally still reaches for the wrong head. The neck is the same scale and width as later Precision basses, but curiously feels smaller and less of a stretch in the lower registers.

The solid body is decorated and protected by an egg shaped scratch plate and at the bridge end is set the double pole, single pickup. This may be raised or lowered by means of three cross head screws. A massive bridge structure affords both height and length adjustment on each string as well as very useful individual foam dampers that are height adjustable. The bridge also has a flat surface that is comfortable for the side of the palm when picking or playing thumb and finger style.

The chrome control panel houses bass, treble, volume knobs and the ¼" output jack. The circuitry of the bass is "active", that is to say it provides bass and treble boost as well as cut. This necessitates the use of a 9v PP3 battery housed in its own compartment in the back of the body.

The tone controls are roughly flat in the middle of their sweep and provide an unsubtle amount of cut and boost either side of this position. With the volume set at maximum and the tones flat, the output level is roughly equal to a regular passive circuit and the bass sounds similar to a Precision, whose users this bass was surely aimed at. A much sharper, cutting sound results when the treble is increased, although the frequency at which this happens is a bit on the high side — a lower one would give a less scratchy noise. Solid body basses have never been favourites for reggae players, but the active bass control gives a great sound for this style or long underpinning throbs. The active circuit also provides a low impedance output allowing the bass to be plugged, with the minimum amount of noise, into virtually any amplifier or mixer input, without transformers, and with any length of cable!

This is a powerful and versatile instrument, and priced reasonably for a professional American product. However, Leo Fender recently left the company and production ceased. This model is therefore likely to become a collector's item.

Price: £439

Body materials: Ash for natural finish, others Poplar

Neck materials: Maple

Fingerboard materials: Maple or rosewood

Machine heads: Early models: Grover, later: Musicman

Pickups: Musicman

Construction:	★★★★
Finish:	★★★
Sound:	★★★★
Playability:	★★★★★
Value For Money:	★★★

Distributed by: Strings and Things, 2 Chappell Road, Portslade, Brighton, Sussex. Tel: 0273-420704.

Overwater OS 050

Another UK maker, but one based this time up in Cumbria. For all that, Overwater guitars and basses are now becoming obtainable in all sorts of areas of the country, with interest apparently growing daily. The appeal of custom, or at lest craftsman-built guitars is obvious. For the price (or a good deal less) of a mass-produced instrument you can get a guitar or bass which has been made by hand — a feeling which carries itself over to somehow inspire the owner with a sense of "rightness" in his instrument. More practically, you can usually order the instrument to your own unique specification and will often find that advanced features cost less than they do on (notably American made) production axes.

This Overwater OS 050 bass came in a black finish. It looked somehow vaguely "Thunderbird"-like, no doubt due to the T-bird derived headstock and offset body shape, but the playing balance was near perfect — a far cry from its Gibson inspiration.

The mahogany body carries a through neck of spliced two-piece mahogany and the fingerboard was of ebony which the makers had used in place of the more usual rosewood. Either can be made to order.

The bought-in bits include Schaller machines, and a Schaller bridge, basically similar to a Bad Ass and a superbly strong and reliable design — one of the very best bass bridges on the market, in fact. The strings, in this case, ride on rotary screws which allow side to side adjustment as well as the usual height functions and intonation making an excellent bridge. The strap buttons are locking types and the nut is bone — certainly a more sensible choice than brass.

The really unique thing about Overwater axes, however, is the use of what is perhaps best called "graduated fretting". This means that the basic fat frets of many good guitars these days are replaced by thinner ones at the 15th/16th fret so that players who like to use the high registers of their instruments can get their fingers comfortably in place for swift runs. It's an odd feel at first but a clever idea which you soon get used to.

Pickups on the Overwater are Bill Lawrence EB 50's, cleverly wired to give a very wide tonal range indeed from this passive bass. There are four rotary pots for the pickups (no switches) and these complement the front pickup (wired in series) and the back pickup in parallel with an extra capacitor inserted to give an extended top range frequency. There is one pot per pickup on this Overwater system, one independently wired tone pot as a master, plus one master pot for volume. Instead of a selector, as such, you use the volumes to mix.

The effect is to give a tonal versatility approaching that of a simple active bass from an instrument with no on-board power whatsoever, a very clever design indeed. The tone is almost Hi-Fi pure at times, with plenty of sustain and some extremely clean and yet rich harmonic overtones. For players who do not appreciate active basses this must be one of the best alternatives to date.

Price: £345

Body materials: Mahogany

Neck materials: Mahogany

Fingerboard materials: Ebony

Machine heads: Schaller

Pickups: Bill Lawrence EB50

Construction:	★★★★★
Finish:	★★★★★
Sound:	★★★★★
Playability:	★★★★★
Value For Money:	★★★★★

Distributed by: The Overwater Guitar Company, The Factory, Nenthead, Alston, Cumbria. Tel: 0498-3873.

Peter Cook Axis Active

Peter Cook is undoubtedly one of Britain's best known custom guitar makers who has the distinction of having been appointed specialist adjuster of all officially imported Gibson guitars into the UK. A job like that speaks volumes for the esteem in which Peter's workmanship is held.

All the while, however, he has continued to offer custom guitars and basses, amongst them the Axis bass which we have chosen to review. The Axis is a handsome instrument, with a maple version, mahogany version and an even better looking rosewood version. Apart from the woods used in production, all active basses are the same. Each features Peter's superlative quality glued neck joint and bodies of multi-laminated wood. The maple sample under review sports two thick rosewood strip insets laminated into the body wood, making the near-white of the maple less visible.

The five piece maple neck (with an applied fingerboard, not an all-in-one type) is beautifully finished, right down to the fretting and the choice of the hardware. Schaller machines are used on this cheaper version of the Axis, the more upmarket variety is fitted with Grovers.

A Bad Ass bridge is fitted to the bass — the design which most professional bass players seem to prefer, a vitally strong unit which offers full adjustment potential while remaining solid and reliable under hard use.

Pickups are Peter's own, wired into a circuit driven by an on-board battery. In some respects, they resemble Thunderbird pickups, but sound very little like them, unless the Axis is run passive. This would be sensible were it not for the provision of one of the best active Eq systems currently on sale.

The three rotary controls govern volume (aided by a pickup selector switch) but the further two tone pots are not in use when the bass is set passive. When active, the final two pots offer cut or boost of +/- 15dB and the frequency selected on, what is in effect, a parametric Eq system. The switches offer pickup selection, pickup phase, and active/passive mode control; which means passive with top cut, full normal passive, and active on. Overall, the frequency range covered is 80Hz to 2KHz. Soundwise, the Axis is possibly the most versatile active bass produced in the UK. A staggering variety of tones is obtainable; a far cry from some of the less than phenomenally ranging active basses of recent years. If you can memorise these functions, and avoid setting unusable tones, then the overall potential is incredible.

The Axis is a bit old fashioned to play, with its glued, fairly fat neck. But it is a neck you'd soon get used to and the tonal potential of this advanced circuitry would be suitable for any gig.

Perhaps not possessing a neck profile which would suit every player, the Axis bass is, nevertheless, a very fine bass indeed. This reviewer can only commend it to the nth degree, leaving the final choice up to you.

Price: £500-£600 (depending on woods used)

Body materials: Maple/rosewood strips (other choices to order)

Neck materials: Maple with mahogany splices inset in back

Fingerboard materials: Maple

Machine heads: Schaller (Grovers on some models)

Pickups: Peter Cook (active circuit powered)

Construction:	★★★★
Finish:	★★★
Sound:	★★★★
Playability:	★½
Value For Money:	★★

Distributed by: Peter Cook, 69 Station Road, Hanwell, Middlesex. Tel: 01-840-1244.

Rickenbacker 4001

Rickenbacker basses are known for their unique shape. Instantly recognisable by the very long cutaway, this is far more than merely an attractive piece of gimmickry because it makes a valuable contribution to the outstanding balance of the instrument.

This makes the guitar one of the most comfortable of all basses to play — no mean feat since it is no lightweight, with neck and body both constructed from seasoned maple. A good balance is essential if intense fatigue is to be avoided during long gigs.

There are certain bass guitars which just shape themselves around your fingers when you pick them up for the first time. The 4001 is not one of these. It is not a beginner's instrument, because something about the way it feels, handles and performs tells you that you should have done this before. There is also a new technique to master before you will be able to achieve the best results.

The 4001 is a bass which inspires tremendous confidence once you are familiar with it. The neck is beautifully playable both at speed and in slower more melodic passages where the superb sustain from that laminated maple neck really begins to sing. The frets are set at the right height, and thanks to the double cutaway design are easily accessible at the top end of the scale. Chords are often a problem for those with short fingers, but on the Rickenbacker they are easy to find.

The sounds available to you are splendidly varied. Individual tone and volume controls for each of the two pickups, plus a triple position pickup selector makes for good versatility. Although if you like to change pickups several times during a song you will find the toggle switch rather a stretch from the strings, particularly if you leave the rear pickup guard in position (most people remove them).

Having selected the kind of sound you want, you can now decide at which end of the playing area to treat your fingers: up by the top of the neck for a deep sing-song sound which is perfect for solo passages, down by the bridge for punch and prominence. This is excellent with the tones set to treble as it give a unique type of sharp penetrating sound which cannot be duplicated on any other guitar. Short stabbing, cross beat lines sound best down here, solid support on beat lines are best further up towards the middle playing area.

A separate kit is required to make the instrument play in stereo, although one finds that only the real specialists demand it. Most players simply plug the jack into the normal socket under the instrument rather than the "Rick-O Sound" socket which gives a pre-set rather nasal tone from one pickup only.

The 4001 is a truly solid and satisfying instrument to own and play with its unique appearance and perfect balance. In time, playing it becomes a acquired habit, a set of different skills are developed and its true personality emerges.

Price: £626

Body materials: Laminated maple

Neck materials: Seasoned maple

Fingerboard materials: Rosewood

Machine heads: Klusons or Grovers

Pickups: 2 Rickenbacker ultra wide range

Construction:	★ ★ ★ ★ ★
Finish:	★ ★ ★ ★ ★
Sound:	★ ★ ★ ★ ★ ½
Playability:	★ ★ ★ ★ ½
Value For Money:	★ ★ ★ ★ ★

Distributed by: Wing Amplification Ltd, 15-15a London Road, Bromley, Kent. Tel: 01-464-3190.

Rickenbacker 4001 Stereo Fretless

Fretless bass guitars require a completely different technique of fingering than standard fret models. They demand absolute precision of placing combined with very accurate striking. Your tightrope is narrower and higher, the safety net less likely to be in position.

Like most other fretless basses, the Rickenbacker is simply a development from the fretted model. There are pearl style dots on the face of the fingerboard in place of each fret. Whichever you use as a guide, you will have to look at your fingers more often!

One of the first things that strikes the seasoned Rickenbacker player is the lightness of the instrument by comparison to its fretted brother. The balance is still perfect, but the loss of 20 frets from the neck gives a featherlight touch. Whereas the fretted model prefers roundwound strings, the fretless responds to the extra depth provided by flatwound strings very nicely. The low frequency responses are absolutely marvellous on this instrument, the rich and deep bass notes from the lower strings reminiscent of pre-CBS Fender basses with added Rickenbacker punch.

The neck, of course is exactly the same as the fretted model; laminated maple with a rosewood fingerboard, but without the frets it gains an additional measure of sustain that makes high notes in particular, sing out. For the fretless player who uses the slide and die technique, this instrument is a joy to use. So highly polished is the neck, even the longer slide loses none of the sustain.

As with the fretted model, some perseverance is required to achieve the best with this instrument. The variety of sounds available is exactly the same because the pickups and circuitry are identical, but generally the most beneficial tones are found with the balance biased towards a more bassier sound. Because the strings have more airspace to resonate in over the neck, the bass pickup is possibly the more effective of the two.

The bridge pickup can be used to give the additional cut required for faster more rhythmic passages where more penetration than texture is required. Again, it is difficult to switch between pickups quickly — but if you combined the use of both the fretted and its fretless brother for different songs, this would alleviate the need to fiddle with the tonal settings.

It is less suited to playing with a plectrum than the fretted model, simply because there is more string movement under the fingers, but one generally plays a fretless bass with fingers anyway. Those who don't beware! You may find your actions rather more clumsy than you are accustomed to!

The general construction remains the same — same machine heads for example which operate very smoothly and not too sensitively. The same excellent bridge with the useful individual mini-bridge for each string built in, which makes the Rickenbackers very easy to set up for individual requirements. Overall, it makes an excellent partner to the fretted, if only for the superb rich, low notes and really long singing high notes it produces from the immaculate neck.

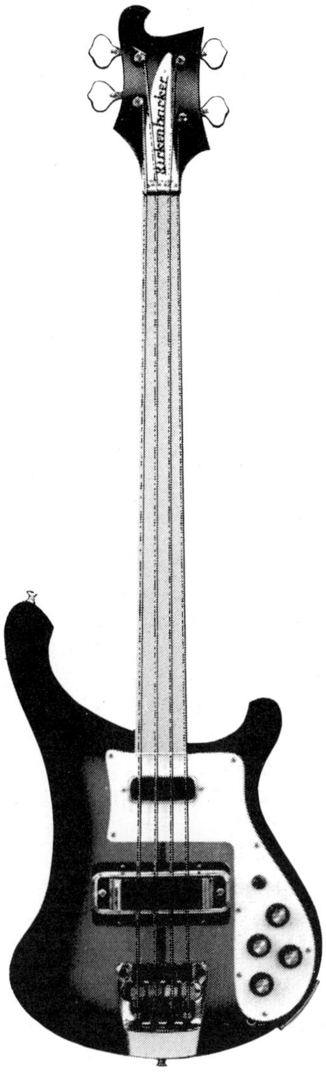

Price: £600	
Body materials: Maple	
Neck materials: Maple/rosewood	
Fingerboard materials: Rosewood	
Machine heads: Klusons or Grovers	
Pickups: Rickenbacker	
Construction:	★★★★★
Finish:	★★★★
Sound:	★★★★★
Playability:	★★★★
Value For Money:	★★★★

Distributed by: Wing Amplification Ltd, 15-15a London Road, Bromley, Kent. Tel: 01-464-3190.

Shergold Marathon Mark II

A frequent criticism of Shergold instruments (although not entirely a justified one) is this manufacturer's use of a body wood known as obechi. This has been mentioned in another review but it bears repetition to say that obechi, whilst it does not seem to render Shergold instruments any less capable of producing a decent sustain or tone than guitars made of other woods, feels very light to hold which has proved offputting to some potential customers.

Shergold heeded this criticism and have introduced this Mark II version of their enduring Marathon bass, with the body wood of American ash (the same as a Precision). The Mark II is thus a heavier guitar to handle, but it is still by no means as heavy to hold as many other basses on the market. Apparently Shergold refuse to make their instruments unnecessarily heavy, and who can blame them? It merits pointing out, however, that this version of the Marathon feels rather more sensible to hold than the older obechi version. To match the new wood, certain other changes have been made, notably to the body contours to help make the bass more comfortable to play. No rub digging here!

As usual, despite having a fairly basic Precision type bridge, the Shergold needed no adjustment whatsoever on arrival. This reviewer maintains that this manufacturer makes the most consistently perfect set-up guitars and basses on the market — this sample was no exception, coming as it did with an almost unbelievable low action and perfect fret height and feel.

The rest of the hardware was typical Shergold, those excellent Schaller bass machines and that regrettably awful looking combination of tiny pots for volume and tone.

In use the Shergold plays like a dream. Yet there is something missing in that sound one can only attribute to a weakness in the pickup output which compares rather poorly with the standard which one might expect from the best of similarly priced Japanese basses. Having said that, the Shergold would work well with a good amp where any such deficiencies could be coped with at the pre-amp stage.

Given that consideration, the sheer playability of the Marathon II, with its new body materials and that phenomenally fast and accurate maple neck, should make it a class winner.

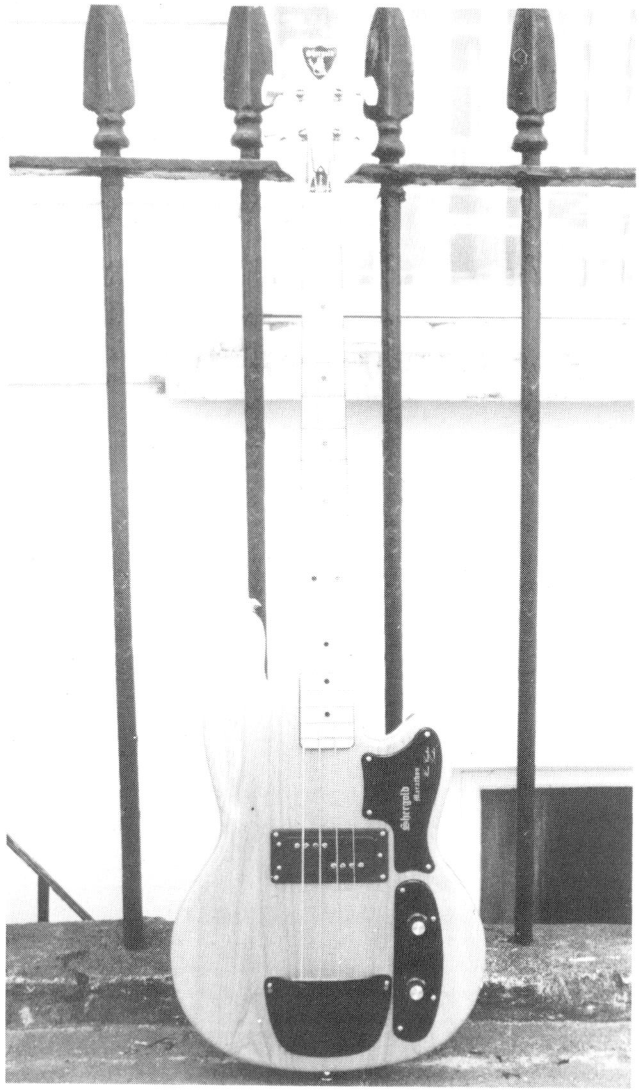

Price: £284

Body materials: American ash

Neck materials: Canadian rock maple

Fingerboard materials: Canadian rock maple

Machine heads: Schaller

Pickups: Shergold

Construction:	★★★★★
Finish:	★★★★★
Sound:	★★★★
Playability:	★★★★
Value For Money:	★★★★

Distributed by: Barnes and Mullins Ltd, 155 Grays Inn Road, London WC1. Tel: 01-278-4631.

Shergold Modulator Six String

Personally this reviewer rather tends to prefer Shergold's basses to their guitars — but how does that affect something as weird and wonderful as a six string bass?

With the Modulator we're back with Shergold's unique use of obechi wood, a very lightweight type which many feel insubstantial compared to more normal woods such as mahogany or maple. Be that as it may, Shergold claim that it is technically as good a wood (better in some respects), and they have tended to stick to their guns with it. All the same, pick up a Modulator Six and you're in for a surprise when you feel the weight.

The body isn't *all* obechi, however, as it is a laminate with a core of maple and three strips of mahogany. The neck is pure Canadian solid rock maple which is rigidly joined to the body by Shergold's unique dovetailed bolt joint.

Overall the guitar is beautifully constructed and finished with that setting up which wins Shergold a personal award as being the best in the business — the action was unbelievably low, and it played with no buzzes at all. Machines on the six stringer are Schallers, and the bridge is basically a Precision type which could, possibly, have been just a shade more substantial although there are no real complaints about it.

Control gear is optional in module form (hence Modulator). There are many different ways of running the two 16-pole pickups and the choice of which of the many different plug-in modules you use is up to you. They offer either/or pickup, volume and tone (M.1.), Phase (M.2.), Coil Taps (M.3.), Stereo (M.4.), Quad (M.5.) and Active Boost (M.6.). Prices of the plug-in modules are very reasonable indeed. The bass comes with the basic No. 1 module.

Obviously, carrying six strings, the bass has a wide neck compared with a normal bass, but no so much so that it's hard to play. Once you get used to the odd feel and the way the runs across the neck differ from those normally played on four strings, it becomes easy to handle. Bass chords come out clean and are easy to play, and the tendency for the tonality to fall to pieces as you play across the neck is offset by the custom made set of Picato strings which come with the bass (and which that maker offers as standard after much development work with Shergold).

Normal guitar players will probably feel immediately at home with this Shergold. Given a good, modern bass amp with a strong speaker (to take the chords) and plenty of Eq control, it should be perfectly usable on stage. Certainly this is the best six string bass this reviewer has ever played, with a good sound and well made feel. Worth experimenting with if you fancy an odd sound.

Price: £348

Body materials: Obechi/maple/mahogany

Neck materials: Canadian rock maple

Fingerboard materials: Maple

Machine heads: Schaller

Pickups: Shergold (a variety of modules available)

Construction:	★★★★★
Finish:	★★★★★
Sound:	★★★½
Playability:	★★★★★
Value For Money:	★★★½

Distributed by: Barnes and Mullins Ltd, 155 Grays Inn Road, London WC1. Tel: 01-278-4631.

Vantage Devil Active Bass

An increasing number of bass players these days are realising the advantages of using active powered basses. As one of the newcomers to these shores, Vantage have done especially well with their passive guitars and basses and the Devil bass represents their attempt to satisfy this new active demand.

The Devil features a maple through neck (typical of the sort of modern trend which players seem to go for these days) which is well spliced into a body of laminated but, regrettably, unidentifiable woods. This doesn't affect one's judgement of the bass, however, as there are many rare, or at least unfamiliar Oriental woods which will do a fine job.

The fingerboard on the Devil, however, is good old familiar rosewood, a well chosen sample, and nicely fretted. Machines comprised four small, enclosed, Japanese types which seemed to be working very well.

The brass nut was well cut and set but the heavy duty bridge, although a very solid design in itself, would have been better if it had taken its basic desire to copy a Fender design one stage further and offered tracking to obviate the tendency of that variety for side slip when played vigorously. Another complaint concerns the awful looking top horn mounted pickup selector which looks clumsy and out of place, although it works well enough.

The twin split pickups are run from three good quality heavy duty rotary pots. There are also three switches: active "on", phase "in", or "out", the third offering single or twin coil operation. The three pots offer master tone (with a centre detent for "flat"), pre-amp volume and master volume. There is also an LED which glows red when the twin PP3's inside the axe run flat.

In use the Vantage has a very pleasant neck profile. It's a long scale instrument, and it tends to feel it, but access to the top is unobscured and the fretting on the sample contributed to an overall feel of ease and comfort.

From a tonal point of view the Devil sounded fine. It does have some tones which one would hate to hit by accident on stage but basically the tonal range is extremely impressive.

The sample tried certainly played well and sounded very versatile indeed. The only objections to it, in fact, were mechanical ones like the occasional clicking through the amp when a switch was thrown, but as this sample was rather an early one, one is inclined not to take this too seriously. At the price the Vantage Devil represents one of the better Japanese active basses currently on the market.

Price: £383

Body materials: Unidentified

Neck materials: Maple spliced with mahogany strips

Fingerboard materials: Rosewood

Machine heads: Vantage

Pickups: Vantage split coil (active powered)

Construction:	★★★★★
Finish:	★★★★★
Sound:	★★★★★
Playability:	★★★★★
Value For Money:	★★★★★

Distributed by: Stack Music Ltd, 9 Stapledon Road, Orton, Southgate, Peterborough, Cambs. Tel: 0733-232440.

Vantage Witch

If the Vantage Devil bass represents just about the "state of the art" in current Japanese mass produced active basses then its little brother (sister?) the Witch bass is very much an archetype of the basic beginner's bass, or at least a very simple instrument for those who value simplicity above all other qualities in bass guitars.

The design of the Vantage is rather cunning in that the walnut body bears a large strip of maple set down the centre so that, from off stage, the instrument looks as though it has that fashionable status symbol, a straight-through neck. In fact the Witch's neck is a bolted-on type, although the join has been very well constructed and there are many players who are perfectly happy with this variety of neck joint.

The fingerboard on this sample was a rather nice rosewood and the bass was well fretted. In fact the neck was, overall, very fast indeed to play on and would be ideal for a younger player who found the ultra-long scales and wide necks of some other basses too much to handle with comfort and ease.

The hardware was a bit of a mixed bag in that the small machines worked very well and the bridge seemed sturdy. Basically this bridge is a good design from a sustain point of view but, regrettably (and very strangely for a Japanese design) it does not provide for individual string height, which, frankly should be offered on all basses, regardless of price.

The pickup is fairly typical for a bass of this type — a split coil design — but one which works better than many of its contemporaries. The sound of the Witch is rather impressive for the money, despite only offering a single volume and tone control and not even the option of a coil tap. It's by no standards an active bass but it plays well and has a versatile tone which basically suits modern rock playing.

For all that, there are quite a few very good basses on the market (some of which have been launched since the Witch made its appearance), which tend to make it look far less good value for money than it did when it first appeared a couple of years ago.

Price: £184

Body materials: Walnut/maple inset

Neck materials: Unspecified

Fingerboard materials: Rosewood

Machine heads: Vantage

Pickups: Vantage split coil type

Construction:	★★★★★
Finish:	★★★½
Sound:	★★★★½
Playability:	★★★★★
Value For Money:	★★★★½

Distributed by: Stack Music Ltd, 9 Stapledon Road, Orton, Southgate, Peterborough, Cambs. Tel: 0733-232440.

Vox Custom

The Custom is not a particularly auspicious looking bass. The body is maple (stained a colour called "honey" in the case of this sample) as is the straight-through neck. The constructional standard of the review model were very high and the instrument looked very well finished indeed.

Great attention has been paid on this Vox to perfecting the vital area of the bridge. Bad bridges (ie. those that move under heavy right-hand styles) are the curse of many players. With this in mind, the designers of this model have opted for a string termination through the body system, leaving the basic bridge saddles as very heavy brass types, vaguely following the Fender pattern by being spring loaded from the rear for intonation setting and with "tracked" grooves to prevent saddle slip. This is not the best bass bridge currently on offer but it will be very reliable in use and would be familiar to players who might otherwise be contemplating a Fender.

Pickups come from the American Di Marzio stable — a P-Bass and a J-Bass fitted like the Fender. These are endowed with one plastic volume pot, one tone pot, one pickup selector and a small three position metal flick switch. This latter is where the Vox is at its best. The settings offer you series, parallel and a strangely wired sort of coil tap. When this is on you have the bottom two strings emphasised in the bottom register and the top two strings accentuated at the top. Unfortunately this implies that should the pickup selector be set so that only one Di Marzio is on, and the coil switch is set to this strange centre marking, either the top two or bottom two strings won't sound at all. If Vox scorn active basses (their catalogue has a swipe at them in passing) then they must be a case of the pot libelling the kettle!

Playing the Vox will be a familiar experience to Fender players, it has that wide-ish neck with a long scale which you either feel at home with or hate. Most players seem to love that Fender feel so they will be happy with this one. Soundwise the Vox is very up to date. It's obviously been designed for the modern stylist who likes that pulling, slapping sound with bags of top and mid without sounding tinny. Certainly those people at Vox who worked on this design have done their homework, and this modern sounding bass is a tribute to their ears. Players who dislike actives and who want a reliable, fashionable sounding bass should most certainly examine one of these.

Having said all that, it is doubtful if the Vox is particularly good value for money. When introduced, this reviewer felt more kindly towards it than now, but since then times have moved on and, undeniably good though this bass is, there are more exciting and better looking basses on the market for less money. Still, it's by no means a bad instrument at all and owners should be very happy with it.

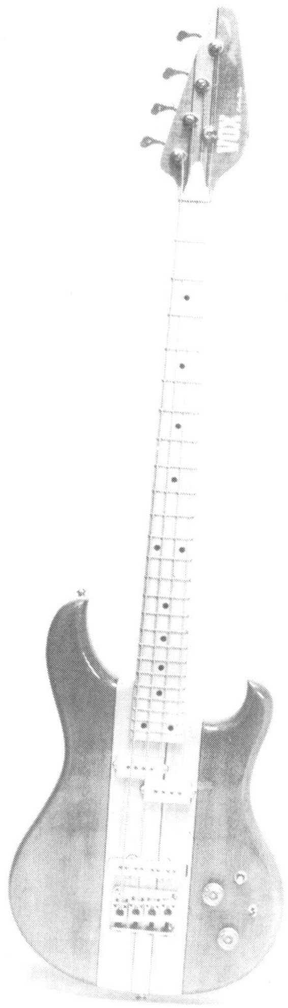

Price: £329

Body materials: Maple

Neck materials: Maple

Fingerboard materials: Maple

Machine heads: Vox

Pickups: DiMarzio P-Bass and J-Bass

Construction:	★ ★ ★ ★
Finish:	★ ★ ★ ★
Sound:	★ ★ ★
Playability:	★ ★ ★ ★
Value For Money:	★ ★ ★

Distributed by: Rose-Morris & Co. Ltd, 32-34 Gordon House Road, Kentish Town, London NW5. Tel: 01-267-5151.

WAL Custom

Of all the custom guitar builders in the UK, Electric Wood and their WAL series of basses have attained a reputation second to none. The body of the new WAL, the Custom, balances very well indeed. Basically each WAL bass has a Brazilian mahogany core but the exterior woods can be chosen from a massive range of exotics including paduak, rosewood, flamed or bird's eye maple, and many others. The bolted-on neck is a fastidious laminate (in six pieces) of maple, hornbean and mukalungu and the fingerboard a light coloured beautifully marked rosewood with an option of ebony.

Hardware on the WAL includes their own splendidly adjustable and stable bridge (in chrome or black finishes) and this is complemented by excellent open backed Schaller machines. Strings supplied with the sample were those superb Superwounds. The pots are specially made for WAL in Germany but British knobs are also specially made to order. Each one is properly black anodised with the scale numbers engraved into them for longevity.

On the electrical front the WAL Custom is a very versatile bass indeed. The eight coil exclusively made pickups are differently wired so that they can function as four discrete units with each string individually pre-amped before mixing. A pan pot replaces the archaic selector of most basses and in this case the centre detented setting alters the relationship of each pickup in balance. Pull the volume/attack pot and a narrow spectrum of high frequencies is boosted — ideal for "slappers" and "pullers".

The bass pickup control is also a push-pull type which offers a low Q boost when pulled out. The treble pickup functions similarly except that when pulled it delivers a high Q boost. The electronics are a low noise type with claimed low power consumption giving around nine months of use before battery change is called for. In addition to the basic controls the WAL Customs also offer two trimpots (buried beneath the backplate) to adjust output volume and attack level.

In use the WAL is something of an education for those who believe that the best basses only come from across the Atlantic. Tonally and constructionally the WAL is as good or better than anything else on the market — improved even further in many small ways since its introduction. It compares tonally with any active on the market and has a naturally exceptional sustain (although both this and tone depends to some extent on which woods the customer orders) and a tonal range from a guttural "clanging" to a deep round bass of positively cabinet-wrecking proportions.

Price: £644

Body materials: Choices of exotic woods/Brazilian mahogany core

Neck materials: Laminate (6 pieces) maple/hornbeam/mukalungu

Fingerboard materials: Rosewood/ebony, available as fretless marked or unmarked.

Machine heads: Schaller

Pickups: WAL Custom 8 coil (active)

Construction:	★ ★ ★ ★ ★
Finish:	★ ★ ★ ★ ★
Sound:	★ ★ ★ ★
Playability:	★ ★ ★ ★
Value For Money:	★ ★ ★ ½

Distributed by: Electric Wood Ltd, Sandown Works, Chairborough Road, High Wycombe, Bucks. Tel: 0494-442925/6.

Washburn B20 Stage Eight String

For players not using the current slap and pull style, eight string basses (whilst sounding unconventional) are actually far easier to play than six string types. The strings are paired, similar to those on a 12 string guitar, and techniques using a pick or normal finger style work so easily on them that most players could adapt to an eight string bass very quickly indeed.

Currently there appear to be three such instruments available on the ready-made market in the UK: a Shergold, a Kramer and the sample under review, a Washburn Stage Series eight string.

The sample had an ash body with a superb looking flame maple top. The straight through maple neck had laminates of rosewood inset and rosewood of different tone had been used, rather luxuriously, to bind the rosewood fingerboard. Despite the asking price, the Washburn is a fantastically built instrument with a great deal of care in its construction. To improve matters, inlays in the fingerboard are of the brass ring type which add to the impression of resolute luxury the instrument gives, despite its fairly low asking price.

Comfort of the Washburn left something to be desired when the bass was played seated but it was fine played standing up. The 22 fret neck, on the other hand, is very well profiled, plays like a veritable dream in fact, and despite that extra set of strings, few players would find it difficult to handle.

The machine placing, however, is odd. One presumes the idea is to offset any problems caused by having an overbalanced headstock, but four of the machines are housed at the opposite end of the body from the headstock in a cutaway at the base of the body. Once one got used to it this should not represent a serious problem but it's pretty confusing after just a brief acquaintance with the instrument! Either way the machines themselves are Japanese Schaller copies which work excellently.

The bridge is, unfortunately, a great disappointment in that it offers intonation setting for each string (even more vital on an eight string bass than normal) but does not offer individual height adjustment which is a great failing on an eight string.

The twin "Jazz Bass" type pickups are run by two tones plus a flick metal pickup selector and these provide the Washburn with an excellent tonal range which would suit the bass to many sorts of music, and makes it an extremely versatile instrument.

If there was a serious flaw in the Washburn it is that this sample was slightly out when played up the neck — a common enough problem with four string basses, let alone eight string models. Having said that, this reviewer was trying it for one day only, in very humid and thundery weather which, as 12 string guitarists can vouch for, will play havoc with the best of instruments.

After weighing this Washburn in the balance it is, despite a few problems, about the best eight string bass on the market in terms of value for money.

Price: £398

Body materials: Ash/maple top

Neck materials: Maple/rosewood

Fingerboard materials: Rosewood

Machine heads: Washburn "Schaller" copies

Pickups: Washburn "Precision" split design/jazz type

Construction:	★★★★★
Finish:	★★★★★
Sound:	★★★★★
Playability:	★★★★★
Value For Money:	★★★★★★

Distributed by: Roland UK, Great West Trading Estate, 983 Great West Road, Brentford, Middlesex. Tel: 01-568-4578.

Washburn SB Wing Vulture

Although built in Japan, the Washburn range of instruments is owned by an American company and apparently designed in America. This theory is bourne out by the noticeable differences in design and playing of Washburns from other Japanese designed instruments.

The Wing Vulture II is a case in point. There is something about the look of this bass, also expressed in the feel of the instrument, which sets it apart. It is fairly extravagant looking, the sample being very well finished in a rich sunburst to dark brown with the grain of the body showing through nicely.

The fingerboard is rosewood, fretted with 21 good quality frets. The headstock bears four large open backed machines and the nut is brass, well cut and set on the model under review.

There have been some fairly recent changes to the Wing Vultures and it is definitely worth noting that earlier versions (such as this sample), had the strings fixed through the back of the body and then passed up over heavy "tracked" saddles which rode on a chromed plate inset into the body. Later Wing Vultures have various changes to them, introduced early in 1982 so it is possible that you could find either type on the market.

This model featured a split Precision type pickup at the neck and a Jazz type at the bridge. All the controls offered were one selector, two volumes and two tones.

The mahogany on the Washburn seemed fine and the playability of this bass is facilitated by one of the best body contouring jobs, up at the point where the straight-through neck enters the body, that this reviewer has ever seen. The result is that the Wing Vulture encourages you to play up high, rather than deters you — the case with far too many basses on the market, even today.

Although the neck is fairly chunky looking, this sample was easy to play and very fast but did suffer from an amplified fret buzz, leading one to suspect that this was not a "doctored" model, and Roland, the UK distributors, had justifiably held back a slightly faulty model for review rather than put it on the market.

The sound of the Washburn is very good indeed — brought alive by that bridge pickup which implies many interesting tones if you juggle properly with it, especially for pullers and slappers. The top output is impressive and the natural resonance of the body enhances these frequencies so that it is very much a "live" sounding instrument, well suited to modern playing styles rather than the old bass thump of the past.

However, despite its excellent qualities, one feels that the instrument is a shade overpriced when compared to others on the market which are equally good and less expensive.

Price: £124

Body materials: Laminated ash/rock maple/walnut

Neck materials: Laminated maple

Fingerboard materials: Rosewood

Machine heads: Westone

Pickups: Westone split type

Construction:	★ ★ ★ ★ ★
Finish:	★ ★ ★ ★ ★
Sound:	★ ★ ★ ★ ½
Playability:	★ ★ ★ ★ ★
Value For Money:	★ ★ ★ ★ ★

Distributed by: Fletcher, Coppock and Newman Ltd, Morley Road, Tonbridge, Kent. Tel: 0732-365217.

Westone Concord Bass One

Bearing in mind the revolutionary low prices of Westone guitars and basses to date, the appearance of one which retails even below the previously bottom level is taking the joke to new levels. Of course, it's only a joke if you are a buyer — distributors of some other Japanese guitars and bass importers might think it more of a tragedy!

This latest Westone is a single pickup bass bearing the ubiquitous split, Precision design, job worn, in the case of the sample, on a jet black body. It was impossible to assess the actual wood the body is made of plastic rather than wood. Apparently it is alder. How well this strangely attractive finish will stand up to life on the road is difficult to assess, but remember that black guitars look awful when they chip!
one wonders whether the body beneath was actually made of plastic rather than wood. Apparently How well this strangely attractive finish will stand up to life on the road it is difficult to assess but remember that black guitars look awful when they chip!

The neck on the Westone is a bolt-on type, rather well done in the case of the sample. The neck itself has 21 frets and simple black dot markers for position. The nut is plastic and the machines are Japanese copies of Schallers which worked very well indeed.

Down at the business end the Concord has a very simple bridge indeed, a straightforward inexpensive copy of one from a Precision. Regrettably this isn't really very good, the height adjusting screws are sharp and can scrape a right hand used to damp the strings and the saddles themselves are not tracked in any way. Despite the very low asking price, one would have hoped for something just a little better, even if it had pushed the price up a couple of pounds or so. Control of the pickup is from volume and tone pots which work splendidly well.

Overall this almost ludicrously cheap guitar is splendid value for money. The fretting on the sample was excellent and the bass played in tune all the way up the neck, which in itself played very comfortably in a similar way to a Fender Precision.

Unfortunately the sample was not well set-up in that the E string was disproportionately loud, driving theamp into a form of overload which counterpointed unpleasantly with the other three strings. Fortunately the pickup height is adjustable and this could have been corrected easily.

Compared with beginners' basses of even five years ago this Westone is superb value for money. Notwithstanding any small criticisms, it represents the best value beginners' bass currently on the UK market.

Price: £120

Body materials: Alder

Neck materials: Maple

Fingerboard materials: Maple

Machine heads: Westone (Schaller copies)

Pickups: Westone split type

Construction:	★★★★
Finish:	★★★★★
Sound:	★★★★★
Playability:	★★★★½
Value For Money:	★★★★★

Distributed by: Fletcher, Coppock and Newman Ltd, Morley Road, Tonbridge, Kent. Tel: 0732-365271.

Westone Thunder I

The launch of the Westone range of guitars and basses in autumn 1981, caused a stir in the electric guitar business in the UK. Not that there was anything special about the Westone range in terms of performance — there were (and still are) many fine imported Japanese guitars and basses on the market, but because importers had slashed margins so that guitars and basses identical in quality to those retailing previously for around £200-£300 were now on the market for just over £100.

One of the first instruments to make its mark was the Thunder I bass. Although only a passive, there aren't that many basses on the market these days at this sort of price which are anything more than pure beginners' instruments. The Thunder I bass doesn't *look* like a beginners' bass. The body is fashioned from Canadian ash, rock maple and walnut, all beautifully laminated together and satin finished. The bolt-on neck (which has been cunningly designed along with the body so that from a distance it looks as though the Thunder I has a straight-through neck) is maple with a rosewood fingerboard applied to it. The sample was very well finished and that fingerboard (which carries 20 frets on its 34" scale length) was nicely fretted, particularly for the price.

The bridge is a basic brass Precision copy which seems to be well made and reasonably stable in use and the pickup also follows the Fender path by being a split Precision type. Regrettably the makers have not stretched their budget to offer tracking on the saddle screws — the only way to overcome that saddle slip sideways which can plague Precision bridges played hard by a finger style bassist — but at the price it hardly seems fair to quibble.

Soundwise the Westone is amazingly good for the money. It's not that far away from a good Precision with that excellent ability to cut through the din made by the rest of the band, one of the many factors which has ensured the success of the basic Fender for so long. The neck on this sample was very fast indeed and excellently proportioned to ensure comfort on long gigs.

The Westone Thunder I may lack originality in sound and design but it is, quite simply, the biggest bargain currently available to the impoverished player in the UK, whether he's an amateur or very hard-up pro.

Price: £121

Body materials: Ash/rock maple/walnut

Neck materials: Maple

Fingerboard materials: Rosewood

Machine heads: Westone

Pickups: Westone "Precision" type

Construction:	★★★★
Finish:	★★★½
Sound:	★★★★
Playability:	★★★★★
Value For Money:	★★★★★

Distributed by: Fletcher, Coppock and Newman Ltd, Morley Road, Tonbridge, Kent. Tel: 0732-365271.

Westone Thunder II Active

As the trend towards basses with active circuitry (i.e. basses with a built-in battery powered pre-amplifier) continues, it is becoming increasingly obvious that they go some way towards answering the traditional complaint of bassists that they can rarely make themselves heard above the rest of the band, and that their instruments are frequently very limited in the variety of sounds which they will produce, however much they've paid for them.

Westone's basic active is the superb looking Thunder II. The Thunder II *looks* every inch a professional bass, despite its price. The body of the sample tested was extremely well finished Canadian Ash and the straight-through neck was of five pieces of hard maple laminated with walnut strips. The finish was very good, even down to the pleasant looking inlays of "snowflake" design inlaid into a fingerboard made of ebony.

The headstock carried four sealed machines of exemplary quality and overall this 24 fret bass looked to be as well constructed and designed as any other active bass on the market, with the possible exception of one or two US and UK custom built models.

Twin Precision type "split" pickups power the bass, controlled by a series of switches as on any active. These comprise three heavy duty knurled brass rotary controls (volume, passive tone and active boost), a pickup selector (on the top horn) and three metal flick switches for "dual tone", phase and active Eq in/out. All are easily accessible although the pickup could perhaps have been moved down to the rest of the controls, rather than set in the traditional place, on the top horn. The bridge is a very solid piece of brass, works like a Fender and, in this case, is properly tracked to prevent saddle slip.

Run passively the Westone is good, but bring in power from the two internally mounted PP3 batteries via the active "on" switch and the bass leaps into very convincing action. This bass is provided with a range of tones, all of which can be used to effect for the adventurous player. The designer of this instrument obviously plays in the modern style!

The neck also facilitates modern playing styles. No longer are bassists relegated to the bottom six or seven frets and the tonal potential of this bass, combined with one of the easiest and fastest bass necks this reviewer has ever played, makes this instrument ideal for the player who is discontented with conventional sounds and styles. Frankly, at the price, this degree of quality is remarkable. Overall, it is probably the best value active bass on the market and no player should pass up the opportunity of trying one.

Price: £272

Body materials: Ash

Neck materials: Laminate: walnut/maple strips

Fingerboard materials: Ebony

Machine heads: Westone

Pickups: Westone split type

Construction:	★ ★ ★ ★ ★
Finish:	★ ★ ★ ★ ★
Sound:	★ ★ ★ ★ ★
Playability:	★ ★ ★ ★ ★
Value For Money:	★ ★ ★ ★ ★

Distributed by: Fletcher, Coppock and Newman Ltd, Morley Road, Tonbridge, Kent. Tel: 0732-365271.

Bass Profiles

Jack Bruce

Jack Bruce was really the first virtuoso electric bass player. Up until his work with Cream from 1966 to 1968, the bass guitar was considered to be simply a part of the rhythm section, but he opened up a whole new world and direction for the instrument.

Bruce's career has encompassed a staggering number of musical styles beginning with pop and blues, then going through the Cream innovation on to avant garde jazz and then to a heavy rock trio. Always restless, he has been at the core of a number of vital musical developments, and is still regarded as a major influence.

Born in Scotland in 1943, his early influences ranged from folk and jazz through to Bach and he later won a scholarship to the Royal Scottish Academy of Music. Jack's rock career began in the early Sixties with the Graham Bond Organisation, and he went on to play with Manfred Mann and John Mayall, before forming Cream with Eric Clapton and Ginger Baker.

Cream were one of the first bands to be taken seriously by intellectuals, and its not hard to see why. In interviews Jack would talk about Bach's bass lines as being some of the greatest ever. With Cream, Jack sang, wrote and even played keyboards on occasion, but it was his bass playing that really grabbed the attention.

To begin with he established a very distinctive bass sound, which was pretty unique for the Sixties. From his Gibson EB3 bass would come a hard trebly tone which really cut through. This was a result of playing too hard with three fingers and a thumb, the distortion seemingly coming from his fingers. Jack really allowed his imagination full rein, and in many cases his bass lines seemed to be competing with Clapton's soaring leads.

Following the demise of Cream, Jack made two critically acclaimed solo albums, and was a member of the phenomenal Tony Williams band Lifetime for a while. He then went to the other extreme by teaming up with guitarist Leslie West and drummer Corky Laing in a heavy rock trio which didn't really work. Following this he formed a new band with Mick Taylor and Carla Bley, but that broke up after a few early gigs.

After laying low for a while, Jack popped up on the John McLaughlin album "Guitar Player" and subsequently went on to do some live work with John and drummer Billy Cobham. More recently he has been working with Robin Trower. He is still able to attract musicians of a very high calibre, and has put together some impressive line ups, but he doesn't seem the kind of person who needs to hold together a steady band.

Although the Jack Bruce bass sound is still as distinctive as ever, there have been many changes in hardware over the last 15 years, and Jack has not been slow to take advantage. He now plays a fretless bass, which he believes he should have done a long time ago, and he's also changed from Gibson basses.

After some time spent checking out a variety of makes, he happened to find an Aria SB1000 in a shop that he really liked. The company built him a fretless ebony model and this is the one which he has been using for live work, preferring a fretted for the studio.

Immensely talented, Jack Bruce is regarded as one of rock's instrumentalinnovators.

Stanley Clarke

When Miles Davis began fusing jazz with elements of rock in the Sixties and early Seventies, his bands became a breeding ground for new young talent like guitarist John McLaughlin and keyboard player Chick Corea. It was inevitable that these young virtuoso musicians would need bass players of the same high technique to continue their high flying music, and thus emerged one in the shape of Stanley Clarke.

Clarke, along with Jaco Pastorius, introduced a whole new dimension to electric bass playing. Jack Bruce had hinted at the kind of things that could be done on the four stringed instrument, but it was really these two young Americans who shook the bass playing world up in the Seventies.

As a child, Clarke learned the violin and then moved on to the cello and finally the double bass. He got his first bass, which was an upright, when he was 15, and the following year acquired his first electric instrument. Playing in a variety of local bands in Philadelphia, he learned to put his technique to good use in addition to gaining the vital experience of actually playing with other musicians.

Stanley played all kinds of music in those early groups, from rock and roll and acid rock through country and western and avant garde jazz. Moving to New York he entered the session world where his career began to take off after a session with drummer Billy Cobham. He worked with artists such as Gato Barbieri, Stan Getz and Pharoah Sanders, developing his own unique style and moving into the free form jazz area.

In 1972 he joined Chick Corea's Return To Forever, and built up an outstanding reputation as a virtuoso bass player. The band were in the forefront of the jazz fusion movement, and over the next four years proved an influential force.

Following the demise of RTF, Clarke embarked on a variety of solo projects which ran the whole gamut of styles from jazz rock fusion to straight rock and roll and funk, featuring the likes of Jeff Beck and Keith Richard. This brought him much criticism from the purists for his self-indulgence and flashy style. One of his latest projects has been a band with keyboards wizard George Duke, and once again it features a diversity of styles.

Whatever Clarke has been doing, however, his incredible technique is always well to the fore. His long boney fingers enable him to rip off notes at great speed, while his technique of plucking the strings results in a sharp, trebly sound which has become his hallmark.

The inevitable collection of instruments include many upright acoustic basses in addition to the electrics. He used to use Gibson and Fender basses, but now he is more likely to use one of his many custom built Alembics. Each has different features, is made of different woods and are different weights. He also has a collection of old European contra-basses dating from the 18th Century.

Despite his critics, Clarke remains an exceptional bass player, and the sight of his long lean figure putting those boney fingers to work on an instrument is to witness the master at work.

Phil Lynott

In the rock business, bass players are essentially heard but very rarely seen. They are very much poor relations to the six string brethren, and are often found in the shadows with the drummer, behind a lead guitarist or singer.

One bass man who does not conform to this pattern is Phil Lynott, the driving force behind Thin Lizzy. Not content with simply playing his instrument well, he also sings, writes and has a hand in the production of the band's recorded output. He has kept Thin Lizzy going for over 10 years, and made them an interesting and exciting band who have escaped many of the clichés which surround heavy rock.

Phil hails from Dublin and began his musical career alternating between the city's folk clubs and singing with a local rock band. Early influences were Dylan, Hendrix and Van Morrison, and he was already writing his own poetry. Life was quite difficult for a singer in the "progressive rock" era, when long guitar solos were the order of the day, so he ended up with a bass guitar and began to practice.

In 1970 he formed Thin Lizzy with drummer Brian Downey and guitarist Eric Bell. After building up a reputation in Dublin, they came over to England to record for Decca. During the sessions, they did a tongue-in-cheek version of the old folk song "Whisky In The Jar". It was destined for a B side, but the record company realised its hit potential, released it and it gave them a Top Ten hit in 1973.

However, this initial success was not without its drawbacks. Although it enabled the band to survive and buy new equipment, it also gave them something of a showband image, and a lot of hard gigging was required to set the record straight. During this time Eric Bell left and instead of finding one replacement, Phil opted for two and thus the twin guitar trade mark of Thin Lizzy was born.

Hard gigging and albums like "Vagabonds Of The Western World" and "Fighting" earned them quite a following and in 1976 they got the kind of break they had been looking for when "The Boys Are Back In Town" was a hit both in Britain and America. Since then they have had a succession of hit albums and singles, and now have a worldwide following.

Phil Lynott is responsible for much of their success, his distinctive vocals and driving bass playing complementing the powerful songs he writes. He doesn't see himself as a musician in the Stanley Clarke, Jaco Pastorius mould, relying more on feel and emotion than fretboard pyrotechnics. Nevertheless he tries to practice a couple of hours a day. Among his many guitars are the inevitable Fender basses, but one particular favourite is an Ibanez.

Phil's writing is unique, often calling upon the romantic images of his native Ireland, or simply translating the anger and frustration of the kids in the street into hard rocking music.

His solo album "Solo In Soho" revealed the true depth of his talent and his writing skills, and he's even found time to have some of his poems published.

Paul McCartney

There can be few people around today who aren't aware of the prodigious talents of Paul McCartney. As a songwriter he ranks with Cole Porter and Irving Berlin, and his part in the Beatles alone has earmarked him for immortality. But how many people are really aware of the musical genius that seems to exude from the man.

The trouble with Paul is that he's so talented and successful on a wide variety of levels, that many of his accomplishments are often overlooked. Bass players, for instance, will take their hats off to his skill on the four stringed instrument, his style maintains a melodic quality which is hard to beat.

Surprisingly, Paul's first instrument was a trumpet because his father happened to play one. He then went on to piano lessons, and while never showing the dexterity of a concert pianist, he learned enough to play tunes. Still, when Paul was growing up in the Fifties, rock and roll was the thing, so he soon sorted himself out a guitar.

When he first met Lennon, John was impressed because Paul knew a few more chords than he did, so they teamed up. Paul originally had a bit of difficulty playing the guitar because he was left handed, but he soon overcame that obstacle and wrote his first song at 14.

Together with John, he would plonk out tunes for hours on end, and eventually they wrote down about a hundred which were the result of sessions round at Paul's house. Very early on they realised the importance of writing their own material, and knew it was the key to real success.

Having formed a group, they went off on those lengendary trips to Hamburg and it was here that Paul switched from guitar to bass. Up till then, bass had been handled by Stuart Sutcliffe, but he couldn't really play, and when he eventually left the group, Paul took over. During the marathon eight hour stints in the clubs, the Beatles were honed to perfection, and it's not really surprising that they began to attract attention when they returned to England. The rest as they say, is history.

Although their live performances were rendered futile because of the screaming and hysteria once they had become famous, it is often forgotten just how good they were live. Apparently, after their return from Germany they were so good on stage that no one could live with them, and many of the standard rock and roll numbers they did were evidently better than the originals.

In those early days, Paul had a Hofner violin bass which he stuck with right up to the time of "Sergeant Pepper" when he acquired a Rickenbacker, although the old Hofner still makes an appearance in the "Let It Be" film. More recently he has been playing a custom built Yamaha, but one gets the impression that no matter what instrument he played, the man would get a nice sound out of it.

Fellow musicians love his playing for its melodic quality although he can pump out some raw high energy stuff when the occasion demands it. Paul's six string guitar playing has also earned plaudits from the musicians who have worked with him. Never a great technician (he still can't read music) he is a shining example of pure musical genius.

Jaco Pastorius

Along with Stanley Clarke, Jaco Pastorius is one of the giants of the modern bass guitar scene. For sheer technique and ability, they are in a class of their own, but whereas Clarke has diversified over the last few years, Jaco, as a member of Weather Report, has kept his playing firmly in the avant garde jazz direction.

He's very, very good and he knows it, which is why in the few interviews he has done, he's earned a reputation for being arrogant. The story goes that he joined Weather Report in 1976 simply by telling leader Joe Zawinul just how good he was — a fact which he was easily able to back up.

Born in Pennsylvania in 1952, he moved to Florida when only seven. Soon after he picked up a bass and taught himself to play and was involved in High School bands playing R&B. From the age of 16 he spent much of his time playing in night clubs backing all kinds of acts.

Jaco never had any formal music lessons, but the long stints he did in the clubs more than compensated, and he taught himself to read music which was a necessity for survival on the club circuit. He worked with everyone, from R&B bands to comedians like Bob Hope, before finally finding his niche with Weather Report.

On the instrument side, Jaco likes Fender Jazz basses, usually old ones. He has a 1962 model from which he removed all the frets and refinished it himself, thus giving him a fretless bass, but he also has a 1960 Jazz bass with the frets left in. The sound he gets, has been described as "R&B with punch".

Pastorius tends to only use the back pickup on the instrument, and compensates for any loss of power by turning the bass on the amplifier all the way up. He is also a master at playing harmonics on the bass. Influences range from jazz giants Charlie Parker and Herbie Hancock through to James Brown and Frank Sinatra! There is no way that Jaco is going to be influenced by other bass players.

Right hand technique is very important in his playing, and he tends to use his first two fingers to pick the strings and the other two fingers and thumb to mute. Jaco has built up a reputation as a great soloist, and when he's working alone on stage he pulls off the most amazing pyrotechnics, and he is able to build up a real wall of sound by using all kinds of effects.

Being the bassman in Weather Report he is never allowed to sit back and take it easy, because leader Zawinul is a hard taskmaster and expects his musicians to have the same high standards and commitment to music that he himself has, which is why the young Jaco has remained on top for so long.

Guitar Hardware — The replacement business

Prior to the mid-Seventies, buying an electric guitar was a pretty straightforward business. You would go into the shop, select one that you liked the sound and feel of and provided you could afford it, take it home and play it to your heart's content. If you became tired with the sound or the guitar, then it was a question of trading it in for another model and hoping that would give you what you wanted — unless, that is, you were a superstar who could afford dozens of guitars. But now things are a little different.

Since the late Sixties, guitarists began to sense a difference between some of the older electrics and their newer counterparts. It became widely accepted that an old Les Paul or Stratocaster, was inherently better than its modern counterpart. However, there were problems involved in opting for old models, the biggest being the lack of spares for these instruments. The big manufacturers had a policy whereby spares were available for current models, but were almost immediately discontinuing parts for models which had gone out of production. For instance, if you had a Fender Stratocaster made before the CBS takeover of the company in 1965, then you would have had great difficulty in replacing the neck, because the design on the newer models had been changed significantly.

Fortunately there sprang up a number of enterprising individuals, who by and large started out catering for the problems of guitar playing friends. It soon transpired there was a vast market in doctoring or customising instruments, and so the replacement industry was born.

One of these early replacement pioneers was a New York guitar player called Larry DiMarzio. A working guitarist, he also had a technical background, particularly in the world of domestic electronics. Larry had a Fender Stratocaster but he really wanted a Les Paul, he couldn't afford one so he set about fiddling around with the pickups on the Strat to try and get the desired sounds.

Soon after, he got a job in a guitar repair shop, and his ideas really began to take shape when he was given a huge box of unwanted pickups by the boss. Larry took the box home and spent many hours taking the pickups apart and finding out what really made them work. By studying old and new pickups closely, he deduced that the major difference between an old guitar and a newer model was the pickups, and the vital part of the pickup was the winding.

So Larry DiMarzio set about winding his own pickups which he sold to his friends. The pickups proved very popular and his business went from a mail order operation to an internatoinal company in a very short time. Today, the name DiMarzio has become synonymous with pickups, and countless guitarists not only insist on their pickups, but also utilise their variety of hardware which ranges from fretwire to guitar bodies.

Apart from making their pickups available over the counter, DiMarzio have also collaborated with several guitar manufacturers whereby their models come ready fitted with DiMarzios. The company have also designed special products, specifically for fitting to guitars in the budget price bracket. Recently, the DiMarzio company themselves have gone into guitar production, by introducing a complete DiMarzio model.

Another of the big names in replacement parts, Schecter, started in much the same way, but their founder, David Schecter, instead of being a guitarist was a concert pianist. However, he was also an extremely good and resourceful toolmaker in addition to having a passion for car hot rodding and customising.

He got into the guitar business by designing an

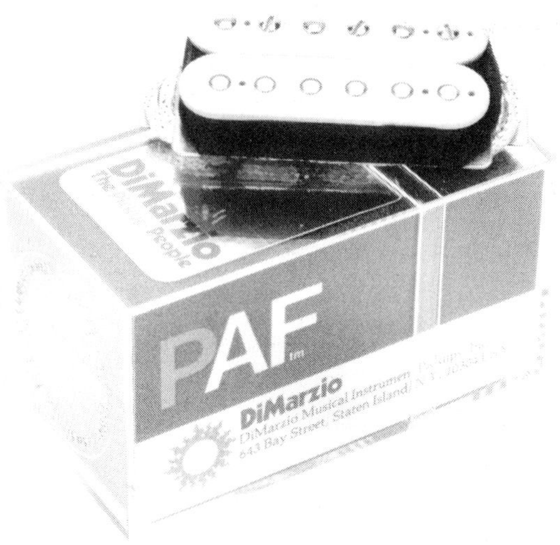

One of the most popular replacement pickups of recent years has been the DiMarzio PAF.

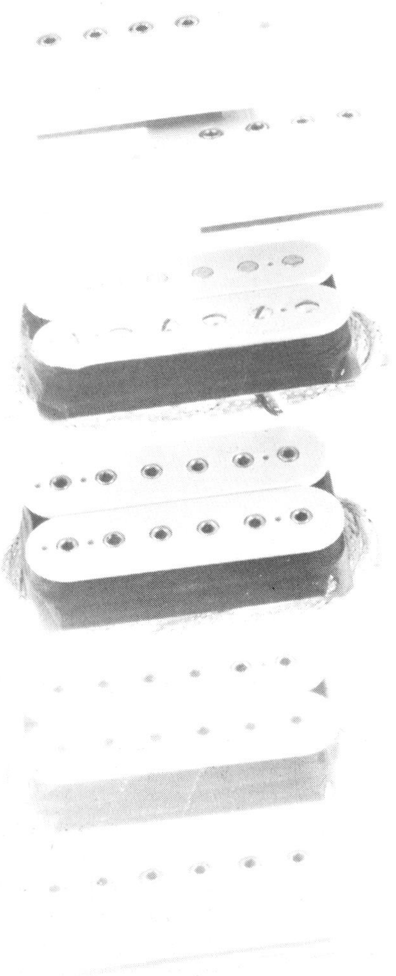

A range of DiMarzio pickups.

extremely effective pickup winding machine, on which he used to do re-winds for a number of Los Angeles musicians. His reputation gradually spread until he began to make complete pickups, the result being the formation of the Schecter company in 1976.

The Schecter business expanded until there was a whole catalogue of wood and metal parts which today stands at around 900 different items. David Schecter still fulfills a vital role in the company, being responsible for the toolmaking side. He programmes the computer controlled lathes which cut all the metal parts, and the guitar necks are made on a machine formerly used to cut gun stocks which he has adapted.

Schecter have a policy of making the great majority of their parts in-house under their control, the only things contracted out being some of the plating processes and the pots and switches. It is probably this aspect which has to a large part guaranteed their success, where many other parts companies have folded. Schecter have also been providing ready made guitars for some years, and their reputation has grown with top guitarists like Mark Knopfler, Jeff Beck and Pete Townshend using them.

Mighty Mite are another of today's leading guitar hardware specialists who began life in the US in the early Seventies. Randy Zacuto began like Larry DiMarzio and David Schecter, by messing about with pickups for friends. Eventually he worked on his own windings, and went into business providing pickups and other hardware.

Randy is generally credited as being one of the first to introduce brass bridges, and he soon expanded operations to include the whole range of replacement hardware and finally bodies and necks. In fact the company scored a first when they offered a complete guitar with straight-through neck but no hardware — the object of the exercise being that the customer could simply put whatever hardware he wanted on it.

Mighty Mite offer the complete range of Do-It-Yourself hardware, with everything from replacement pickups for Fenders and Gibsons, through to pick guards, bridges, switches and knobs. The company also provide two "limited edition" guitars, which are hand assembled in this country for Rosetti by master craftsman Peter Cook. The Rock I lead guitar and Rock II bass are made up completely of Mighty Mite hardware.

Some companies merely specialise in replacement pickups, almost all dating from the early Seventies, and offering their own particular sounds; names like Seymour Duncan, Bill Lawrence and Bartolini. Invariably they provide replacement pickups for Gibsons and Fenders, and it is very much up to the individual and the sound you want, as to which one to choose.

However, each manufacturer will offer something a little different. Seymour Duncan, for instance, do a range of pickups for some of the more unfamiliar old guitars, like Guilds and Epiphones, while Bartolini make a particularly impressive acoustic pickup.

More and more of the guitar manufacturers have become aware of this increasing trend towards customising, and are themselves offering guitar hardware and replacement parts. This is good news for the guitarists in that the range of parts is increasing, but it also makes for even greater difficulty in choosing the hardware which is suitable.

The foundation of the replacement parts business is based on the premise that the hardware that these companies are offering will exactly fit the model they are designed to replace. For instance, it is possible to purchase pickups from a number of different manufacturers which will fit exactly onto a Fifties Les Paul, or an early Sixties Fender.

However, if you have a Japanese copy which you want to hot up by fitting some modern pickups, then you have to tread very carefully. The basic problem is that Japan and (now Britain, through the EEC) work to metric measurements, while the Americans are still working to imperial measure. No matter how similar your copy may look to its famous American counterpart, the minute screw holes are often slightly different, and this would make customising a very difficult task.

Some Japanese companies are getting round this by making imperial parts, but the Americans are

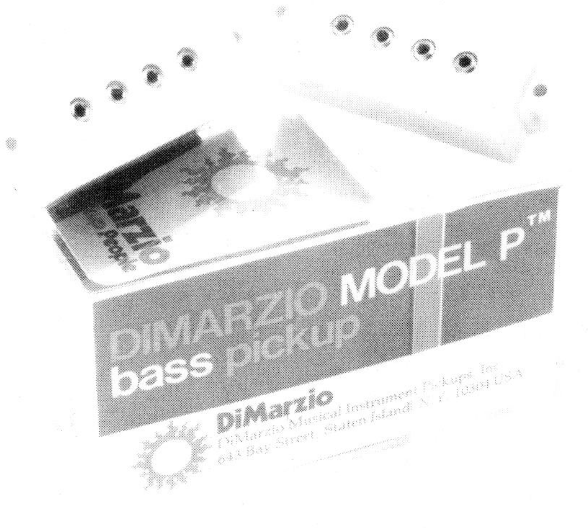

Basses too can be customised. This is a DiMarzio Model P bass replacement pickup.

The DiMarzio SDS I is designed specifically for Stratocasters.

unlikely to go over to metric because their home market is sufficiently large not to warrant it. Generally speaking, you should have no difficulty fitting replacement parts to an American guitar, but with instruments made outside the US, it is best to check the mountings very carefully.

Another important point is that the pickups from the various manufacturers, despite the fact that they may all be designed to fit the same guitar, will sound different. All the various replacement manufacturers have different construction techniques, and different design principles, and in the case of pickups, different windings. So with the vast array of pickups available today, it is possible to simply choose the type of sound you want by merely choosing the right pickups, or combination of pickups.

Doug Chandler is the UK representative for Schecter, and knows more than most about the guitar parts business. He started out as a customiser and repairer of guitars, and began making some replacement parts, however he had problems getting the right screws. So he jumped on a plane to America in search of imperial size screws, met David Schecter, and became Schecter's UK distributor.

Doug has seen the whole parts industry blossom, an industry which many of the large manufacturers ignored. "It's changed to the extent that you can sell someone a brand new Stratocaster, and you open up a whole new market which could be anything from selling him a 50 pence string retainer to complete pickup assemblies for around £150. We've had experiences where people have come in with a brand new guitar, and spent almost as much money on customising the instrument as they have on the original purchase."

With a company like Schecter who make 900 different guitars, it is possible to make an endless variety of guitars. And making these "kit component" guitars has become an increasingly large part of the business.

Doug explains, "The guy looks at the catalogue and sees all the stuff he wants. He sees that it's pretty pointless buying a guitar or using an existing instrument when he can build one exactly to his own tastes from scratch. The choices are now fairly limitless, within what is basically a Fender body shape. The reason it's a Fender and not a Gibson is that the Fender is essentially a bolt-on guitar and therefore easier to customise. It's not so easy with a Gibson due to the assembly techniques and design criteria.

"You can, in fact, get yourself the nearest equivalent to a Gibson Les Paul with something that looks like a Strat. You can have a wide flat neck, a rear-routed humbucking body with binding and a flame maple top. The fact is that it just looks like a Strat, and it is one of our most popular guitars.

"You can also go to the other extreme and have virtually a replica of a 1954 Stratocaster, and that's all within the bounds of just one manufacturer's catalogue."

Such is Schecter's faith in Doug Chandler's operation, that they are now the only Schecter custom station outside the US who are authorised to put together these guitars with the Schecter logo. In fact they assemble the guitars which go out to dealers all over Europe.

Anyone who wants such a guitar put together, is given a form to fill out which lists every aspect of the equipment from finish through to colour and pickups. Some of the requests have been fairly outlandish, and some of the more bizarre ones are actively discouraged because apart from the problems of putting them together, such an instrument is likely to have a lower re-sale value.

The reputation of the Schecter guitars has caused a

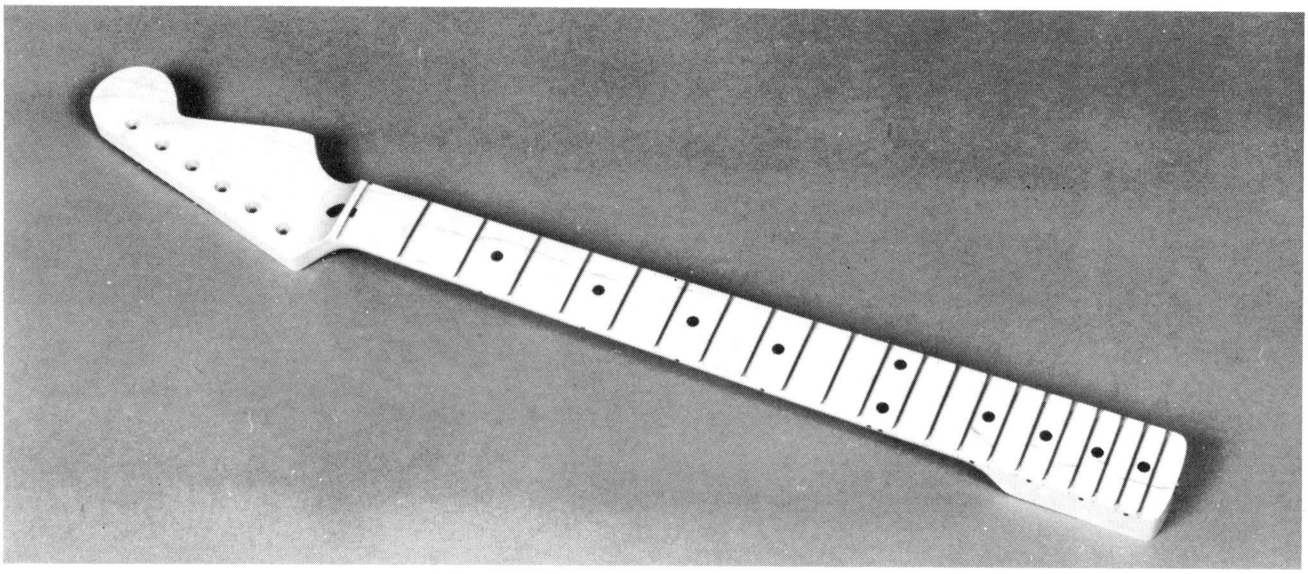

In addition to replacement pickups, companies began supplying necks and bodies like this handmade neck from DiMarzio.

number of top players to abandon instruments which they have been faithful to for many years. Pete Townshend, for example, has played a Gibson Les Paul for a long, long time, but recently he has taken to playing Schecter Telecasters.

Apparently he likes their durability and the sound of the pickups, and currently has a collection of seven, all of which he uses on stage.

Scott Gorham of Thin Lizzy is another Schecter convert, as is the current master of the Strat, Mark Knopfler. Schecter also do a Van Halen model, which is characterised by the Strat shape, single humbucking pickup, single volume control and tremolo arm.

However, it is important to remember that much of the parts appeal lies in the amateur or semi-pro player being able to customise his own instrument. Anyone who can use a soldering iron reasonably well should be able to fit replacement pickups, and DiMarzio are one company who have actually produced a booklet which is a practical guide to replacing pickups. Still much care has to be taken, and about half of customising work is usually done by an expert.

The guitar market, and its offshoot spare parts business, is subject to fashions and trends. One of the trends of recent years was for brass hardware, and there was an upsurge of companies offering everything from brass bridges and nuts to scratchplates. However, only a brass bridge was likely to improve the sound of the guitar, the rest was purely cosmetic.

Brass also tends to turn green after a while if it isn't treated properly, and many companies who invested heavily in the brass parts market found themselves in trouble. The trend now seems to be back to chrome,and in some cases manufacturers have returned to making faithful reproductions of original hardware found on early Fifties guitars.

The parts business has undoubtedly become an important aspect of the guitar industry, and it seems likely that these parts companies will be in the forefront of research and development. Doug Chandler thinks that these developments will make an important contribution to guitar technology over the next few years.

"In the long term, there'll be a lot of work put into making low impedance pickups really perform well. They work at the moment, and are an extremely practical way of making guitar pickups because they are cheaper and you don't get much signal loss, but they don't sound as good as the high impedance pickup. There's going to be a lot of work done on making them sound good.

"Active electronics aren't going to happen, guitarists don't like them, and they don't improve the guitar's sound. Graphite necks are extremely good, they make guitars sound very good and are very practical and don't warp. At the moment they are phenomenally expensive but I think the Japanese will get to work on them.

"Major things like that, which are a long term contribution to guitars, will happen, but all this has to be within the light of the current economic climate. Guitars are losing ground to keyboards, so you will probably find further developments in guitar synthesizers and guitar processors."

Manufacturers and distributors of replacement parts

1) DiMarzio: Rose-Morris & Co, 32/34 Gordon House Road, London NW5. Tel: 01-267-5151.
2) Schecter: Chandler Guitars, 199 Sandycombe Road, Kew, Richmond, Surrey Tel: 01-940-5874.
3) Mighty Mite: Rosetti (EMI) Ltd., 138/140 Old Street, London EC1. Tel: 01-253-7294.
4) Seymour Duncan: Summerfields, Saltmeadows Road, Gateshead, Tyne and Wear. Tel: 0632-770431.
5) Bill Lawrence: FCN Music, Morley Road, Tonbridge, Kent. Tel: 0732-366421.
6) Bartolini: No UK distributor at time of going to press.

Introduction to playing the guitar

Learning to play the guitar is probably more difficult than you think. It may look simple when you see the stars on television strumming away, but even mastering the basics takes a fair amount of hard work and perseverance.

Learning any musical instrument requires constant practice, and the guitar is no exception, but the instrument is different in that it involves a fair amount of discomfort in the early stages. The notes of the guitar are made by pressing down on the strings, and this pressure can make the fingertips sore. Don't let this put you off, however, because the tips will soon become hard and you'll have no trouble at all.

It is always a matter of intense frustration after having bought a guitar, not being able to get some kind of tune out of it. Remember, it is not a toy and if you are going to buy one, you should be determined to sit down and learn to play the instrument properly.

Methods of teaching

There are many and varied ways of learning to play the guitar. One of the best ways is to go to a teacher and have proper lessons, although this isn't always practical or desirable. At one time, most guitar teachers were solely concerned with a formal classical tuition, but these days there seems to be less dogma and more enjoyment.

Another development over the past few years has been the number of schools who run guitar courses for pupils. These are usually excellent because they combine the right amount of theory with practice and the class atmosphere is often a help to younger players. For the older beginner, there will invariably be a series of night classes run by the local adult education centre.

Starting off with formal private tuition can sometimes be a little offputting for youngsters just starting, so it may well be worth waiting to see if they really are interested in learning the instrument before booking a series of lessons.

Most guitar players, at some time or another, have used one of the many tuition books that are available, and selecting and using the right book can be a great help.

Things have come a long way since Bert Weedon's *Play In A Day* book of 20 years ago. Now you can buy records and cassettes to compliment the written material, and the books themselves can run to whole volumes, covering a variety of styles.

You should look carefully through a number of books before selecting one to help you learn. Make sure that each step is explained fully and in easy to follow language with clear diagrams. It is also worth noting which songs are used in the teaching — there's nothing worse than slaving away over your chords only to arrive at some obscure folk song that no one's ever heard of.

A good book will always come in handy because you can use it as a point of reference, particularly if it contains a whole range of chord shapes which you are likely to use from time to time.

Finally, if you aren't fortunate to have a guitar teacher, try and find someone who plays and to whom you can go for pointers or advice. This can be a great help and improve your playing enormously. Listening to records and watching performers, whatever kind of music they're playing is also important because you can usually learn something from every guitarist.

Tuning

As it has already been covered in a previous chapter, we'll assume you have bought the right instrument to learn on — which will probably be a nylon strung Spanish guitar.

One of the first problems to wrestle with is how to tune the instrument. The guitar is bound to go out of tune sometime, due to a variety of factors from constant playing, to changes in the room temperature. Remember that the strings are subject to a tremendous amount of pressure, and worn strings will distort the sound.

To tune the guitar you will need to know the name of each string. See Fig 1 overleaf.

The sixth string, which is the lowest and thickest, is tuned to E, the fifth to A, the fourth to D, the third to G, the second to B and the first to E again.

There are various ways of tuning the guitar, one of the most popular for beginners is with the aid of pitch pipes. All you have to do is try and match the sound which comes out of the pipe as near as possible to that of the corresponding guitar string. The same applies to a piano: locate the notes which correspond to those of the guitar strings and tune your guitar accordingly. See Fig 2 overleaf.

It may be difficult at first to get the correct sound, but after a while your ear will become accustomed to it, and tuning should only take a matter of minutes.

Fig 1

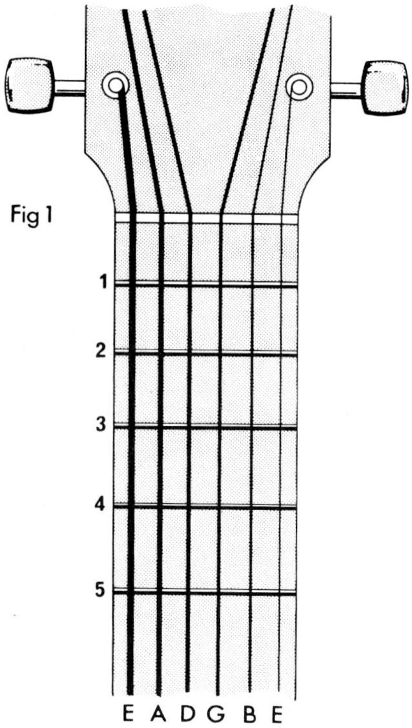

Fig 3

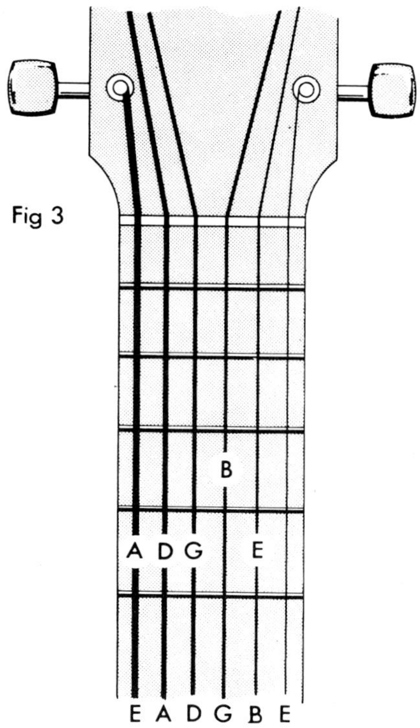

As you become more proficient you can use a method of guitar tuning which is much quicker. All you need to do is get the correct tuning for one string, the top E, and then you can tune the rest of the strings to this.

Once you have tuned the E, put your finger on the second string at the fifth fret. When you pluck it, it should give the same note as the E played open. If it doesn't, tighten or loosen it until it does. Similarly, to tune the fourth string put your finger on the string at the fourth fret and tune it to the fifth string played open. The third string is tuned to the open fourth by playing the note at the fifth fret, and you do the same with the rest of the strings. See Fig 3 above.

More recently, electronic guitar tuners have been introduced but these are quite costly, and are hardly a beginner's tool.

Beginning to play

The guitar may feel quite awkward and cumbersome to begin with, but it is important to adopt the right stance for playing from the start. The best way to play the guitar is to cross your right knee over your left and let the body of the instrument rest over your thigh. Try and keep the guitar in a vertical position so that the frets are always at right angles to the way you are

Fig 2

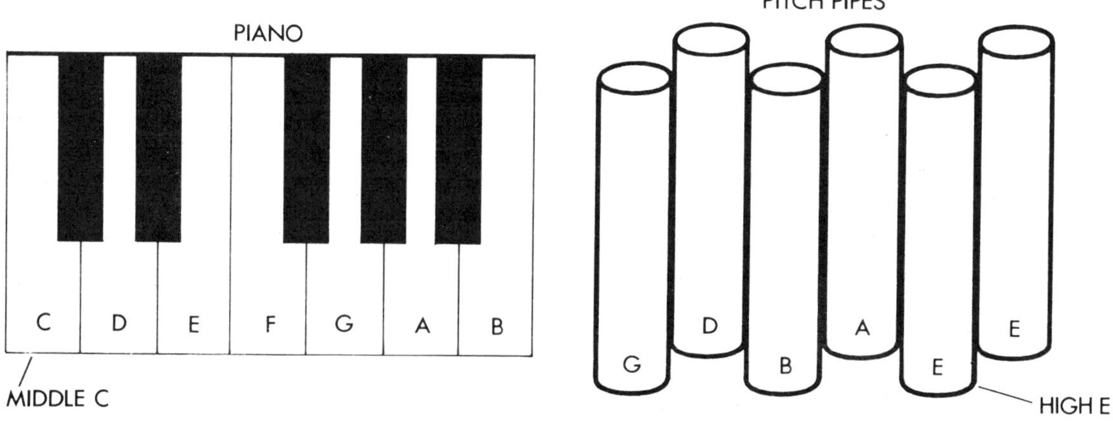

playing. Don't be tempted to play it at an angle, and avoid trying to hold the guitar up with your left hand, you should always be able to play comfortably.

In order to facilitate teaching, the fingers of the hand are numbered. See Fig 4 below.

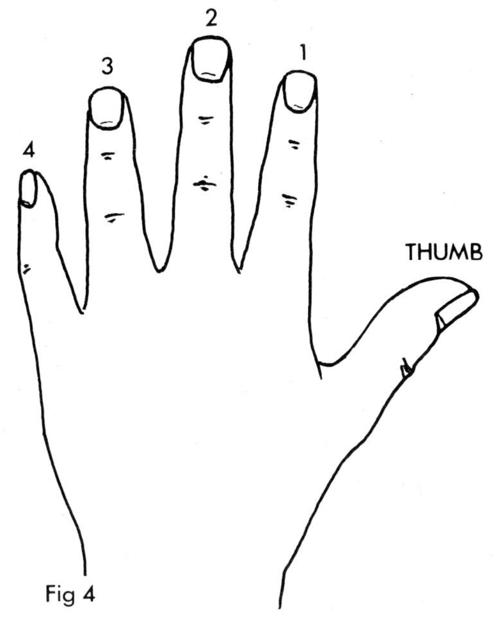

Fig 4

To play notes properly on the guitar the fingers are bent at right angles at the joints and the string should be pressed down with the tip of the finger. If you don't get this angle right, there is a tendency for it to lie across other strings and so interfere with the way they are played.

The notes you play should be clear and crisp. If they sound muffled or buzz then you should look closely at the positioning of your fingers. It is also worth noting that the nails of the left hand should be kept short, as long nails could interfere with your playing.

The thumb should be behind the neck about halfway round. Don't be tempted to have it poking over the top of the fretboard, as this could lead to difficulties when stretching for notes. It may all seem impossible at first, and your joints may creak a little, but you'll soon have them trained to go into these positions.

Chords

Chords form the basis of much of your learning. A chord is two or more notes played together, but they are invariably three or four. It is an old saying that you can play almost anything with three chords and it's not too far from the truth.

In order to learn chords we have a chord chart which tells you where to put your fingers and which notes to play. On the chord chart:—

The black dots represent the notes.
The numbers tell you which fingers to put on the strings.
The double line at the top represents the nut of the guitar.
The rest of the horizontal lines represent the frets.
The vertical lines represent the strings. (l to r EADGBE).

A small circle at the top of the string tells you that it has to be played open i.e. no notes fretted. If there is no circle or note indicated, then the string is simply not played.

One of the basic chords is C. The diagram tells you that the first finger is placed on the second string at the first fret, the second finger on the fourth string at the second fret and the third finger on the fifth string at the third fret. See Fig 5 below.

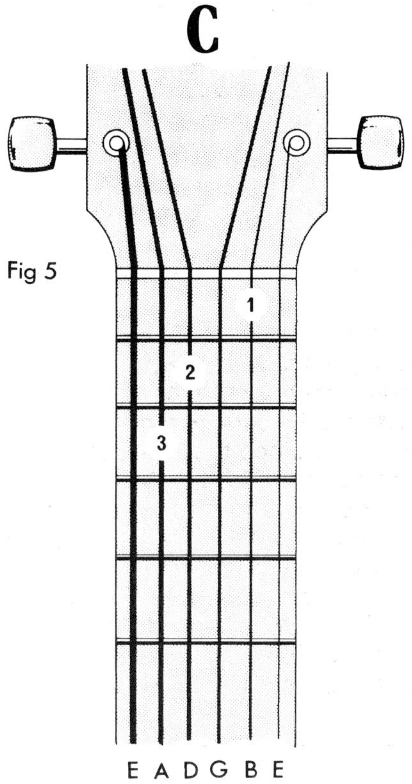

Fig 5

You will notice that the third and first strings are played open, while the sixth isn't played at all. Strum all the strings with your thumb in a downward action. Listen for any muffled notes or buzzes and check that the strings are being held down correctly.

Another basic chord is G7, which as you can see from the diagram, uses all the strings. You may find the stretching a little awkward to begin with, but you will soon get used to it. See Fig 6 overleaf.

When you are satisfied that your fingering is correct, try changing from C to G7 and back again. It may seem impossible to begin with, but after practice it will soon become automatic.

Once you have mastered those two, a useful one to learn is the F chord. This introduces a further tricky

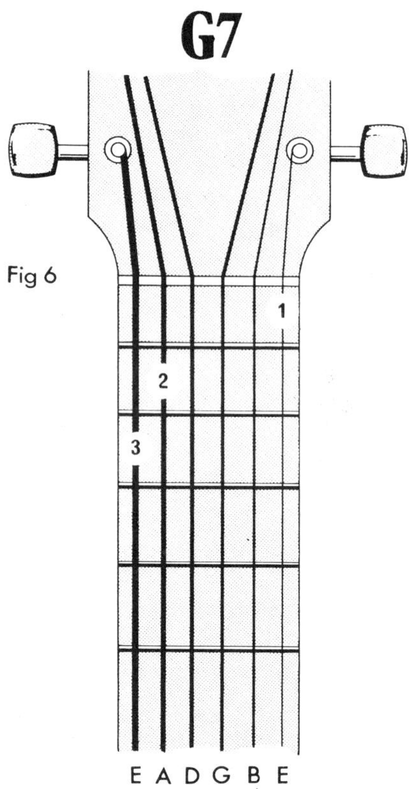

Fig 6

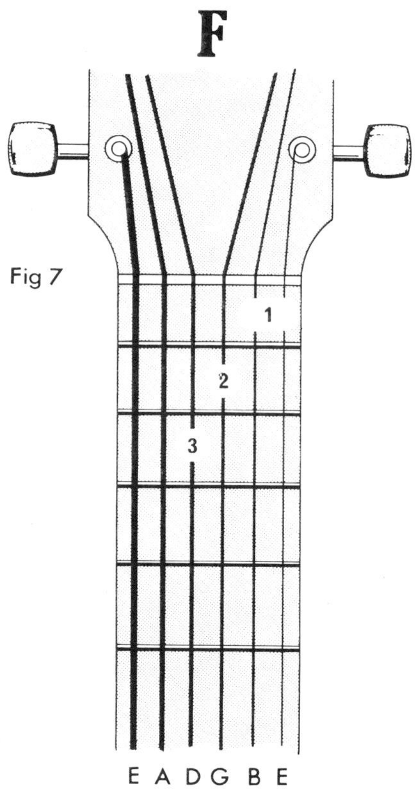

Fig 7

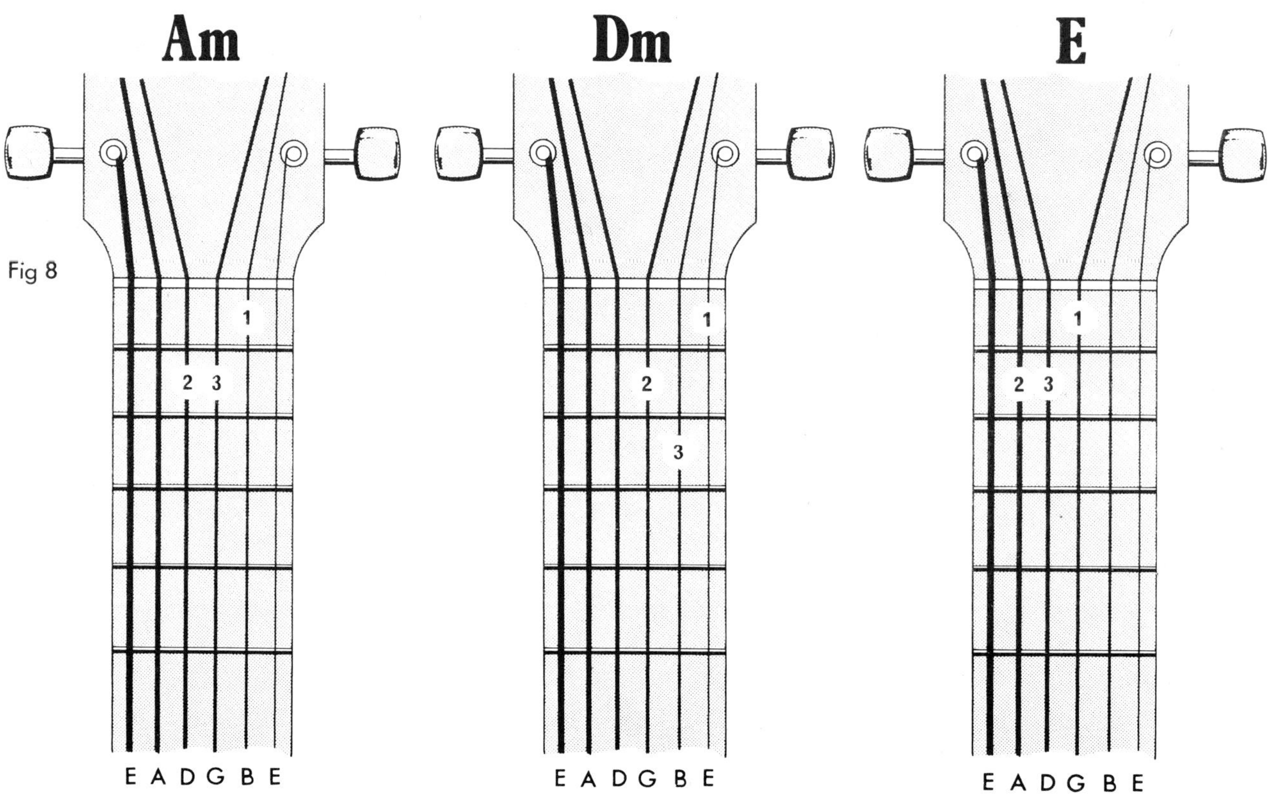

Fig 8

element because it requires two strings to be played by one finger. This requires a little extra pressure by the first finger, but once again it is purely a question of practice. See Fig 7 on preceding page.

When you can play C, G7 and F effectively then you will have mastered the basic chords of many songs, and can consider yourself over the first hurdle of guitar playing.

Some other basic chords you will find useful are Am, Dm and E. See Fig 8 on preceding page.

Once you've mastered these chords, there's really only one basic technique to be overcome and that is the bar or *barré*, to give it its correct name.

The bar enables you to play an infinite number of chords and variations along the entire length of the fretboard and must be learned if you are to progress as a guitarist. This technique is probably the most difficult to master, so don't become dispirited if you find it difficult.

The bar involves getting your first finger across the entire width of the fretboard, pressing down on all the strings, and forming a chord with the rest of your fingers. The first bar chord is F. See Fig 9.

The bar chord involves a fair amount of pressure from the fingers, and the thumb which should be pressed against the back of the neck. As with all chords, check that all the notes are being played cleanly, and give your hand plenty of rest in between practicing this bar chord or else it will become stiff and sore.

There is much more to be learned about the guitar, but this chapter has merely served as an introduction. As has been mentioned earlier there are numerous books and courses you can follow if your appetite has been whetted. The watchword for learning the guitar is to keep practicing and don't become dispirited, it's worth enduring the hardship to reap the reward of being able to make your own music.

Fig 9

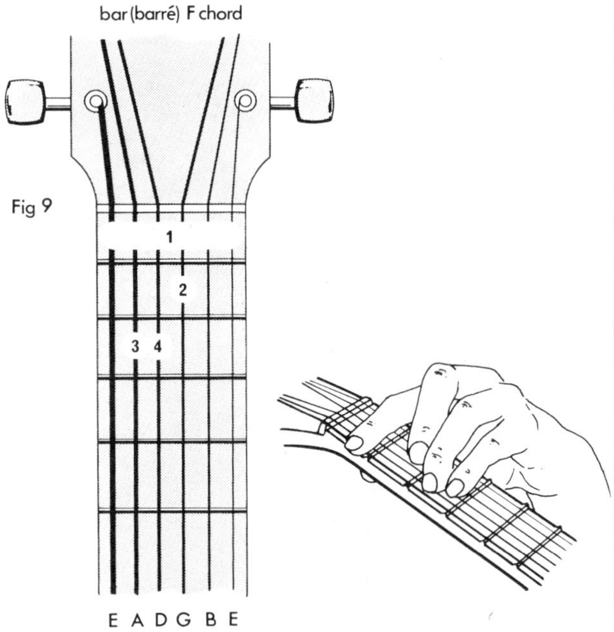

Some books you may find useful

The Complete Guitar Player, Books 1 — 4 by Russ Shipton (Music Sales). Also available, a cassette to go with each book.
Folk Guitar Styles For Beginners by Russ Shipton (Music Sales).
Guitarists' Picture Chord Encyclopaedia by John Pearse (Music Sales).
How To Improvise Lead Guitar by Palmer and Hughes (Music Sales).
Electric Bass Guitar — A Complete Guide by Laurence Canty (Chappell).

Glossary

Action — The distance between the strings and the fretboard.

Active circuitry — The inclusion of a battery operated pre-amp which gives a wider variety cut and boost to an electric guitar.

Binding — The edging around a guitar which can be made of wood or plastic.

Bolt-on neck — A guitar which comes in two pieces: the neck and the body, the neck is bolted onto the body.

Carved top — A guitar body with a carved, as opposed to flat, top.

Coil tap — This enables a pickup to be changed from single to humbucking mode at the flick of a switch.

Custom — Usually applied to an electric guitar which boasts an improvement or extra facility over the basic model in the range.

Cutaway — Refers to the part of the guitar where the body joins the neck, which is cut away to form a horn. This facilitates access to the upper frets. Cutaways can either be single (Fender Telecaster) or double (Gibson SG).

Dot inlays — The dots on the fingerboard used as markers and often made from mother-of-pearl.

Feedback — A high pitched whistling sound produced when part of the sound output from a speaker is returned to an instrument or microphone.

F-Hole — A particularly shaped sound-hole, usually seen on semi-acoustic guitars.

Fingerboard — The thin layer of wood on the neck of the guitar which forms the playing surface.

Flat top — A term used to describe a steel strung folk type acoustic.

Fretless — A bass guitar possessing no metal frets on the fingerboard.

Frets — The areas on the fingerboard which are divided by strips of wire, enabling specific notes to be played.

Harmonic — The overtones of a fundamental note, as produced by lightly touching the strings.

Headstock — The part of the guitar which carries the machine heads.

Heel-less — A method by which the neck is fitted to the body which reduces thickness and allows for easier access to the top frets.

Humbucking — Referring to a particular type of pickup with hum cancelling properties. It involves two coils wound in opposite directons but wired in parallel.

Intonation — The capacity to play in tune.

Jack — Short for jack plug which connects via a lead, the electric guitar with an amplifier.

Laminate — A joining of two or more thin sheets of material.

Machines — The machine heads by which the strings are wound and held at the headstock.

Natural finish — A finish which allows the natural colour of the wood to come through.

Nut — Grooved strip of either plastic, brass, bone or ivory over which the strings pass at the beginning of the fretboard.

Overdrive — Overloading the components of an amplifier to deliberately produce distortion.

Phasing — In relationship to pickups, the positive and negative poles can be wired up in different ways to produce different sounds, i.e. an out-of-phase sound.

Pick — A name for a plectrum which is used for striking the strings and is usually made of plastic.

Pickup — An electro-magnetic transducer which converts the vibration of steel strings into electric signals.

Pot — Abbreviation for potentiometer, meaning tone and volume controls.

Purfling — Strips of complex binding.

Run — A collection of notes put together in sequence.

Saddles — The parts of the bridge over which the strings pass.

Screening — Electrical insulation against unwanted interference.

Selector switch — A switch on the guitar which enables the player to select various pickups and combinations of each.

Set up — To set up the action of a guitar ready for playing.

Solid body — A guitar made froma solid block of wood which has no sound-hole and needs to be amplified.

Sound-hole — The hole on the top of an acoustic guitar body from which the sound emanates.

Strings through-the-body — Developed for easy string replacement, the strings are threaded through the guitar and then over the bridge saddles.

Sunburst — A type of finish on guitar bodies which is dark around the edges and gradually becomes lighter around the centre of the guitar.

Sustain — The length of the notes emanating from the guitar.

Tailpiece — Where the strings are harnessed after passing through the bridge.

Through-neck — The neck of the guitar continues straight through the body of the instrument on which the pickups and the bridge are mounted.

Transducer — A device used to amplify acoustic instruments.

Tremolo arm — A short metal arm, attached to the bridge which gives vibrato affect on the strings when pulled.

Truss rod — Usually a metal bar inserted in the neck of a guitar to strengthen it and allow some degree of adjustment.

Tune-O-Matic — The name given to a specific type of bridge developed by Gibson.

Violining — A way of playing which involves hitting notes on the fretboard with one hand, and turning the volume control very quickly with the other; thus producing notes without the usual striking of the strings.

Index

Acoustic Guitars

Acoustic Profiles

Lead Guitars

Lead Profiles

Bass Guitars

Bass Profiles

Take your pick!

With 6 string or 12 string electric or 6 string acoustic, the New MATRIX Roundbacks have a great deal to offer.

At the heart of every MATRIX is one feature that sets it apart from all other guitars in its class – an aluminium neck core. Based on the Kaman Bar, this strong yet lightweight design renders the MATRIX neck virtually impervious to temperature and humidity changes that can warp an ordinary neck.

A solid rosewood fingerboard and long wearing nickel silver frets help you play fast and accurately, note after note. Combined with the proven Lyramold roundback design and the natural strength of a laminated spruce top with superior bracing pattern, the new MATRIX is a worthy stable mate to those other great Kaman guitars – Ovation and Adamas.

So take your pick, and try a MATRIX today. Rose, Morris will be pleased to advise you of your nearest dealer.

Rose-Morris
MATRIX

Rose, Morris & Co, Ltd
32-34 Gordon House Road London NW5 INE
Telephone: 01-267 5151

- FENDER – MUSICMAN – ARIA – IBANEZ – GORDON SMITH – RICKENBACKER – WAL – SHERGOLD – GUILD – C
ON – SIGMA – COLUMBUS – WESTBURY – WESTONE – DOUBLE EAGLE – B & M CLASSIC – GIBSON –
AN – ARIA – IBANEZ – GORDON SMITH – RICKENBACKER – WAL – SHERGOLD – GUILD – C F MARTIN – OVATIO
BUS – WESTBURY – WESTONE – DOUBLE EAGLE – B & M CLASSIC – GIBSON – FENDER – MUSICMAN – ARIA –
SMITH – RICKENBACKER – WAL – SHERGOLD – GUILD – C F MARTIN – OVATION – SIGMA – COLUMBUS – WE
E – DOUBLE EAGLE – B & M CLASSIC – GIBSON – FENDER – MUSICMAN – ARIA – IBANEZ – GORDON
ACKER – WAL – SHERGOLD – GUILD – C F MARTIN – OVATION – SIGMA – COLUMBUS – WESTBURY – W
EAGLE – B & M CLASSIC – GIBSON – FENDER – MUSICMAN – ARIA – IBANEZ – GORDON SMITH – RICKENBACKE
LD – GUILD – C F MARTIN – OVATION – SIGMA – COLUMBUS – WESTBURY – WESTONE – DOUBLE EAGL
– GIBSON – FENDER – MUSICMAN – ARIA – IBANEZ – GORDON SMITH – RICKENBACKER – WAL – SHERGOLD
TIN – OVATION – SIGMA – COLUMBUS – WESTBURY – WESTONE – DOUBLE EAGLE – B & M CLASSIC – GIBSON
MAN – ARIA – IBANEZ – GORDON SMITH – RICKENBACKER – WAL – SHERGOLD – GUILD – C F MARTIN – C
COLUMBUS – WESTBURY – WESTONE – DOUBLE EAGLE – B & M CLASSIC – GIBSON – FENDER – MUSICMA
– GORDON SMITH – RICKENBACKER – WAL – SHERGOLD – GUILD – C F MARTIN – OVATION – SIGMA – COL
RY – WESTONE – DOUBLE EAGLE – B & M CLASSIC – GIBSON – FENDER – MUSICMAN – ARIA – IBANEZ – GORD
BACKER – WAL – SHERGOLD – GUILD – C F MARTIN – OVATION – SIGMA – COLUMBUS – WESTBURY – W

Tim Gentle music
Dare you go anywhere else?

. . . for Guitars & Drums
. . . for Amps & Cabs
. . . for PAs & Accessories
. . . for Keyboards
. . . for Personal Multitrack Recording Equipment

TIM GENTLE MUSIC 1420 LONDON ROAD, LEIGH-ON-SEA, ESSEX, ENGLAND.
TEL (0702) 72926

H.P P/EX Buy it with Access BARCLAYCARD VISA

SHOP OPEN 10-6, 6 DAYS A WEEK.

MAIL ORDER MUSIC

For Guitar

AC/DC The BEST OF £5.25
AC/DC BACK IN BLACK £5.25
AEROSMITH COMPLETE £7.25
BAD COMPANY RUN WITH THE PACK .. £3.99
BAD COMPANY DESOLATION ANGELS . £3.99
FRANK ZAPPA SONGBOOK £6.25
LED ZEPPELIN BEST OF £3.99
LED ZEPPELIN THROUGH THE YEARS .. £8.25
GENESIS ABACAB £3.49
CROSBY STILLS & NASH £5.25
GEORGE BENSON COMPLETE £6.25
POLICE GHOST IN THE MACHINE £2.99
PINK FLOYD COMPLETE £6.99
MEATLOAF DEADRINGER £3.99
SONGS OF DAVID BOWIE £5.25
BOWIE STATION TO STATION £5.25
BEATLES SONGBOOK £6.49
HUMAN LEAGUE DARE £3.25
STEELY DAN GAUCHO £5.25
TED NUGENT COMPLETE £5.25
THE WHO SONGBOOK £6.99
HAIRCUT 100 .... £3.99
THE COMPLETE JIMI HENDRIX £6.99
JOHN LENNON SONGBOOK £6.25
RUSH MOVING PICTURES £5.25
SIMON & GARFUNKEL £6.25
THE JAM REST OF THE BEST £3.99
HEAVY METAL SONGBOOK £4.25
SPRINGSTEEN THE RIVER £6.25
ULTRAVOX RAGE IN EDEN £3.50
NEIL YOUNG COMPLETE £8.99
ROLLING STONES TATTOO YOU £3.99
BEST OF NEW WAVE ROCK £6.25
JUDAS PRIEST SAD WINGS £3.50
DOORS COMPLETE £8.99
ALICE COOPER COMPLETE £5.99
ALICE COOPER LACE & WHISKEY £4.25
ELVIS COSTELLO SINGING DICTIONARY £10.99
ELP ANTHOLOGY £6.50

MYSTIQUE MUSIC BOOKS
58 Westbourne Terrace, London W11
Postage 75p one book
+ 35p each additional book
MAIL ORDER ONLY
Trade Enquiries Welcome

All Customers Please Allow 28 Days For Delivery

GIGSVILLE distribute other things besides

Aria

ELECTRIC GUITARS WHICH MUSICIANS KEEP TELLING US ARE THE BEST VALUE IN THE BUSINESS. — SO APPLY EYEBALL TO THESE GOODIES — IT'S PAINLESS!

JJ-6
Designed by John Joyce Gigsville's Guitar Consultant and distributed world wide by Aria.
Solid Spruce top, Mahogany back and sides, Rosewood fingerboard, Tortoise-shell type binding with herringbone purfling in red. Hand carved Rosewood bridge.
12-string model available.
(S.R.P. £265.60)

FE 70
Solid Spruce top. Sycamore back and sides. Rosewood fingerboard with Mother of Pearl inlays. Rosewood bridge. Tone and Volume controls. Built-in pre amp.
Colour: Violin finish.
Jack socket acts as on/off switch for pre amp circuit.
(S.R.P. £292.68)

Aria *Elecord*
with built-in pickup

AE90
Special pickup strip is mounted in the bridge beneath the saddle and produces a good clean balanced sound.
Body. Solid arched Spruce top. Rosewood back and sides. Rosewood fingerboard with Mother of Pearl inlays. Rosewood bridge. Tone and Volume controls.
Colours: Natural or Tobacco Brown.
(S.R.P. £353.82)

LOCO BOX ANALOG DELAY

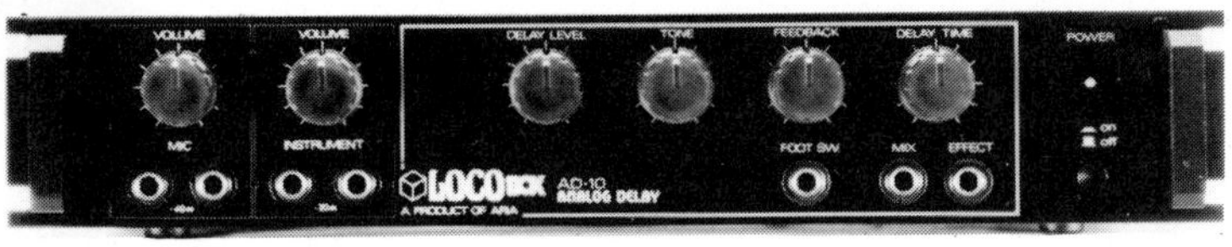

.D 10
Mic and 2 instrument inputs. ›ntrols, delay level. Tone, Echo ›eat, delay time. Peak level :D Indicator. Foot switch cket.
;.R.P. £133.50)

AD 15
2 Mic and 2 instrument inputs. Controls, bass. Treble. Echo Repeat. Delay time. Reverb. Peak Level LED Indicator. Foot switch socket.
(S.R.P. £169.33)

SAME HIGH QUALITY AS LOCO AMPS & EFFECTS SAY NO MORE!

erested in ______________________

ss ______________________

____

to Gigsville Dept. IM4

Aria Guitars ☐
LOCO Effects ☐
Shadow Pickups ☐
Tick info required

GIGSVILLE
Phoenix Way, Heston
Middx. 01 897 3792

PICKUP

YOUR ACOUSTIC GUITAR.

2500E Concealed Permanent Mount Guitar Transducer

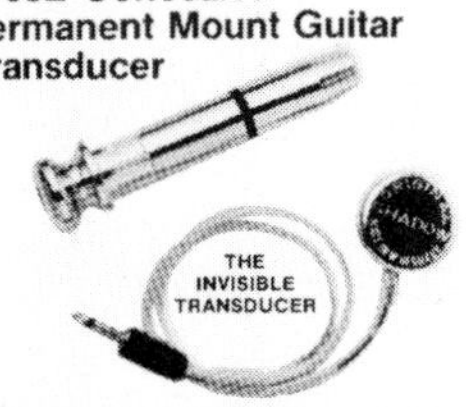

A concealed permanent mount transducer for acoustic guitar makes a lot of sense—especially when its Shadow's Model 2500E with the industry's widest frequency range (1-30,000 Hz).
It installs in minutes, invisibly, inside your guitar where it never interferes with acoustic playing; but plug the 2500E into an amp and it boosts every lick and chord without changing your acoustic sound to electric. It's conveniently out of the way, eliminates cord noise, can't mar guitar finish and never needs preamps. Maybe that's why its one of America's leading sellers.
Shadow's 2500E. The invisible transducer with the impact you can see and hear.

shadow
PICKUPS

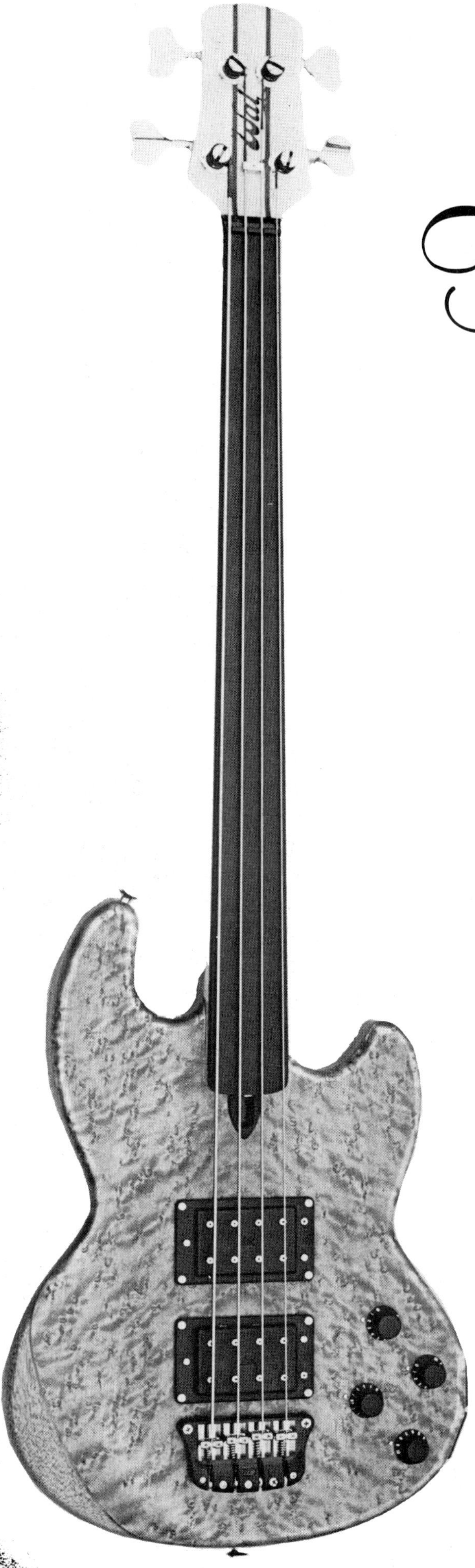

The Professiona Choice!

Wal®

Electric Wood Ltd.,
Sandown Works, Chairborough Road,
High Wycombe, Bucks HP12 3HH England
Tel: 0494 - 442925/6

GIBSON GUITARS ARE DISTRIBUTED EXCLUSIVELY IN THE U.K. BY ROSETTI LTD
138 - 140 OLD STREET · LONDON EC1V 9BL · TEL: 01-253 7294

Peter Cook Guitars Basses England

PC

NOT ONLY
the ultimate customizing and
repair service

BUT ALSO
a selection of the most
playable new and vintage
instruments in the UK

Peter Cook Guitars
69 Station Rd, Hanwell W.7
Tel. 01-840 1244

Eccleshall
LONDON

GUITARS, BANJOS
MANDOLINS AND
DULCIMERS

We specialize in making musical
instruments, individually designed and
made to customers requirements.
Please send any details to

Chris Eccleshall Guitars
17c, Station Pde, Ealing Common
London W5. England. 01-992-4741

Through sound and vision to-days
'Rock and Soul' is powerfully projected
by PAUL WELLER and BRUCE FOXTON
who, for every performance, swear by
'ROTOSOUND' guitar strings, in particular
the **GAUGE SELECTION ·010"**
and **SWING BASS** sets.

GREAT BRITISH SOUNDS COME FROM ROTOSOUND

JAMES HOW INDUSTRIES LTD. 20, UPLAND ROAD,
BEXLEYHEATH, KENT DA7 4NR Telephone: 01 304 4711

John Thomas of Budgie has loved guitars since he was knee high to a treme[lo] arm, and now has one of the finest guitar collections around. He has used every conceivable brand of strings under the sun, searching to find something special. That search ended when he discovered the difference between Superwound and ordinary strings.

John says, "The thing I like about Superwound is that they really are different. They are unbelievably responsive whereas ordinary strings just do a job. I also like the way they tune up easily and hold their tuning even throug[h] heavy tremelo use. In a word they are just 'perfect' ".

Sole Manufacturers
SUPERWOUND LTD
Unit 1, Morewood Close, Sevenoaks, Kent, England.
Tel: Sevenoaks (0732) 50838 Telex: 898031